DATE DUE

Christmas in the Old West

BACK COVER:
Christmas tree photograph courtesy of Colorado Historical Society;
photograph of party courtesy of World Museum of Mining, Butte,
Montana; Irma Hotel menu courtesy of Buffalo Bill Historical Center

Library of Congress Cataloging-in-Publication Data

Travers, Sam, 1959–
    Christmas in the Old West / Travers.
        p. cm.
    Includes bibliographical references and indexes.
    ISBN 0-87842-460-1 (alk. paper)
    1. Christmas—West (U.S.)—History. 2. West (U.S.)—Social life
and customs—19th century. I. Title.

GT4986.W47T73 2003
394.2663'0978—dc21

                                                    2003046423

PRINTED IN HONG KONG BY MANTEC PRODUCTION COMPANY

Mountain Press Publishing Company
Missoula, Montana
2003

For the Scharmann Brothers

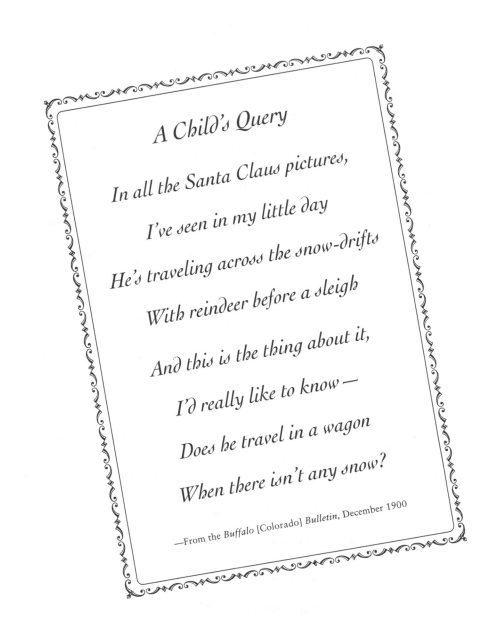

A Child's Query

In all the Santa Claus pictures,

I've seen in my little day

He's traveling across the snow-drifts

With reindeer before a sleigh

And this is the thing about it,

I'd really like to know—

Does he travel in a wagon

When there isn't any snow?

—From the *Buffalo* [Colorado] *Bulletin,* December 1900

Contents

Dear Reader,

An author is little more than an invisible tour guide through a world made of pages. With this in mind, I want you to get your bearings so if later I let go of your hand, you will be safe to wander on your own and not feel lost.

This volume was designed to be more of a treasure box than a book. It is not intended to be an imposing volume on the history of western holidays. While you may read sequentially from page one, it is just as easy to reach in and pull out a recipe, story, or slice of history that suits your fancy at the moment and leave the remainder for another day. There is no true beginning or end. The chapters are organized roughly according to level of "civilization," reflected in the stories, menus, poems, pictures, etc. My words may be few at times, and it might even seem as if I have abandoned you, but this is not so. I have simply stepped aside so you may let these long-ago voices tell their own stories.

This book explores Christmas as it was celebrated in the American West. In it, I hope to share with today's westerners the Christmas heritage they may not know they have. My goal is to present to you the opportunity to see into a Christmas past beyond plum pudding and old lace—not only as an onlooker, but as a welcome holiday guest. I hope this book inspires you and your family to explore the world of Christmas frontier style together.

Let us begin our tour. We have quite a distance to cover.

Your humble guide,

SAM TRAVERS

A Western Christmas Timeline

DECEMBER 24

1809 Kit Carson born

1813 Davy Crockett returns home from the Creek War for Christmas

1814 Treaty of Ghent signed

1849 The first great San Francisco fire

1852 First Texas locomotive, *The General Sherman*, goes into service

1853 The S.S. *San Francisco* sinks on its way to California; 240 drown

1855 The *Weekly Sunday Times* established in San Francisco

1859 The First Dragoons battle the Apache in New Mexico; six Apache killed

1861 Waco University chartered in Texas

1864 Boise named state capital of Idaho

1879 Mormon colonists celebrate Christmas at Hole in the Rock, Utah

1880 Billy the Kid arrested at Fort Sumner

1881 Jesse James rents 1318 Lafayette Street in St. Joseph, Missouri, and dresses up as Santa Claus for his two daughters

1889 Butch Cassidy, age 23, pulls his first holdup, at San Miguel Bank in Telluride, Colorado

DECEMBER 25

1804 First documented Rocky Mountain Christmas, celebrated at Fort Mandan in present-day North Dakota

1806 Lt. Zebulon Pike and his men spend Christmas in Colorado

1848 John C. Frémont and his men spend Christmas in southern Colorado

1853 First gas-lit theater opens in San Francisco

1854 Ute Indians avenging an outbreak of smallpox destroy the settlement of Fort Pueblo, Colorado

1858 "Uncle Dick" Wooten brings the first alcohol ("Taos Lightning") to the small mining camp that later would become known as Denver

1860 Pony Express founder William Russell arrested for fraud

1865 Chicago's Union Stockyards open

1868 Battle of Soldier Spring: U.S. troops defeat a band of Kiowa and Comanche Indians and destroy their village

1877 Sam Bass robs Fort Worth Cleburne stagecoach; his booty is $11.25

1891 In Texas, Mexican revolutionary Catarino Garza fails in attempt to over take Fort Ringgold

1894 Kid Curry (Harvey Logan) shoots up Landusky, Montana, killing its founder, Pike Landusky

1894 Popular San Francisco resort Cliff House burns down

*Gifts and other Christmas goods could be
ordered from back East via mail.* —Courtesy
Park County Historical Society

Introduction

Christmas on the Wild Frontier

THE CHRISTMAS TRADITIONS WE KNOW—trimmed trees, colorful packages, and the guy with the bright red suit—were already in place by the middle of the nineteenth century, the time of the great westward migration in America. Many of our now-cherished customs first came to the New World with Dutch settlers in the 1620s, and soon immigrants from all over Europe were adding their own yuletide traditions to the celebration. With the growth of the young nation during the nineteenth century, Victorian ideals of charity, good will, and close family life inspired a newfound interest in the Christmas holiday. The Industrial Revolution fueled the fire with mass-produced goods ready for wrapping.

In the West, early in the nineteenth century, Jesuit missionaries brought Christmas to the Indians as a joyous yet solemn ocassion. As the century progressed and a more elaborate and festive approach to Christmas came to be embraced in the United States, emigrants carried the new attitude to the western territories. For the settlers, Christmas provided an occasion to rejoice in an often harsh and isolated environment, as well as a tie to traditions of a home otherwise abandoned. For this reason, Christmas was often a bittersweet time, especially for those far from loved ones left behind. Yet with true pioneer determination, these westerners sustained and in some cases reinvented the holiday, even in the absence of silver bells and pretty bows.

Because isolated westerners had fewer resources than their eastern counterparts for obtaining material goods with which to celebrate the holiday—the gifts, the special foods, the decorations, and in some cases, even the tree—they had to be resourceful and creative when it came to Christmas. Gifts and decorations were often homemade. Items that had to be purchased, including holiday musts like sugar and alcohol, were either saved from one's most recent trip to a town or ordered through catalogs. In areas devoid of evergreens, a stick of cottonwood or a sagebrush might be dressed up to serve as a Christmas tree.

As the West became more and more developed—that is, more and more like the East—the challenges of the early settlers in keeping Christmas were largely forgotten. Yet these humble but meaningful celebrations represent an important part of our western American heritage.

Undaunted Christmas

Explorers, Fur Traders, and Other Trailblazers

CHRISTMAS HAS BEEN CELEBRATED in the American West since the time of the first white explorers and fur traders in the late 1700s. For this book, we'll begin with Lewis and Clark's first Christmas at Fort Mandan and examine the Christmas observances—or lack thereof—of early western trailblazers who went into uncharted territory, bringing the notion of Christmas with them. These intrepid adventurers included explorers and surveyors; early missionaries who came into western areas before they were settled; and fur traders, trappers, and mountain men who lived among the natives and cut their own paths through the unmapped frontier.

Council between Whites and Indians *by William Henry Jackson*
—Courtesy Scotts Bluff National Monument

LEWIS AND CLARK and their Corps of Discovery spent the first winter of the expedition, in 1804, just outside a Mandan village at the mouth of the Knife River, in present-day North Dakota. The journals the men kept described their Christmas at Fort Mandan, celebrated with "taffia" (brandy) and gunfire:

William Clark —From *Lewis and Clarke's Journey to the Rocky Mountains . . . as Related by Patrick Gass*

December, Christmass, 1804. I was awakened before Day by a discharge of 3 platoons from the party and the french. The men merrily Disposed, I give them all a little Taffia and permitted 3 Cannon fired, at raising of Our flag. Some men Went out to hunt and others to Danceing and Continued untill 9 oClock P.M., when the frolick ended.

—William Clark

Meriwether Lewis —From *Lewis and Clarke's Journey to the Rocky Mountains . . . as Related by Patrick Gass*

Tuesday 25th [1804]. The morning was ushered in by two discharges of a swivel, and a round of small arms by the whole corps. Captain Clarke then presented to each man a glass of brandy, and we hoisted the American flag in the garrison, and its first waving in fort Mandan was celebrated with another glass.— The men then cleared out one of the rooms and commenced dancing. At 10 o'clock we had another glass of brandy, and at 1 a gun was fired as a signal for dinner. At half past 2 another gun was fired, as a notice to assemble at the dance, which was continued in a jovial manner till 8 at night; and without the presence of any females, except three squaws, wives to our interpreter, who took no other part than the amusement of looking on. None of the natives came to the garrison this day; the commanding officers having requested they should not, which was strictly attended to.

—Patrick Gass

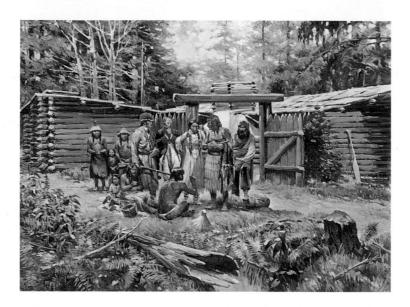

Fort Clatsop, Oregon,
by Newman Myrah
—Courtesy Fort Clatsop
National Memorial

[December 25, 1804] *cloudy. we fired the Swivels at day break & each man fired one round. our officers Gave the party a drink of Taffee. we had the Best to eat that could be had, & continued firing dancing & frolicking dureing the whole day. the Savages did not Trouble us as we had requested them not to come as it was a Great medician day with us. we enjoyed a merry cristmas dureing the day & evening untill nine oClock — all in peace & quietness.*

—John Ordway

25ᵗʰ December, 1804, Christmas. *we ushred the morning with a discharge of the Swivvel, and one round of Small arms of all the party, then another from the Swivel. then Capt. Clark presented a glass of brandy to each man of the party. we hoisted the american flag, and each man had another Glass of brandy. the men prepared one of the rooms and commenced dancing. at 10 oC we had another Glass of brandy, at one oC a gun was fired as a Signal for diner. half past two another gun was fired to assembl at the dance. and So we kept it up in a jovel manner untill eight oC at night, all without the compy of the female Seck, except three Squaws, the intreptirs wives, and they took no part with us, only to look on. agreeble to the officers request, the natives all Stayed at their villages all day.*

—Joseph Whitehouse

By Christmas 1805, the Corps had reached the Pacific Ocean. The men erected a winter camp, Fort Clatsop, at the mouth of the Columbia River, near present-day Astoria, Oregon. Their Christmas at Fort Clatsop was considerably less festive than the holiday they spent at Fort Mandan, yet they remained cheerful and optimistic:

Christmas, Wednesday, 25th December, 1805—*at day light this morning we we[re] awoke by the discharge of the fire arm[s] of all our party & a Selute, Shouts, and a Song which the whole party joined in under our windows, after which they retired to their rooms were chearful all the morning. after brackfast we divided our Tobacco, which amounted to 12 carrots, one half of which we gave to the men of the party who used tobacco, and to those who doe not use it we make a present of a hendkerchief. The Indians leave us in the evening, all the party Snugly fixed in their huts.*

I recved a presnt of Cap. L. of a fleece hosrie, Shirt, Draws and Socks, a pr. Mockersons of Whitehouse, a small Indian basket of Gutherich, two dozen white weazils tails of the Indian Woman, & some black root of the Indians before their departure. . . . The day proved Showery, wet and disagreeable.

We would have Spent this day, the nativity of Christ, in feasting, had we any thing either to raise our Sperits or even gratify our appetites. our Dinner concisted of pore Elk, so much Spoiled that we eate it thro' mear necessity, Some Spoiled pounded fish and a few roots.

—*William Clark*

Noisemaking was a common part of some Christmas celebrations. Today, noisemaking is associated with New Year's, but in early America, as in parts of Europe, it was a popular custom to shoot guns in the air to salute Christmas morning. Early western explorers and missionaries often shot guns off this way, and a firearm salute was part of nearly every Christmas celebration at trading posts and military forts throughout the West.

Wednesday 25th [1805]. Was another cloudy wet day.— This morning we left our camp and moved into our huts. At daybreak all the men paraded and fired a round of small arms, wishing the Commanding Officers a merry Christmas. In the course of the day Capt. Lewis and Capt. Clarke collected what tobacco remained and divided it among those who used tobacco as a Christmas-gift; to the others they gave handkerchiefs in lieu of it. We had no spirituous liquors to elevate our spirits this Christmas; but of this we had but little need, as we were all in very good health. Our living is not very good; meat is plenty, but of an ordinary quality, as the elk are poor in this part of the country. We have no kind of provisions but meat, and we are without salt to season that.

—*Patrick Gass*

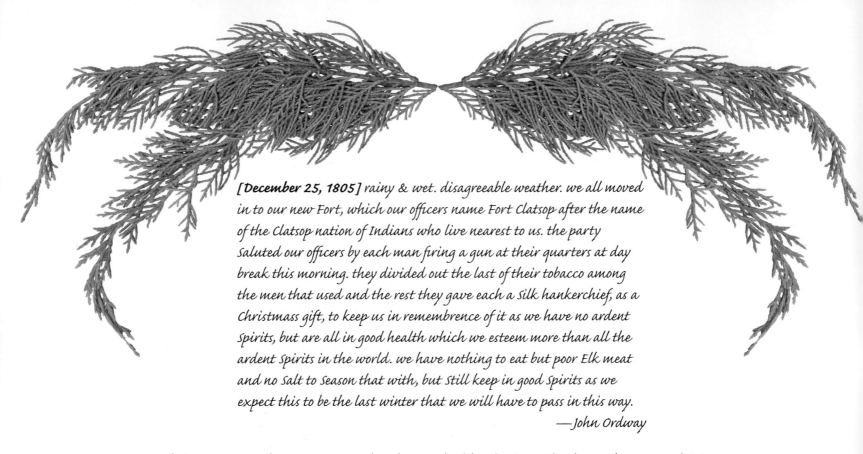

[December 25, 1805] rainy & wet. disagreeable weather. we all moved in to our new Fort, which our officers name Fort Clatsop after the name of the Clatsop nation of Indians who live nearest to us. the party Saluted our officers by each man firing a gun at their quarters at day break this morning. they divided out the last of their tobacco among the men that used and the rest they gave each a Silk hankerchief, as a Christmass gift, to keep us in remembrence of it as we have no ardent Spirits, but are all in good health which we esteem more than all the ardent Spirits in the world. we have nothing to eat but poor Elk meat and no Salt to Season that with, but Still keep in good Spirits as we expect this to be the last winter that we will have to pass in this way.

—John Ordway

Christmas, December 25, 1805, Wednesday. We had hard rain & Cloudy weather as usual. We all moved into our new Garrison or Fort, which our Officers named after a nation of Indians who resided near us, called the Clatsop Nation; Fort Clatsop. We found our huts comfortable, excepting smoaking a little.

We saluted our officers, by each of our party firing off his gun at day break in honor to the day (Christmass). Our Officers in return presented to each of the party that used Tobacco a part of what Tobacco they had remaining; and to those who did not make use of it, they gave a handkerchief or some other article in rememberance of Christmass.

We had no ardent spirit of any kind among us; but are mostly in good health, a blessing which we esteem more than all the luxuries this life can afford, and the party are all thankful to the Supreme Being, for his goodness toward us, hoping he will preserve us in the same, & enable us to return to the United States in safety. We have at present nothing to eat but lean Elk meat & that without Salt, but the whole of our party are content with this life.

—Joseph Whitehouse

IN 1806, TWENTY-FOUR SOLDIERS under the command of Lt. Zebulon Pike set out to navigate the Arkansas and Red Rivers. Christmas Eve found the company near present-day Salida, Colorado. The snow was deep and food was scarce, so it was with great relief and joy they heard the news that their hunting party had shot eight buffalo. On Christmas Day the men shivered and thought of home. The following is an excerpt from Pike's journal:

Zebulon M. Pike
—Courtesy Independence
National Historical Park

[December 24, 1806] We now again find ourselves all assembled together on Christmas Eve. and appeared generally to be content, although all the refreshment we had to celebrate the holiday with was buffalo meat, without any salt, or any other thing whatever.

[December 25, 1806] Here I must take the liberty of observing that this situation, the hardships and privations we underwent, were on this day brought more fully to our mind. Having been accustomed in the past to some degree of relaxation; but here 800 miles from the frontiers of our country, in the most inclement season of the year; not one person clothed for the winter, many without blankets (having cut them up for socks, etc.) and now laying down at night on the snow or wet ground; one side burning whilst the other was pierced with the cold wind; this was in part the situation of the party whilst some were endeavoring to make a miserable substitute of raw buffalo hide for shoes. I will not speak of diet, as I conceive that to be benieth the serious consideration of a man on a voyage of such nature. We spent the day as agreeably as could be expected from men in our situation.

BISON STEAK.

Render some fat in a hot skillet. Add sirloin of bison and sear on both sides. At lower heat, cook as beefsteak until done.

For gravy, add a tablespoon of flour to pan drippings and cook until brown. Stir in a cup of milk and bring to a boil. Salt to taste. (Pioneer recipe)

Thomas Breckenridge, member of John C. Frémont's fourth western expedition, recorded this Christmas dinner menu:

Menu
Camp Desolation
Christmas 1848

Soup
Mule Tail

Meats
Mule Steak, Fried Mule, Mule Chops,
Boiled Mule, Stewed Mule,
Scrambled Mule, Shirred Mule,
French-Fried Mule, Minced Mule,
Damned Mule, Mule on Toast
(without toast),
Short Ribs of Mule with Apple Sauce (without apple sauce)

Beverages
Snow, Snow Water, Water

"We suffered greatly for the want of salt; but by burning our mule steaks, and sprinkling a little gunpowder upon them, it did not require a very extensive stretch of the imagination to fancy the presence of both salt and pepper."

—Capt. Randolph B. Marcy,
from The Prairie Traveler, 1859

IN *ROADSIDE HISTORY OF ARIZONA,* author Marshall Trimble tells of an extraordinary Christmas with explorer Amiel W. Whipple's expedition into present-day Arizona:

On November 29, 1853, . . . [an Army Corps of Topographical Engineers survey expedition under Lt. Amiel W.] Whipple left Zuni, New Mexico, and headed west. . . . The expedition followed [the Colorado River] to Sunset Crossing, near today's Winslow, and headed west to the San Francisco Mountains, where they spent a chilly Christmas camped at the foot of those majestic peaks. . . .

By the time the party reached the mountains [on December 24], slogging through heavy snows had left the pack animals exhausted. Whipple decided to call a halt to allow the stock to recoup and to give the men a chance to celebrate Christmas. [One of the men, artist and writer Heinrich Baldwin Möllhausen, described the peaceful evening]:

As night came on, our company was seated in picturesque groups round the fires, which glowed larger and brighter in the darkness. The cooks were running about busily with their hissing frying-pans and bubbling coffee-pots, some were singing, some cheerfully gossiping, some only wrapped in their blankets and calmly smoking their pipes.

All, however, were relaxing in the warming Christmas spirit, which was about the only tepid thing, save the blazing fire, in that snowy woodland.

Much of the next morning was spent "in perfect quiet, in thinking over past times and our distant homes, where church bells were now summoning all to the religious celebration of the season. . . . We looked up at the sublime summits of the San Francisco Mountains and needed no temple made with hands within to worship our Creator."

Later, while opening up the packs, the men uncovered "some well preserved bottles of what makes glad the heart of the traveling man."

One pack included eggs that by some miracle had survived the journey. The wine and food were turned over to the cooks "for the glorification of our Christmas dinner in the Wilderness."

While the cooks were preparing venison, wild turkey, and other tasty delights, Lieutenant John, a resourceful young officer in the party, took the eggs and liquor and conjured up a punch. . . .

All gentlemen [were] requested to assemble after supper before Lieutenant John's tent, and to bring with them their tin drinking mugs.

No one had a previous engagement, nor was it at all tempting to decline, and as soon as the night set in and the stars began to flitter in the deep blue firmament, and to look down upon us between the snowy branches, the company began to assemble at the appointed spot. . . .

MULLED WINE.

Grate one half Nutmeg into a Pint of Wine and Sweeten to your Taste with Loaf-sugar. Set it over the fire and when it boils take it off the fire to cool. Beat the yolks of four eggs very well, strain them and add to them a little cold wine, them mix them with hot wine gradually. Pour it backward and forward several times till it looks fine and light, then set it on the fire and heat it very gradually till it is quite hot and pretty thick, and pour it up and down several times. Put it in chocolate cups and serve it with long, narrow toast. (1801)

HAUNCH OF VENISON.

If the outside be hard, wash off and rub with fresh butter or lard. Cover it on the top and sides with a thick paste of flour and water, nearly inch thick. Lay upon this a large sheet of thin white wrapping paper well buttered, and above this thick foolscap. Keep all in place by greased pack-thread, then put down to roast with a little water in the dripping pan. Let the fire be steady and strong. Pour a few ladlefuls of butter and water over the meat now and then to prevent the paper from scorching. About 1 hour before you take it up, remove the papers and paste and baste every few minutes with claret and melted butter. At the last, baste with butter, dredge with flour to make a light broth, and dish. Send this to table in a tureen. Send around currant jelly with venison always. (1893)

Lieutenant John was busy with his brewage and that fragrant steaming pail, with the inviting froth at the top, was a most agreeable sight to men who had been so long limited to water. Lieutenant John made a speech, as nearly as I can remember to this effect:

"Let us now forget for a few hours our hardships and privations, the object of our journey, and the labours still before us; and here, under a roof of boughs, and on the spotless white carpet that God Almighty has spread for us, for as we are far from our homes, let us think of our friends, who, very likely, are thinking of us as they sit around their firesides; and drowning our cares in a social glass of toddy, drink to their health, and to our own happy return."

The Winter Campaign *by Frederic Remington*
—Courtesy Rockwell Museum of Western Art, Corning, New York

We sat in a circle, smoked, drank, toasted and told jokes—hearts became lighter, blood ran more swirly in veins, and all joined in a hearty songfest that echoed through ravines and mountains and must have sadly interfered with the night's rest of the sleeping turkeys.

[The local] Mexicans made their contribution to the festival by throwing firebrands into the cedar thickets:

The pointed leaves, or needles, rich in resin, caught fire immediately; the flames blazed over the tops of the trees and sent millions of sparks up to the sky. It was a most beautiful spectacle!

Snow glittered with magic splendor. All objects were suffused in a red glow. Most exquisite effects of light and shade were produced among the neighboring rocks and mountains. The splendor of the sight served to enhance the gaiety of the company till it reached an almost perilous pitch.

The evening festivities climaxed in joyous singing. The Americans sang Negro spirituals and the Mexicans shared their traditional Christmas songs. This multicultural event . . . was given an added dimension when two men, former prisoners of the Navajo, performed native dances.

[Expedition guide] Antoine Leroux was the only one who remained vigilant during the festivities. The old scout had lived in the mountains by his wits too long to let his guard down for a Christmas party. He was heard to mutter between sips, "What a splendid opportunity it would be for the Indians to surprise us tonight."

To old Antoine's relief, no attacks came that night. This occasion marked the first recorded Christmas in Arizona north of the Gila River.

IN 1841, JESUIT MISSIONARY Father Pierre-Jean de Smet spent Christmas among the Salish at St. Mary's Mission in present-day Montana, having arrived on December 8. In his journal he described the remarkable Christmas Eve vision of a young Indian boy:

> On Christmas Day I added 150 new baptisms . . . and thirty-two rehabilitations of marriage. . . .
>
> Accordingly, on Christmas Eve, a few hours before the midnight mass, the village of St. Mary was deemed worthy of a special mark of heaven's favor. The Blessed Virgin appeared to a little orphan boy named Paul, in the hut of an aged and truly pious woman. The youth, piety, and sincerity of this child, joined to the nature of the fact which he related, forbade us to doubt the truth of his statement."
>
> The boy described a beautiful woman dressed in white, with a star over her head, a serpent under her feet, and rays of light beaming from her heart.

In 1842, Father Nicholas Point traveled with Father de Smet to present-day Idaho to help bring Christianity to the Coeur d'Alene Indians. Father Point painted a watercolor of the interior of the church at the Sacred Heart Mission as it was decorated for Christmas and made a note of the celebration in his journal:

> A little before midnight the firing of muskets announced that the church had just been opened. Waves of worshipers hurried toward the palace of the infant God and, at the sight of the night suddenly changed into splendid day, they were moved to cry, "Jesus, I give you my heart."

*Father Nicholas Point's watercolor of the interior of Sacred Heart Church, from
the papers of Pierre-Jean de Smet* —Courtesy Washington State University Library

Father de Smet was with the Kalispel tribe, in present-day Washington, in
1844. Upon his arrival on December 17, the Indians began building a church,
finishing it in two days. In his journal, Father de Smet wrote a detailed description of the Christmas celebration:

> *The great festival of Christmas, the day on which the little band was to be
> added to the number of the true children of God, will never be effaced from the
> memory of our good Indians. The manner in which we celebrated midnight
> mass may give you an idea of our festival. The signal for rising, which was to
> be given a few minutes before midnight, was the firing of a pistol, announcing
> to the Indians that the house of prayer would soon be open. This was followed
> by a general discharge of guns, in honor of the birth of the Infant Savior, and
> 300 voices rose spontaneously from the midst of the forest, and entoned in the*

language of the Pend d'Oreilles the beautiful canticle, "The Almighty's glory all things proclaim." In a moment a multitude of adorers were seen wending their way to the humble temple of the Lord—resembling, indeed, the manger in which the Messiah was born.

Of what was our little church of the wilderness constructed? Of posts fresh cut in the woods, covered over with mats and bark; these were the only materials. On the eve, the church was embellished with garlands and wreaths of green boughs, forming, as it were, the frame for the images which represent the affecting mysteries of Christmas night. The altar was neatly decorated, bespangled with stars of various brightness, and covered with a profusion of ribbons—things exceedingly attractive to the eye of an Indian. At midnight I celebrated a solemn mass; the Indians sang several canticles suitable to the occasion.

A grand banquet, according to the Indian custom, followed the first mass. Some choice pieces of the animals slain in the chase had been set apart for the occasion. I ordered half a sack of flour and a large boiler of sweetened coffee to be added. The union, the contentment, the joy and charity, which prevaded the whole assembly, might well be compared to the agape of the primitive Christians. . . . The recitation of prayers and the chanting of hymns were heard in all the lodges of the camp till the night was far advanced.

FOR MANY EARLY TRAPPERS and traders, Christmas was just another workday. Many who kept journals made no special mention of the holiday on December 25, or made only a passing reference. In fur trader David Thompson's *Narrative*, he wrote, "Christmas and New Years day came and passed. We could not honour them, the occupations of every day demanded our attentions; and time passed on, employed in hunting for a livelihood." Of another Christmas, he noted, "Christmas when it comes finds us glad to see it and pass; we have nothing to welcome it with."

Most of these isolated men, if they commemorated the day at all, indulged in a few drinks if they had liquor, and perhaps treated themselves to an extra ration of food if they could spare it. The factor at the Hudson's Bay Company trading post Nisqually House mentioned modest celebrations:

Wednesday 25th [1833]. This being Christmas day I gave the men a liberal Regale of eatables and drinkables, to make up in some measure for the bad living they have had all year here, and they enjoyed the feast as might be expected men would do who lived solely on Soup since they came here. Weather still very cold.

[December] 25th [1834]. Thursday. Christmas. All hands were allowed the best I had in the Fort say, ducks, venison, and each half pint of rum. All quiet and no Indians. Mild weather but clowdy.

There was a bit more food and drink for Christmas at Saleesh House in present-day Montana in 1813, as trader Ross Cox notes:

Our hunters killed a few mountain sheep, and I brought up a bag of flour, a bag of rice, plenty of tea and coffee, some arrowroot, and fifteen gallons of prime rum. We spent a comparatively happy Christmas and, by the side of a blazing fire in a warm room, forgot the sufferings we endured in our dreary progress through the woods.

DRIED MEAT.

Cut meat into thin strips. Hang on a rack to dry, turning often until meat is thoroughly dry. (Native American recipe)

PEMMICAN.

Pound dried meat into a fine powder, then combine with lard, cherries or berries, and sweetner if desired. Form into cakes.
(Native American Recipe)

"Gave 30lb flour and 30lb tallow to the boys for regaling themselves tomorrow. . . . This evening the boys had a treat of whisky and made merry fired 3 guns at sunset in honor of the approaching night."

—From the December 24, 1812, journal of John C. Luttig, clerk for the Missouri Fur Company

"Same camp, gale S.S.W. Snow and rain all day a miserable Christmas. Worked what little we could on the canoes."

—From the December 25, 1834, journal of trader Nathaniel Jarvis Wyeth

Thanksgiving Dinner for the Ranch *by Frederic Remington*
—From *Harper's Weekly*, November 24, 1888

At better established posts, traders' journals report somewhat more elaborate celebrations. In the journals of John Owen, owner of the Montana trading post Fort Owen, we learn of regular Christmas celebrations held there during the 1850s and 1860s. He mentions visitors including Peter Skene Ogden and other fur men of the day, along with their wives. The company enjoy mince pies, brandy, egg nog, mutton, chicken, and other treats. In December 1864, for example, Owen reports:

> The Christmas passed off as usual. Calls, Salutes of Small Arms, Egg Nogg, etc. etc. Mr. Harris last Night gave us a Salute from the four-lb. Brass Howitzer. Mr. Banty and Lady, Mr. Peters and Lady Called and took dinner with us, and the day wound up with a dance.

EGG NOGG.

Beat separately the yolks and whites of six eggs. Stir the yolks into a quart of rich milk, or thin cream, and add half a pound of sugar. Then mix in half a pint of rum or brandy. Flavour it with a grated nutmeg. Lastly, stir in gently the beaten whites of three eggs. (1851)

Sketch of a deer hunter's shack by Charles Graham
—From *Harper's Weekly*, April 19, 1890

WHILE TRADERS LIVED with relative comfort and companionship in a trading post, trappers often lived alone in tents or crudely built cabins in the wilderness. Yet even they sometimes came together and used their limited resources to cele-brate the holiday. Mountain man Rufus B. Sage describes a cheerful Christmas in 1842 in the White River region of Colorado:

Christmas Greeting *by Sandy Ingersoll*
—Image from a Christmas card

This great annual feast is observed with all the exhilaration hilarity and good cheer that circumstances will allow. Several little extras for the occasion have been procured from the Indians, which prove quite wholesome and pleasant-tasted. One of these, called washena, consists of dried meat pulverized and mixed with marrow; another is a preparation of cherries, preserved when first picked by pounding and sun drying them (they are served by mixing them with bouille, or the liquor of fresh boiled meat, thus giving to it an agreeable winesh taste); a third is a marrow fat, an article in many respects superior to butter; and lastly, we obtained a kind of flour made from the pomme blanc (white apple), answering very well as a substitute for that of grain.

The above assortment, with a small supply of sugar and coffee, as well as several other dainties variously prepared, affords an excellent dinner, and though different in kind, by no means inferior in quality to the generality of dinners for which the day is noted in more civilized communities.

THE MOUNTAIN MAN'S KITCHEN: A GLOSSARY

appalos: camp version of shish kabob, alternating pieces of lean meat and fat on a stick and roasting over a low fire

boudins: sausages made with casings of buffalo intestines

buffalo cider: a liquid found in the stomach of a buffalo, drank as a beverage

bull cheese: buffalo jerky

fizz-pop: an early version of soda pop made by mixing a little vinegar and a spoonful of sugar in a glass of fresh water, then adding about a quarter spoonful of baking soda

fly-blowed meat: rancid meat

gordos: flapjacks

gras: animal fat

grease and beans: food

grease hunger: hungry for meat

hump ribs: the small ribs that support the buffalo's hump

larruping good: fine flavor

lumpy dick: a pudding made of hot milk thickened with flour and served with sweet milk and molasses or sugar

made dog of: made a feast of

meat bag: the human stomach

I N *JOURNAL OF A TRAPPER*, Osborne Russell recorded the events of Christmas 1839, which he spent in an encampment of Snake Indians near the present site of Ogden [Utah]. Russell was lodging with a Frenchman and his Flathead Indian wife and child. The neighboring lodges housed a mixture of Indians of various tribes, and an additional fifteen lodges belonged to Snake Indians. Russell described the Christmas dinner they all ate together:

The first dish was a large tin pan, 18 inches in diameter, rounded full of stewed elk meat. The next dish was similar, heaped with boiled deer meat. The third and fourth dishes were equal in size and contained boiled flour pudding, prepared with dried fruit, accompanied by four quarts of sauce made of the juice of sour berries and sugar. Then came cakes followed by about six gallons of strong coffee already sweetened.

—From *Roadside History of Utah* by Cynthia Larsen Bennett

SIMMERED BEAR PAW.

2 bear paws
cup red wine
flour
garlic
sage, rosemary & cloves
salt and pepper

Roll meat in flour seasoned with salt and pepper. Brown on all sides in a dutch oven in a little bacon grease. Add wine herbs and minced garlic and enough water to reach halfway up the meat as it cooks, cover and bake in moderate oven until tender, turning from time to time.
(Pioneer recipe)

—From *Harper's Monthly Magazine*, June 1869

Christmas Menu
Utah, 1839

Stewed Elk Meat

Boiled Deer Meat

Boiled Flour Pudding with
Dried Fruit and Sour Berry Sauce

Cakes

Strong Coffee, Sweetened

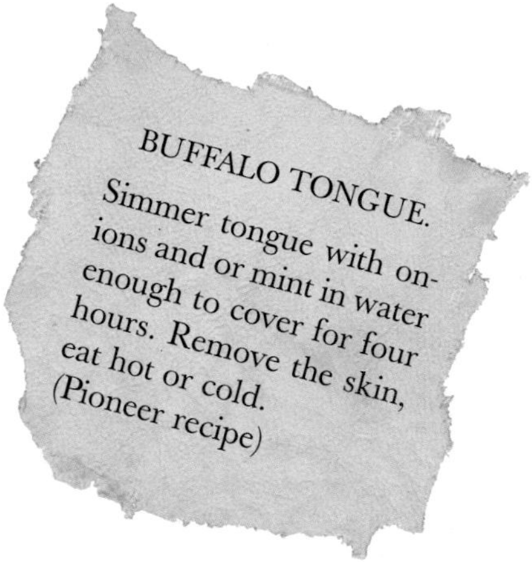

BUFFALO TONGUE.
Simmer tongue with on-
ions and or mint in water
enough to cover for four
hours. Remove the skin,
eat hot or cold.
(Pioneer recipe)

Russell refers to after-dinner discussions concerning political activities, the state of governments among the different tribes, and the characteristics of distinguished warrior chiefs. "Dinner being over," he recorded, "the tobacco pipes were filled and lighted while the squaws and children cleared away the remains of the feast to one side of the lodge where they held a sociable tit-a-tit over the fragments."

A NOTHER MOUNTAIN MAN Christmas party, this one in Taos in 1841, is described in this 1911 story from *Field and Farm*:

DINNER WITH KIT CARSON

A great Christmas dinner was given by and among the few English speaking residents of the Rocky Mountains in the year 1841. . . . O. P. Wiggins, the aged scout and trapper, who still resides in Denver, is credited with having been a participant in that holiday feast and is the sole survivor as far as we have information. . . .

Kit Carson
—Courtesy Taos Historic Museums

SANTA FE GIN COCKTAIL.

Mix 3 oz gin, dash of bitters, 2 dashes maraschino liquer, 2 dashes white vermouth, 2 small ice cubes. Lemon slice for garnish. Stir all ingredients, strain, and serve with lemon slice. (1848)

Some days in advance he sent out runners to invite the guests. When the day arrived great curiosity existed among the entire population of the Taos region. Months before, the trappers had sent a fine season's catch of furs to the Missouri river. In return they had received an unprecedented cargo of the goods of civilization—blankets, gold coin, tobacco and not least a barrel of old Mizzoo whiskey or Taos lightning as the trappers called it on that occasion. Jim Beckwourth, a colored trapper, was the cook who prepared the feast. He entered into the spirit of the occasion, and for days neglected his traps in the interest of the dinner.

Kit Carson's home in Taos, by A. D. Richardson
—From *Frank Leslie's Illustrated Newspaper*, December 8, 1860

Pits were dug and a great variety of meats was prepared in barbecue style—bear meat, buffalo, venison, wild turkey, fat beaver and that marvelous delicacy of the old trappers, fat tails of beaver, sliced and pickled. No bread was served, but the lean meats answered instead. Of buffalo meat only the hump was considered fit for the lords who sat at the first table. The other cuts were relegated to the common Indians

PICKLED MEAT.

For 100 pounds of meat: 8 pounds salt, 4½ gallons water, 10 pounds brown sugar, 1 pound saltpeter, 4 tablespoons baking soda.

Lay meat in salt 24 hours, then soak in fresh water 24 hours, which draws out all the blood. Place in keg and pour above pickling over meat. Keep under a weight.

To prepare pickling, put water in a boiler with the salt, sugar and saltpeter and let boil, stirring often. After it is boiling stir in soda and skim off all the scum off liquid. Let stand overnight before using. (1852)

who thronged the outskirts of the circle in great numbers. In the forenoon an old fashioned shooting match was pulled off by the pioneers. In this competition they shot at a mark with rifles and glasses of booze were the prizes.

Dinner was called at noon. Kit Carson sat at the head of the table. On his right were three Mexican alcaldes. On his left were seated five Indian chiefs, wearing their state uniforms of head dress, paint and feathers. Among the trappers present, tradition mentions Ceran St. Vrain, William Simpson, Jack McGaa, Dick Wooton, Bill Williams, Chamberlain, Wiggins and others. There were many courses, mostly all of meats. The coffee contained genuine sugar and milk. Three hours were spent at the table. The glasses of spirits were voted unusually fine. Cook Beckwourth became intoxicated, after which event the program was less formal. That Christmas day was in all the region about Taos voted the greatest known to that date and Kit Carson the chief over all. The different tribes ate, drank and smoked together and fraternal peace was pledged for at least another year.

The Spirit of Christmas Posts

Forts and Military Camps

THE DICTIONARY'S DEFINITION OF "fort" is "a fortified place or position stationed with troops," but early westerners had a more robust and less restrictive definition. In the West of the 1800s, "fort" referred not just to military posts but to any fortified encampment, including trading posts, stagecoach stations, settlements, even missions. In this chapter, we focus on military forts alone.

In the early nineteenth century, the U.S. Army established forts west of the Mississippi to protect traders. Later outposts had a variety of purposes, serving as watch posts and way stations for emigrants and as guardians for settlers. Toward these goals, concern for the aesthetics and comfort of the structures was secondary. The forts were often makeshift, made of logs or stucco or sod, sometimes jerry-rigged onto existing buildings. Others were almost luxurious.

*Fort Stevenson;
painting by Col.
Phillipe Regis de
Trobriand, 1867*
—Courtesy State Historical
Society of North Dakota

Fort Laramie's Officers' Quarters A (left) were modern and comfortable, while Fort Rawlins's Officers' Quarters were almost primitive. Both forts were in Wyoming Territory. —Fort Laramie, author photo; Fort Rawlins, courtesy National Archives

Forts varied considerably not only in their structure but also in their character, conditions, surroundings, and inhabitants. A surprising number of garrisons housed women and children, mostly officers' families. Other forts were lonely outposts. The types and quality of food and supplies available at any given fort depended largely on its proximity to a town, railroad, or stage line. Larger posts were practically self-sufficient, with their own livestock, gardens, shops, and services. Some soldiers might have fresh meat and vegetables on a regular basis—perhaps even lobster at Christmas—while others had to subsist on mostly beans and jerky every day of the year.

For all their differences, there were considerable similarities among the forts as well. The writings in this chapter remind us that many soldiers stationed at military posts out West passed the holiday on active duty: working, obeying orders, preparing for battle, even fighting. The somber news of felled comrades respects no holiday.

Most forts, though constructed for efficiency rather than comfort, were not miserable wastelands inhabited solely by hardened warriors. For career soldiers, the posts were home to them and their families. At Christmas, army wives and children were all the more appreciated. For the sake of their own families and that of the homesick soldiers, the women made extra efforts to bring Christmas joy and gaiety to the garrison.

Nearly every aspect of life at a fort was subject to army rules, and many of these applied to the wives as well as the soldiers. But once a year, the barriers came down, drink was allowed, and the food was the best that personal funds and local resources could provide. Festivities such as concerts, plays, sleigh rides, and dances were not uncommon, as even mess halls dressed up for the occasion. And most posts, especially if children lived there, had a tree (or a reasonable substitute).

When all is said and done, we find a fort was nothing more or less than a small town, and Christmas was, as in other towns on the frontier, a chance to come together and celebrate.

Families enjoying a warm afternoon at Fort Bridger, Wyoming, circa 1873
—Courtesy National Archives

LIBBY CUSTER, wife of the ill-fated George A. Custer, wrote fondly of Christmases spent at western forts. This reminiscence appeared in *The American West* magazine.

Sometimes I think our Christmas on the Frontier was a greater event to us than to any one in the states. We had to do so much to make it a success.

One universal custom was for all of us to spend all the time we could together. All day long the officers were running in and out of every door, the "wish you Merry Christmas" rang out over the parade ground after any man who was crossing to attend to some duty. . . . We usually had a sleigh ride and everybody sang and laughed as we sped over the country where there were no neighbors to be disturbed by our gaiety. If it was warm enough there poured out of the garrison a

Officers pose before their quarters at Fort Maginnis in Montana.
—Courtesy Mrs. Tom Lefferts and Lewistown Public Library

Elizabeth Bacon Custer
—Courtesy Custer Battlefield Museum

cavalcade vehemently talking, gesticulating, laughing or humming bars of Christmas carols remembered from childhood, or starting some wild or convivial chorus where everybody announced that they "wouldn't go home till morning" in notes very emphatic if not entirely musical.

The feast of the day over, we adjourned from our dinner to play some games of our childhood in order to make the states and our homes seem a little nearer. Later in the evening, when the music came up from the band quarters, we all went to the house of the commanding officer to dance.

With a garrison full of perfectly healthful people with a determination to be merry, notwithstanding the isolated life and utterly dreary surroundings, the holidays were made something to look forward to the whole year round.

Forts closest to the railroads fared best when it came to Christmas goodies, since anything from lobsters to lace could be delivered in fairly short order, sometimes arriving within ten days. Camp Sheridan, Wyoming, was an example, as we see from army wife Fanny Corbuiser's letter home in 1877.

Our Christmas Day and dinner were all that could be desired. We had sent a wagon to the railroad, 162 miles, as we did about once a month, for supplies that we ordered at Grand Isle Neb. There, many articles are quite reasonable—eggs 10c a dozen—butter 15c a pound—chickens 10c a pound—turkeys and ducks 12c. We sent to Chicago for Booths oysters which came in flat tin cans, packed in ice so that the dinner we sat down to was a sumptuous one. . . .

FRIED OYSTERS.

Drain the oysters in a colander. Then put them in a dish of beaten egg, seasoned with pepper and salt. One egg is sufficient for a quart of oysters. Have ready a bowl of sifted cracker crumbs or finely pounded dried breadcrumbs. Take five or six oysters, and with the hand, pat them into a cake, and sprinkle crumbs over them. Fry in butter, taking care that the butter is hot before putting the oysters in the frying pan. When one side is firm, turn with cake turner, and fry the other. (1885)

"Christmas at Fetterman. A brighter or more glorious day never dawned in the south of France than the one now passed: a clear blue sky with a soft haziness in the air equaled only by a June day. The ground, however covered with snow, did not seem in the least to affect the air."

—Ada A. Vodges, wife of Lt. Anthony W. Vodges

Fort Fetterman, 1869
Christmas Menu
Roasted Rabbit, Chicken, Tongue, Chicken Salad
Jellies, Raisins, Sardines, Almonds
Candy, Cake
Coffee, Tea, Wine

CHICKEN SALAD.

Cut one well boiled hen into dice, add an equal quantity of celery cut into small pieces the whites of four boiled eggs chopped rather fine. Mix the ingredients well together, just before the salad is to be made, then serve the dressing with it.

DRESSING.

Yolks of four eggs, one gill of good vinegar (or juice of lemon if that is preferred), one gill of olive oil, one and one half teaspoonfuls of salt, one quarter teaspoonful of cayenne pepper, one large tablespoon of mixed mustard, a little sugar to give a piquant zest to the vinegar. Beat the yolks of four eggs to a light cream, then stir the vinegar into them, beating hard all the time. Stir mixture over the fire until it thickens, then remove, and beat gradually into it the sugar, salt and pepper and oil. Do not fail to beat it well. When very smooth set it upon ice to become well chilled. (Undated recipe)

SOME OF THE MOST ELABORATE holiday celebrations occurred at Fort Laramie, and Christmas 1863 was no exception, as Mrs. Catherine Collins notes in a letter to her fifteen-year-old daughter back home. Mrs. Collins was at the fort visiting her husband, William Collins, then commanding the Eleventh Ohio Volunteer Cavalry, and her son Caspar Collins, who was doing clerical work.

Fort Laramie, Christmas, 1863

My dear Josie,

. . . Having returned from the dinner given by Co D, I thought I might . . . give you an account of the dinner. . . .

The tables, three long ones, accommodated about 75. Mrs. Van Winkle, Mrs. Dr. Smith, Mrs. Captain Love, Mrs. Wright and myself were the ladies present, and the rest of the places were taken up by officers, commissioned and non-commissioned, and guests. They had roast pig, roast beef and cold boiled ham, jellies, pickles, coffee, tea, peaches, cake, mince pie and ice cream. The tables looked very handsomely. I cannot think where they got all their table-cloths, but everything was arranged with taste and judgment. A large cake, nicely iced and a basket of flowers on it with the inscription Co D 11 O.V.C. in large raised letters was much admired. Co D. was pretty much in abeyance only represented by its officers, one of whom a gentleman of intelligence and very superior education. Lieut. Boalt did the honors and did them well, not eating at all but moving from one table to another, and by his bright smile and genial manner doing much to pass off everything well. The little Van winkles were there—and so was Mrs. Wright's baby. As soon as we were fairly through, we moved off and out to give way to others. 8 or ten pleasant young fellows waited on table looking as if they thoroughly enjoyed the success of their entertainment. . . .

While I have been away, John baked the bread that I made up, and has made and is now baking some cake. I hope it will prove good, as we wish some day next week to have a reception or something of the kind. We have another invitation for this evening for cake and egg-nog at Mr. Bullock's. I told Mr. B. I would call and take some cake if he would excuse me about the egg-nogg.

Christmas night—I have been to two entertainments since I wrote the above—the first at Mr. Bullock's. He has a very pretty house, and the parlor is a beautiful though not large room with handsome curtains to the three windows, a beautiful brussels carpet, a few pictures, and other nice furniture. In one corner two very elegant bowls filled with egg-nogg, and two fine cakes, with goblets and small china plates were placed on a circular table. One of the cakes was a superb fruit—the other jelly. Mrs. Van Winkle ladled out the egg-nogg. I cut the cake, and Mr. B— passed it round himself. All the ladies who were at the dinner, with the exception of Mrs. Wright, were there, and Captains Van Winkle, Marshall, Love, Koehne, and Lieutenants Glenn, Reeves Boalt, Brown, Waters and Collins. There were a few songs sung, and I was sorry to have to leave and go to the other supper. However, go we did, and you should have seen the table. It was furnished with the greatest abundance, and our "glorious banner" festooned above it. After supper, your father drank to the health of Sergeant Lewis, a fine looking gentlemanly young fellow who responded in quite a happy little speech. Then Sergeant Blades and Sergeant Cochran were called for, each replying in a short but patriotic manner. They afterwards called for your father, who replied briefly but gracefully to the compliment when we took our leave, as we supposed many of

Fort Laramie, Company D
Christmas Dinner, 1863
Roast Pig, Roast Beef, Cold Boiled Ham
Jellies, Pickles
Peaches, Cake, Mince Pie, Ice Cream
Coffee, Tea

CHRISTMAS CAKE.

Wash one pound and a quarter of butter in water, beat it to a cream; beat ten eggs, yolks and whites separately, half an hour each; have ready a pound and a quarter of flour well dried and kept hot, also three-quarters of a pound of sugar, half an ounce of pounded mixed spice, a pound and a half of currants washed, picked, and dried, a quarter of a pound of almonds blanched and sliced, and four ounces of candied peel, also sliced. Mix all these, and keep them by the fire. Strain the eggs, and mix them with the butter; add to them a teacupful of sweet wine, and a wineglassful of brandy. Then add the dry ingredients by degrees, and a quarter of a pound of chopped raisins. Beat all together for a full hour. Butter a piece of white paper, and line the moulds with it, and fill them about three parts full. Bake in a quick oven two hours. (1868)

the Company were yet to eat. Last night we had a serenade from the Band, who played "Home Sweet Home," "Oft in the Stilly Night." . . . I write by every mail to one or both of you girls and if you should fail to hear from me, once in each week, you may attribute it to storms or snow or some accident detained our mail.

God bless you, my beloved child prays

Yr. Affect. Mother

"Oft in the Stilly Night"

Oft in the stilly night

Ere slumber's chain has bound me,

Fond memory brings the light

Of other days around me.

The smiles, the tears of boyhood's years,

The words of love then spoken,

The eyes that shone, now dimmed and gone,

The cheerful hearts now broken.

When I remember all

The friends so linked together

I've seen around me fall

Like leaves in wintry weather,

I feel like one who treads alone

Some banquet hall deserted,

Whose lights have fled, whose garland's dead,

And all but me departed.

A few weeks later Mrs. Collins sent her daughter a sketch of the fort that Josie's brother had drawn.

Jany 16, 1864

Dear Josie,

I send you a drawing of Ft Laramie done by Casper. It is a very correct one, but does not include the entire post, the Quarter Master and Commissary buildings and stables, which are very extensive being on the right and outside.

—Letters from *An Army Wife Comes West*

Sketch of Fort Laramie by Caspar W. Collins, 1864 —Courtesy Colorado Historical Society

T HIS FREDERIC REMINGTON STORY, which originally appeared in *Harper's*, describes a less luxurious army Christmas.

A MERRY CHRISTMAS IN A SIBLEY TEPEE
By Frederic Remington

"Eat, drink, and be merry, for to-morrow we die." Not a good excuse, but it has been sufficient on many occasions to be true. The soldier on campaign passes life easily. He holds it in no strong grip, and the Merry Christmas evening is as liable to be spent in the saddle in fierce contact with the blizzard as in his cosey tepee with his comrades and his scant cheer. The jug containing the spirits of the occasion may have been gotten from a town fifty miles away on the railroad. It is certainly not the distillation of the summer sunlight, and is probably "tough" enough stuff to mingle naturally with its surroundings; but if one "drinks no more than a sponge" he may not have the jaded, retrospective feeling and the moral mending on the day to come. To sit on a camp chest, and to try and forget that the soldier's quart cup is not filled with best in the market, and then to enter into the full appreciation of the picturesque occasion, is to forget that long marches, "bull meat," and sleepless, freezing nights are in the background. Pleasant hours sit so nicely in their complemental surrounding of hard ones, since everything in the world is relative. As to the eating in a cavalry camp on campaign, it is not overdone, for beans and coffee and bacon and bacon and coffee and beans come round with sufficient regularity to forestall all gormandizing. The drinking is not the prominent feature either, but helps to soften the asperities of a Dakota blizzard which is raging on the other side of the "ducking."

The Sibley tent weaves and moans and tugs frantically at its pegs. The Sibley stove sighs like a furnace while the cruel wind seeks out the holes and crevices. The soldiers sit in their camp drawing-room buttoned up to the chin in their big canvas overcoats, and the muskrat

The toast: "Merry Christmas!"
Illustration by Frederic Remington
—Courtesy 21 Club, New York

caps are not removed. The freemasonry of the army makes strong friend-ships, and soldiers are all good fellows, that being a part of their business. There are just enough exceptions to prove the rule. The cold, bloodless, compound-interest snarler is not in the army, and if he were he would be as cheerless on a damp evening as he would in a fight. One man is from Arizona, another from Washington, and the rest from the other corners of Uncle Sam's tract of land. They have met before, and memory after memory comes up with its laughter and pathos of the old cam-paigns. One by one the "shoulder-straps" crawl in through the hole in the tepee. And, mind you, they do not walk in like a stage hero, with dash and abandon and head in the air; they prostrate themselves like a Turk at prayer, and come crawling. If they raise the flap ever so much, and bring company of the Dakota winds, they are met with a howl of protests. After gaining erectness, they brush the snow from their clothes, borrow a tin cup, and say, "How! how!"

The chief of scouts buttons up to his eyes, and must go look after his "Inguns"; the officer of the day comes in to make his papers, and if he keeps the flying jokes out of his statistics, he does well enough. The second lieutenant, fresh from West Point, doesn't hesitate to address the grizzled colonel of twenty campaigns—nay, he may even deign to advise him on the art of war; but that is unsatisfactory—the advising of colonels—because the colonel's advice to the sub has always to be acted upon, whereas the sub's advice to the colonel is mostly nullified by the

Cavalry troop caught in a blizzard; sketch by
R. F. Zogbaum —From Harper's Weekly, *January 28, 1888*

great powers of discretion which are vested in the superior rank. The life-study of a sub should be to appear like the cuckoo-bird in a German clock—at the proper moment; and when he appears at wrong intervals, he is repaired. Colonels are terrible creatures, with vast powers for promoting happiness or inflicting misery. If he will lend the moderating influence of his presence, it is well; but if he sends his man around to "present his compliments, and say that the d—— row will immediately cease," his wishes if not his personality are generally respected.

It is never a late evening, such a one as this; it's just a few stolen moments from the "demnition grind." The last arrival may be a youngster just in from patrol, who explains that he just "cut the trail of forty or fifty Sioux five miles below, on the crossing of the White River"; and you may hear the bugle, and the bugle may blow quick and often, and if the bugle does mingle its notes with the howling of the blizzard, you will discover that the occasion is not one of merriment. But let us hope that it will not blow.

The toasts go around, and you use your tobacco in a miserly way, because you can't get any more, since only to-day you have offered a dollar for a small plug to a trooper, and he had refused to negotiate, although he had pared off a small piece as a gift, and intimated that generosity could go no further. Then you go to your tepee, half a mile down the creek at the scout camp, and you stumble through the snow-laden willows and face the cutting blast, while the crash and "Halt!" of the sentinel stop you here and there. You pull off your boots and crawl into your blankets quickly before the infernal Sibley stove gives its sigh as the last departing spark goes up the chimney, and leaves the winds and drifting snows to bellow and scream over the wild wastes.

I N SPITE OF A FAIRLY FESTIVE CHRISTMAS at Fort Bridger in 1857, Capt. Jesse Gove of the Tenth Infantry was homesick, as we can see in this letter to his wife in New Hampshire.

Friday December 25

It is Christmas and my thoughts fly to you in Concord. I imagine I see Charlie wishing his Papa a Merry Christmas. Well, today I went up to camp. Called on Colonel Johnston. Several of the officers and myself then started out for calls. Went to Mrs. Canby's, who is living as comfortable as a heart could wish, and on Mrs. Burns, then on Governor Cumming and lady. She is a small pert woman, looks like Miss Retchie, wears spectacles, very agreeable and affable. Comfortable as

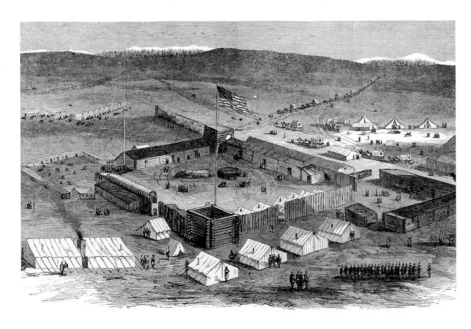

Camp Supply on the Canadian River
—From *Harper's Weekly*, February 27, 1869

Fort Ringgold, Texas, 1886
Christmas Menu

Meat
Turkey, Cranberry Sauce
Venison, Mayonnaise Sauce
Chicken, Roast Pork

Vegetables
Cabbage, Mashed Potatoes, French Peas
Mashed Turnips, Green Corn, Tomatoes

Pastry
Apple Pie, Cranberry Pie, Mince Pie, Lemon Pie

Dessert
Marble Cake, Jelly Cake, Gold Cake, Silver Cake
Oranges, Soft Shell Almonds

GREEN CORN.
Grate the corn from 12 ears of corn, boiled. Beat up five eggs, stir them with the corn, season with salt and pepper and fry the mixture brown. Fry in small cakes with a little flour and milk, stirred in to form a batter. (1860s)

LEMON PIE.
Take three large fresh lemons; grate off the rind; pare off every bit of the white skin of the lemon (as it toughens while cooking); then cut up the lemon into very thin slices with a sharp knife, and take out the seeds; add two cupfuls of sugar, three tablespoonfuls of water, and two of sifted flour. Put into the pie a layer of lemon then one of sugar then one of grated rind, and, lastly of flour, and so on until the ingredients are used; sprinkle the water over all, and cover with upper-crust. Be sure to have the under-crust lap over the upper, and pinch it well, as the syrup will cook all out if care is not taken when finishing the edge of the crust. Bake in moderate oven. This quantity makes one medium size pie. (1837)

could be desired, took some wine, et cetra. All these people have comfortable homes and tents, and in this delightful climate everybody is happy and cheerful. At 4:00 PM, I dined with Captain Dickerson. During the evening the soldiers had a ballet in two large hospital tents. Most of the officers went in and took a glass of wine with the managers. Last night the 10th Infantry and 5th Infantry bands were out all night playing throughout the camp. A Merry and Happy Christmas to you and the dear ones.

—Courtesy Fort Laramie Archives

S OME ARMY POSTS apparently did not celebrate the holiday at all, leaving the soldiers feeling quite forlorn.

Christmas Eve. No Christmas supper for us. Everyone stays in his hut, probably dreaming of past memories that this date recalls. Outside, after a stormy day, the night is clear; the stars twinkle. Inside, the lonely lamp burns until the customary hour of retiring. Nothing marks this night from all the others. And if the calendar did not indicate that today is the twenty fourth of December, no sign in heaven or on earth would reveal to us here that tonight the Christian world is festive. . . .

—Col. Phillipe Regis de Trobriand
Fort Stevenson, Dakota Territory, 1867

Dec. 25, 1868. *. . . . Today is Christmas Day and I have only two hard tacks for my dinner and a quart of bean soup that a hog would not eat if he were starving. This is the kind of a dinner I have to sit down to today, alright. Everything is lovely.*

—Diary of Winfield Scott Haney, Custer's 7th Cavalry

This is Christmas Eve and we lie on our bed and tell what we would likely be doing if we were at home. I told them I would very likely be at some church's Christmas tree and have a good time.

—David L. Spotts, 19th
Volunteer Cavalry, Kansas

An army home —From *Harper's New Monthly Magazine*, June 1869

I N 1871 L T . F AYETTE W. R OE and his wife Frances spent Christmas at Fort Lyon in Colorado Territory. In the following letter to a family member, Mrs. Roe wrote of pleasant holiday visits, laboring over a fruitcake, and the magic of dancing with a man in uniform. She also expressed her frustration at the belated delivery of the much anticipated Christmas box from home.

Our first Christmas on the frontier was ever so pleasant, but it certainly was most vexatious not to have that box from home. And I expect that it has been at [Fort] Kit Carson for days, waiting to be brought down. We had quite a little Christmas without it, however, for a number of things came from the girls, and several women of the garrison sent pretty little gifts to me. It

Christmas tree at a lieutenant's home at Fort Huachuca, Arizona, 1894
—Courtesy Fort Huachuca Museum

was so kind and thoughtful of them to remember that I might be a bit homesick just now. All the little presents were spread out on a table, and in a way to make them present as fine an appearance as possible. Then I printed in large letters on a piece of cardboard, "One box-contents unknown!" and stood it up on the back of the table. I did this to let everyone know that we had not been forgotten by home people. My beautiful new saddle was brought in, also, for although I had had it several weeks, it was really one of Faye's Christmas gifts to me.

Troop & 1st U.S. Cavalry, Fort Custer, Montana
Christmas, 1889

Soup, Oyster, Macaroni, Broiled Prairie Chicken

Roast
Porterhouse Beef, Natural Sauce
Venison, Apple Sauce, Pig
Turkey, Cranberry Sauce
Oyster Dressing

Salads
Lobster, French Slaw, Shrimp

Vegetables
Mashed Potatoes, Stewed Onions
Sugar Corn, Beets
Roasted Potatoes, Stewed Tomatoes

Relishes
Worcestershire Sauce, Chow Chow
French Mustard
Pickled Cucumbers, Pickled Onions

Pastry
Mince Pie, Cranberry Pie, Apple Pie

Dessert
Preserved Peaches, Preserved Pears
Apples, Raisins, Nuts

Tea, Coffee, Chocolate

PRAIRIE CHICKEN.
Cut out all shot, wash thoroughly but quickly, using some soda in the water, rinse and dry, fill with dressing, sew up with cotton thread, and tie down the legs and wings; place in a steamer over hot water till done, remove to a dripping-pan, cover with butter, sprinkle with salt and pepper, dredge with flour, place in the oven and baste with the melted butter until a nice brown. (1876)

MACARONI.
Pour one pint boiling water over five ounces macaroni, let stand half an hour; drain and put in a custard-kettle with boiling milk or milk and water to cover, cook until tender, drain, add a table-spoon butter, and a tea-cup cream, and season with salt and pepper; grate cheese over the top and serve. (1876)

They have such a charming custom in the Army of going along the line Christmas morning and giving each other pleasant greetings and looking at the pretty things everyone has received. This is a rare treat out here, where we are so far from shops and beautiful Christmas displays. We all went to the bachelors' quarters, almost everyone taking over some little remembrance— homemade candy, cakes, or something of that sort.

I had a splendid cake to send over that morning, and I will tell you just what happened to it. At home we always had a large fruit cake made for the holidays, long in advance, and I thought I would have one this year as near like it as possible. But it seemed that the only way to get it was to make it. So, about four weeks ago, I commenced. It was quite an undertaking for me, as I had never done anything of the kind, and perhaps I did not go about it the easiest way, but I knew how it should look when done, and of course I knew precisely how it should taste. Eliza makes delicious every-day cake, but was no assistance whatever with the fruit cake, beyond encouraging me with the assurance that it would not matter in the least if it should be heavy.

Well, for two long, tiresome days I worked over that cake, preparing with my own fingers every bit of the fruit, which I consider was a fine test of perseverance and staying qualities. After the ingredients were all mixed together there seemed to be enough for a whole regiment, so we decided to make two cakes of it. They looked lovely when baked, and just right, and smelled so good, too. I wrapped them in nice white paper that had been wet with brandy, and put them carefully away—one in a stone jar, the other in a tin box—and felt that I had done a remark-ably fine bit of housekeeping. The bachelors have been exceedingly kind to me, and I rejoiced at having a nice cake to send them Christmas morning. But alas I forgot that the little house was fragrant with the odor of spice and fruit, and that there was a man about who was ever on the lookout for good things to eat. It is a shame that those cadets at West Point are so starved. They seem to be simply famished for months after they graduate.

It so happened that there was choir practice that very evening, and that I was at the chapel an hour or so. When I returned, I found the three bachelors sitting around the open fire, smoking, and looking very comfortable indeed. Before I was quite in the room they all stood up

It's likely that Mrs. Roe got her fruitcake ingredients from Denver. This ad is from 1877.

FRUITCAKE.

1 pound butter

1 pound sugar

1 pound flour

1 teaspoon soda

4 pounds raisins

3 pounds currants

1 pound citron

1 pound almonds

1 pound candied cherries

1½ pounds dried figs

1 pound candied pineapple

2 squares chocolate

2 teaspoons cinnamon

1 teaspoon cloves

1 teaspoon mace

1 teaspoon nutmeg

1 gill rosewater

juice of 2 oranges

12 eggs

Bake in a slow oven for three hours. After cooling, wrap in cloth soaked in brandy or bourbon, resoaking when cloth dries out. (late 1800s)

and began to praise the cake. I think Faye was the first to mention it, saying it was a "great success"; then the others said "perfectly delicious," and so on, but at the same time assuring me that a large piece had been left for me.

For one minute I stood still, not in the least grasping their meaning; but finally I suspected mischief, they all looked so serenely contented. So I passed on to the dining room, and there, on the table, was one of the precious cakes—at least what was left of it, the very small piece that had been so generously saved for me. And there were plates with crumbs, and napkins, that told the rest of the sad tale—and there was wine and empty glasses, also. Oh, yes! Their early Christmas had been a fine one. There was nothing for me to say or do—at least not just then—so I went back to the little living-room and forced myself to be halfway pleasant to the four men who were there, each one looking precisely like the cat after it had eaten the canary! The cake was scarcely cold, and must have been horribly sticky—and I remember wondering, as I sat there, which one would need the doctor first, and what the doctor would do if they were all seized with cramps at the same time. But they were not ill—not in the least—which proved that the cake was well baked. If they had discovered the other one, however, there is no telling what might have happened.

At half after ten yesterday the chaplain held service, and the little chapel was crowded—so many of the enlisted men were present. We sang our Christmas music, and received many compliments. Our little choir is really very good. Both General Phillips and Major Pierce have fine voices. One of the infantry sergeants plays the organ now, for it was quite too hard for me to sing and work those old pedals. Once I forgot them entirely, and everybody smiled—even the chaplain!

From the chapel we—that is, the company officers and their wives—went to the company barracks to see the men's dinner tables. When we entered the dining hall we found the entire company standing in two lines, one down each side, every man in his best inspection uniform, and every button shining. With eyes to the front and hands down their sides they looked absurdly like wax figures waiting to be "wound up," and I did want so much to tell the little son of General Phillips to pinch one and make him jump. He would have done it, too, and then put all the blame upon me, without loss of time.

Christmas dinner at Fort Riley, Kansas, in 1904
—Courtesy University of Kansas Libraries

The first sergeant came to meet us, and went around with us. There were three long tables, fairly groaning with things upon them: buffalo, antelope, boiled ham, several kinds of vegetables, pies, cakes, quantities of pickles, dried "apple-duff," and coffee; and in the center of each table, high up, was a huge cake thickly covered with icing. These were the cakes that Mrs. Phillips, Mrs. Barker, and I had sent over that morning. It is the custom in the regiment for the wives of the officers every Christmas to send the enlisted men of their husbands' companies large plum cakes, rich with fruit and sugar. Eliza made the cake I sent over, a fact I made known from its very beginning, to keep it from being devoured by those it was not intended for.

The hall was very prettily decorated with flags and accoutrements, but one missed the greens. There are no evergreen trees here, only cottonwood. Before coming out, General Phillips said a few pleasant words to the men, wishing them a "Merry Christmas" for all of us. Judging from the laughing and shuffling of feet as soon as we got outside, the men were glad to be allowed to relax once more.

At six o'clock Faye and I, Lieutenant Baldwin, and Lieutenant Alden dined with Doctor and Mrs. Wilder. It was a beautiful little dinner, very delicious, and served in the daintiest manner possible. But out here one is never quite sure of what one is eating, for sometimes the most tempting dishes are made of almost nothing. At holiday time, however, it seems that the post trader sends to St. Louis for turkeys, celery, canned oysters, and other things. We have no fresh vegetables here, except potatoes, and have to depend upon canned stores in the commissary for a variety, and our meat consists entirely of beef, except now and then, when we may have a treat to buffalo or antelope.

The commanding officer gave a dancing party Friday evening that was most enjoyable. He is a widower, you know. His house is large, and the rooms of good size, so that dancing was comfortable. The music consisted of one violin with accordion accompaniment. This would seem absurd in the East, but I can assure you that one accordion, when played well by a German, is an orchestra in itself. And Doos plays very well. The girls in the East may have better music to dance by, and polished waxed floors to slip down upon, but they cannot have the excellent partners one has at an army post, and I choose the partners!

The officers are excellent dancers—every one of them—and when you are gliding around, your chin, or perhaps your nose, getting a scratch now and then from a gorgeous gold epaulet, you feel as light as a feather, and imagine yourself with a fairy prince. Of course the officers were in full-dress uniform Friday night, so I know just what I am talking about, scratches and all. Every woman appeared in her finest gown. I wore my nile-green silk, which I am afraid showed off my splendid coat of tan only too well.

The party was given for Dr. and Mrs. Anderson, who are guests of General Bourke for a few days. They are en route to Fort Union, New Mexico. Mrs. Anderson was very handsome in an elegant gown of London-smoke silk. I am to assist Mrs. Phillips in receiving New Years day, and shall wear my pearl colored Irish poplin. We are going out now for a little ride.

—From *Army Letters from an Officer's Wife, 1871–1888* by Frances Roe

D RIVING WAGONS OF SUPPLIES across rough western terrain could be challenging, especially in winter. In this story, friendly Oglala Indians help a party of stranded freighters during the Christmas of 1856. The account appeared in *The Denver Field and Farm* on December 19, 1908, and the narrator was identified as an "old timer now living in Denver."

In 1856 a train of military supplies for the United States government was sent from Fort Leavenworth, Kansas, to Fort Laramie, in the Rocky mountains. It was in early October when we started and winter begun to show itself, while the Cheyenne Indians were hostile on the plains of Nebraska also. It took us two months going from Fort Leavenworth to deliver our supplies to the quartermaster at Fort Laramie. We left our

Montana Winter Scene *by Harvey Thomas Dunn*
—Courtesy Rockwell Museum of Western Art, Corning, New York

oxen and freight wagons there—starting back to Leavenworth with a light two-horse wagon and four extra horses, when we were caught in a terrible blizzard at Ash Hollow, a cannon of hills striking the North Platt valley northwest of the present town of Ogalalla.

The blizzard left the whole country covered with a deep fall of snow which prevented further travel on the land for that winter, leaving our party in a very precarious, exposed and destitute condition, with a prospect of perishing from cold and hunger. We took only enough provisions to last us to Fort Kearney. After the storm the provisions were about used up and the weather was thirty degrees below zero. It happened providentially, however, that we were within but a few miles of chief High Bear's band of Ogalalla Sioux Indians who proved to be quite friendly and with whom we had to stay seven weeks before we could move from there. Then we had to travel for sixteen days 160 miles on the ice bound surface of the Platte.

Indian village in winter —From *Harper's New Monthly Magazine*, June 1869

Christmas day found us in the midst of the Ogalalla Sioux camp with only buffalo meat as our main food and that without any salt to season it with—for there was no salt in the whole Sioux camp. We did however for a time and as a luxury have one very small piece of bread with our morning and evening meal for flour was so scarce and Indian traders could not spare us more than a sack, for which we had to pay $20. We had to make that sack of flour last our whole party nine weeks through that bitter cold weather. Sugar was out of the question as it was fifty cents a pound. So we took our hot coffee straight and was very thankful to get it. Our party of eleven men had only a thin canvas tent to sleep in at night. As soon as we could get to the Indian village, however, through the snowdrifts, we got a little corn meal from the trader and some sugar and made a mush feast for the Indians. Some of them in return for our kindness came together and gave us one of their Indian dances, while some squaws showed their appreciation of our gifts and their good will by sticking up our two wagon sheets into a wigwam.

Thanks to the Indians' kindness, the freighters survived until the weather allowed them to move their wagons out.

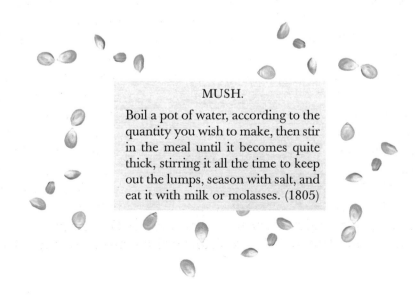

MUSH.

Boil a pot of water, according to the quantity you wish to make, then stir in the meal until it becomes quite thick, stirring it all the time to keep out the lumps, season with salt, and eat it with milk or molasses. (1805)

From the Fort Laramie Historical Society archives comes another story of the rugged and dangerous duty of driving a freight wagon. When the freight is for Christmas, determination can overcome anything Mother Nature dishes out.

The Christmas Wagon, 1882
Or, How I became a Sergeant

By Martin J. Weber, 5th Cav., 1879-84

In December, 1882, I was a Corporal in Troop H, 5th Cav., at Ft. Robinson, Neb. I was ordered on detached service by the Commanding Officer. My orders were to report to the Quartermaster at Fort Sidney, the nearest railroad point, to get the Christmas goods for the Fort. A driver and a six mule team were [also] detailed for the service.

We started about December 10th—a six day journey. The weather was nice clear, sunny days and we arrived at Fort Sidney on time, but was delayed two days owing to the non-arrival of the goods that was coming over the Union Pacific Railroad. They finally arrived the morning of the 18th. We loaded our wagon at once and pulled out for Fort Robinson, one hundred and twenty-five miles to the North. The weather had turned cold and frost began to fly through the air—sure sign of a storm. We made good time that first afternoon, camping just before dark. The next morning the storm broke in all its fury, a regular blizzard raging. We had to face, or head, into the storm. We made Camp Clark, where the Sidney-Black Hills Trail crossed the Platte River. A toll bridge, general store, and post office were being kept at this point. Here we obtained shelter for ourselves, mules and horses. The lady had a hot breakfast and coffee ready for us about day break. The storm had increased during the night. I mailed a report of the storm and that we would try and make the fort if possible, to the Commanding Officer. The bridge tender and his wife advised us to stay until the storm should pass, as they did not think we could make it in such a blizzard. As much as we disliked to leave the snug quarters and hot meals, we were to enjoy for the next four days only a ration of frozen hard bread and bacon, we bid them goodbye and headed into the storm.

Without shelter or fire three days and two nights, when we thought each day would be our last, we traveled over an open country for about eighty miles and had to break trail all the way, it being 30 to 40 degrees below zero. The mules was going home was the only reason we was able to make them face the blizzard. We had plenty of corn and oats for mules and horse, and at night we tied them so the wagon would act as a wind break and covered them with blanket lined covers. We would spread our tent on the snow, roll out our bed and pull part of the tent over us and let the storm howl.

Wagons on snowy Togwotee Trail, Wyoming, circa early 1900s —Courtesy Wyoming State Archives

We got to the stage station on the Running Water after dark the night of the 23rd. Here we had hay for the mules and horse and a good fire and warm place to cook our supper. Boy, how good that coffee tasted! The stage from the Black Hills and Deadwood arrived about 3 a.m., the first in 4 days. The stock tender awakened us about 4 a.m., and had the coffee hot, it gave us new life and courage for the last twenty miles of our journey. The stage had broken the trail to the top of Breakneck Hill, the storm had passed, the sky was clear, and the sun shown brightly and the Valley of the White River lay before us. The Fort was only five miles away. We got safely down Breakneck, crossed the Creek and broke trail across the Valley, arriving at the Fort about 2:30 o'clock the afternoon of the 24th.

I rode ahead to report to the Commanding Officer. When I passed the Officers quarters the kiddies were all out running up and down the

COFFEE.

Pour hot water into your coffee pot, and then stir in your coffee, a spoonful at a time, allowing three to every pint of water; this makes strong coffee. Stir it to prevent the mixture from boiling over, as the coffee swells, and to force it to combine with the water. This will be done after it has boiled gently a few minutes. Then let it stand and boil slowly for half an hour; remove it from the fire, and pour in a tea-cup of cold water, and set it in the corner to settle. As soon as it is clear, it is to be poured, gently, into a clean coffee pot for the table.

Made in this manner it may be kept two or three days in summer, a week in winter; you need only heat it over when wanted. (1841)

A freight wagon braves the snow to deliver goods in Silver City, Idaho.
—Courtesy Idaho State Historical Society

board walks for the first time in five days, having been housed up on account of the storm. When they saw me they began to shout "The Christmas wagon has come!" The officers and men hearing them came out and asked if it was true. They could hardly believe it until the teamster drove his six weary mules up and we began to unload the Christmas goods. Even the officers were willing to help!

So old Santa arrived and there was a Merry Christmas after all had given up hope of seeing the Christmas wagon, or Santa. A rocking horse was one of the presents for one of the youngsters, who is now a Colonel in Washington. I was snow blind and had to wear dark glasses for some time after that trip. . . .

I was promoted to Sergeant and a year later to 1st Sergeant.

A Christmas Tragedy, 1866

MRS. **E**LIZABETH **B**URT, wife of Captain Andrew S. Burt, wrote of Christmas at her home, Fort Laramie, in 1866.

As Christmas approached, for our boy's sake, we made as great an effort as possible to enter into the spirit of the season. We made different kinds of candy. . . . Judge Carter had brought a small supply of gifts in his ox train. . . . The stockings were hung in the wide, open fireplace, down which Santa Claus could descend with ease. My six Sunday School scholars were made happy by home-made candy, ice cream, cookies and doughnuts.

The holiday activities Mrs. Burt described could have occurred at any of the western forts that year. But "The holiday time thus happily begun was of short duration, for . . . we began to hear mysterious rumors of a fight that had taken place near Fort Phil Kearny. . . ."

Fort Phil Kearny, 236 miles northwest of Fort Laramie, had been built that summer to guard travelers on the Bozeman Trail from Indian attacks. The wagon road ran right through Sioux lands, angering the Indians into action.

Old Fort Kearny by William Henry Jackson
—Courtesy Scotts Bluff National Monument

Sioux leader Red Cloud promised to destroy the trail; the government vowed to keep it open. The situation was doomed to erupt. On December 21, Captain William Fetterman, boasting he could wipe out the entire Sioux nation with eighty men, rode out from Fort Phil Kearny with that number of soldiers to check on a work party that had not returned. Two thousand Sioux, led by Red Cloud, Crazy Horse, and others, proved the brazen young captain wrong. None of Fetterman's command survived.

When people back at the fort realized what had happened, they were not only shocked, but nervous; if the large warrior force attacked again, they were vulnerable. The fort needed reinforcements immediately—but the nearest help was at Fort Laramie, many bitterly cold, snowy miles away. The commander of the fort, Colonel Henry Carrington, hired two civilians, John "Portugee"

John "Portugee" Phillips at Horseshoe Station; drawing by M. D. Houghton
—Courtesy Wyoming State Museum

Phillips and Daniel Dixon, to go. John Phillips—of Portuguese descent, hence the moniker—was an employee of the quartermaster. For reasons we don't know, Dixon traveled part of the way with Phillips, but didn't complete the trip.

No one knew whether the Sioux were still in the area, or whether the messengers would make it. Earlier parties had been killed. That night, Colonel Carrington walked Phillips to the gate, and sent him off saying, "May God help you."

Legends about Portugee Phillips's ride abound. Some say Phillips rode the same horse all the way to Laramie, and that the horse dropped dead upon arrival. Another story has it that Phillips took Colonel Carrington's own thoroughbred, Grey Eagle. More likely, Phillips changed mounts when he stopped to rest, once at Fort Reno, and again at Horseshoe Station, near present-day Glendo, Wyoming, where he sent his news ahead by telegraph.

Only four days and nights after leaving Fort Phil Kearny, on Christmas night, Phillips entered a party in Old Bedlam, the officers' quarters at Laramie. The incredible ride made Phillips a Wyoming hero. Captain David Gordon wrote of Phillips's arrival:

It was Christmas night 11 P.M. . . . A full dress garrison ball was progressing, and everybody appeared superlatively happy, enjoying the dance, notwithstanding the snow was from ten to fifteen inches deep on level, and the thermometer registered twenty-five degrees below zero, when a huge form, dressed in buffalo overcoat, pants, gauntlets and cap, accompanied by an orderly, desired to see the commanding officer. The dress of the man, and at this hour looking for the commanding officer, made a deep impression upon the officers and others that happened to get a glimpse of him . . . dropping into our full-dress garrison ball at this unseasonable hour.

After the news came, Mrs. Burt wrote,

In our fear we [had] little realized the actual truth, so when the official report arrived we were only partially prepared for the heartbreaking news—Captain William J. Fetterman, Captain Frederick Brown, 18th Infantry, Lieutenant George W. Grummond, 2nd Cavalry, and 78 men massacred near Fort Phil Kearny on December 21st; this was a shock that reached the very soul of comradeship and from which it seemed we could not recover. These were among the friends from whom we had parted on the Platte River the previous June when they separated from us to go with Colonel Carrington to build Fort Phil Kearny in what is now Wyoming. Little did we imagine the horrible fate awaiting them when we said goodbye that peaceful June evening.

Back at Phil Kearny, Margaret Carrington, wife of Colonel Carrington, and others at the fort passed an anxious and sober Christmas while waiting for the reinforcements to arrive—which they finally did in mid-January.

The holidays were as sad as they were cold. Lights burned in all quarters, and one non-commissioned officer was always on duty in each building, so that in case of alarm, there could not be an instant's delay in the use of the whole command. The whole garrison shared the gloom. Charades, tableaus, Shakespearian readings . . . and all the social reunions that had been anticipated were dropped as unseasonable and almost unholy.

—Quotes from Fort Laramie Archives

I Won't Be Home for Christmas

Yuletide in the Middle of Nowhere

THERE IS SOMETHING ABOUT the boundless western sky that makes you feel you've reached the top of the earth and have been swallowed up by God. But glorious as it is, for the homesick, that vast expanse of color can highlight a lonesome heart.

For many, Christmas is about home and family, so it's natural to pause and reflect on joys or hardships of the present, on memories of the past, and on dreams of the future. Such reflections hit harder and deeper "in the middle of nowhere"—when nothing is familiar and survival itself may be difficult.

In the Old West, there was movement everywhere: miners, cowboys, railroad men; settlers relocating for a chance at a better life; young people drawn by dime-store novel images; even outlaws looking for a new hideout. Among non-Indians, men outnumbered women. Although entire families came West, it was also common for men to go first, alone, and ready a home. Many men also arrived as bachelors—and stayed that way.

Some of the people whose stories appear in this chapter have chosen to be where they are and to forego family and home. For them, the holiday may give way to a moment of regret. Others have found themselves stranded at Christmastime due to circumstances outside their control. Many of the people here were visited by memories—of Christmases past, full of comfort, security, and love. For some, these memories were their best—sometimes their only—Christmas gift.

In all these writings, people paused on Christmas Day and thought about it—if only to "wonder," as Charles Russell writes, "what day is today." Most, with very little to work with, found some way to celebrate; privation and difficult circumstances only made the day more meaningful. They may have prepared some special food, reread letters from home, or decorated an evergreen bough or a cottonwood, often banding together with others to make the day brighter. By celebrating Christmas, they transcended, at least for a time, the strangeness of their surroundings. Far from home, they found home within themselves. Christmas reminded them of aspects of being human that were easy to forget in adversity, in rough company, or in an unfamiliar place. Most emerged with spirits refreshed—ready to keep on going.

—Paul Klieben drawing, courtesy Knotts Berry Farm

IT WAS ALREADY late September when the Sand Company of emigrants departed Provo, Utah, and headed south on the Old Spanish Trail to Los Angeles. Although this route had the advantages of having no threat of snow and no major mountain ranges to cross, it also had little water or grass. The journey was to have taken nine weeks, but after five, the company had traveled only one-third of the way.

—From *Harper's Weekly,* April 4, 1874

On November 4, the emigrants met up with a company of bachelors, calling themselves the Jayhawkers, headed west on the Walker Cutoff. The Jayhawkers claimed the cutoff would save them hundreds of miles. Ninety-eight of the Sand

Company's 105 wagons opted to take the new trail, but within four days, seventy-five had returned to the Old Spanish Trail, and under the guidance of their original captain arrived in Los Angeles seven weeks later. By December 2, only one family, the Briers, remained with the Jayhawkers on the Walker Cutoff. Christmas found the party tortuously plodding through Death Valley. Mrs. Julia Brier's recollection of that fateful holiday appeared in the *San Francisco Call* on December 25, 1898.

First Christmas in Death Valley

I don't know how to tell you about our struggle through Death Valley in 1849 and the Christmas we spent amid its horrors. . . . I was the only woman in the party—Mr. Brier, our three boys, Columbus, John and Kirk, the oldest being nine years, and two young men, John and Patrick, made up "our mess," as we called it.

We reached the top of the divide between Death and Ash valleys, and oh, what a desolate country we looked down into. The next morning we started down. The men said they could see what looked like springs out in the valley. Mr. Brier was always ahead to explore and find water, so I left with our three boys to help bring up the cattle. We expected to reach the springs in a few hours and the men pushed ahead. I was sick and weary, and the hope of a good camping place was all that kept me up. Poor little Kirk gave out and I carried him on my back, barely seeing where I was going, until he would say, "Mother, I can walk now." Poor little fellow! He would stumble on a little way over the salty marsh and sink down, crying, "I can't go any farther." Then I would carry him again, and soothe him as best I could.

Many times I felt I should faint, and as my strength departed I would sink on my knees. The boys would ask for water, but there was not a drop. Thus we staggered on over many salty wastes, trying to keep the company in view and hoping at every step to come to the springs. Oh, such a day! If we had stopped I know the men would come back at night for us, but I didn't want to be thought a drag or hindrance.

Night came down and we lost all track of those ahead. I would get down on my knees and look in the starlight for the ox tracks and then we could stumble on. There was not a sound and I didn't know whether we would ever reach camp or not.

—From *Harper's New Monthly Magazine*, October 1874

About midnight we came around a big rock and there was my husband at a small fire.

"Is this camp?" I asked.

"No, it's six miles farther," he said.

I was ready to drop and Kirk was almost unconscious, moaning for a drink. Mr. Brier took him on his back and hastened to camp to save his little life. It was 3 o'clock Christmas morning when we reached the springs. I only wanted to sleep, but my husband said I must eat and drink or I would never wake up. Oh, such a horrible day and night.

We found hot and cold springs there and washed and scrubbed and rested.

That was a Christmas none could ever forget.

Music or singing? My no. We were too far gone for that. Nobody spoke much, but I knew we were all thinking of home back East and all the cheer and good things there. Men would sit looking into the fire or stand gazing away silently over the mountains, and it was easy to read their thoughts. Poor fellows! Having no other woman there I felt lonesome at times, but I was glad too, that no other was there to suffer.

The men killed an ox and we had Christmas dinner of fresh meat, black coffee and very little bread. I had one small biscuit. You see, we were on short rations then and didn't know how long we would have to make provisions last. We did not know we were in California. Nobody knew what untold misery the morrow might bring, so there was no occasion for cheer.

Fred Carr said to me that night, "Don't you think you and the children had better remain here and let us send back for you?"

—From *Harper's New Monthly Magazine*, October 1874

I knew what was on his mind. "No," I said, "I have never been a hindrance, I have never kept the company waiting, neither have my children, and every step I take will be toward California."

Then I was troubled no more. As the men gathered around the blazing campfire they asked Mr. Brier to speak to them—remind them of home—though they were thinking of home fast enough anyway. So he made them a speech. It was a solemn gathering in a strange place.

So ended, I believe, the first Christmas ever celebrated in Death Valley.

IN ANOTHER, more notorious story of a shortcut regretted, the Donner-Reed Party of twenty wagons spent Christmas of 1846 snowbound in the Sierra Nevada. Out of the eighty-one souls who started out on the Hastings Cutoff, only forty-six would survive the winter. Virginia Reed Murphy, age thirteen at the time of the tragedy, described her family's harrowing experience in *The Century Illustrated Magazine*, July 1891.

The Donners were camped in Alder creek valley below the lake, and were, if possible, in a worse condition than ourselves. The snow came on so suddenly that they had no time to build cabins, but hastily put up brush sheds, covering them with pine boughs. Three double cabins were built at Donner Lake, which were known as the Breen Cabin, the Murphy Cabin, and the Reed-Graves Cabin. The cattle were all killed, and the meat was placed in snow for preservation. My mother had no cattle to kill, but she made arrangements for some, promising to give two for one in California. Stanton and the Indians made their home in my mother's cabin. . . .

The misery endured during those four months at Donner Lake in our little dark cabins under the snow would fill pages and make the coldest heart ache. Christmas was near, but to the starving its memory gave no comfort. It came and passed without observance, but my mother had determined weeks before that her children should have a treat on this one day. She had laid away a few dried apples, some beans, a bit of tripe, and a small piece

—From *Harper's New Monthly Magazine*, June 1869

of bacon. When this hoarded store was brought out, the delight of the little ones knew no bounds. The cooking was watched carefully, and when we sat down to our Christmas dinner mother said, "Children, eat slowly, for this one day you can have all you wish." So bitter was the misery relieved by that one bright day, that I have never since sat down to a Christmas dinner without my thoughts going back to Donner Lake.

A LESS GRUESOME TALE of a snowbound Christmas occurred in 1859, when a party of Iowa missionaries, traveling with a military expedition, miscalculated the extent of their journey and became temporarily stranded on Deer Creek in present day Wyoming (then part of Nebraska Territory). Not willing to allow this unexpected stoppage to ruin their holiday, they brought a pine from the bluffs four miles away and dressed it with all the adornments they had carried with them for their first Christmas tree, not knowing it would be in the wilderness of the Big Horn Basin. Here is one member's account of this modest celebration:

At 7 o'clock in the evening everything was ready. But we thought we were to be disappointed as our invited guests, Major Twiss and family and Dejer and his people, had already gone to bed. However, Reverend Braeuninger went to one of the members of the expedition and as a result brought with him several Indians and children as well as members of the expedition. They were all exceedingly glad when they saw the tree with its decorations. One man, a lieutenant, stated again and again as his confession of faith, "Glory to God in the highest, and on earth peace, good will toward men."

Really it was a great joy to me to see the man thus. Then we sang *"Von Himmel Hock da Komm ich Her."* Missionary Braeuninger read the Christmas gospel in German and Captain Raynolds read it in English. These two men also played several selections. Reverend Braeuninger played the violin and Captain Raynolds the flute.

Next we distributed gifts from the first Christmas tree in the territory of Nebraska. The lieutenant, already referred to, who spoke the language of the Indians very well, told the Indians that these gifts were from the Great Spirit and that these missionaries were sent by Him. One of the Indian squaws, in a most naïve manner, asked why the Great Spirit, while he was at it, did not send full sacks of sugar and flour. Why such small amounts? Finally, we gave the Indians some bread and coffee and then dismissed the assembly. . . .

On the evening of Christmas Day, various members of the expedition came in. They sang in the English language while we sang in German. . . . Everyone had a good time and enjoyed himself.

—Courtesy Wyoming State Archives

MUTTON.
To roast mutton, make a brisk fire, and allow fifteen or twenty minutes to the pound. Paper the fat parts. Baste and froth it the same as beef. (1841)

Granville Stuart's First Christmas
in Montana, 1857
Menu
Roast mountain mutton
Black coffee
Sourdough bread

Stuart was an early Montana prospector and one of the region's first white settlers.

SOURDOUGH STARTER.
Take 4 cups water in which potatoes have been boiled. Add 4 cups flour, 2 teaspoons salt, and 2 teaspoons sugar. Mix well and put in crock, cover. Let stand several days in a warm place until fermented. (Undated recipe)

Camp by the Yellowstone River, 1871; photo by William Henry Jackson
—Courtesy U.S. Geological Survey

IN 1857 PRESIDENT JAMES BUCHANAN appointed Alfred Cumming to replace Brigham Young as governor of Utah. Cumming and his wife, Elizabeth, joined General Johnston on the "Utah Expedition" traveling from the Missouri River to the Salt Lake Valley. With winter coming on, the party decided to set up camp on Black's Fork of the Green River near Fort Bridger, in present-day Wyoming. The governor and Mrs. Cumming occupied five tent "rooms." The following is from a letter Mrs. Cumming wrote to her sister-in-law:

January 3, 1858

I told you, I know, of our restrictions in food, but I did not add, as I intended, that everybody has as much to eat as they wish, though perhaps they would like a little more variety. On New Year's Eve a thousand pounds of salt arrived here from Fort Laramie, and two thousand more were sent, but from loss of animals and the usual winter troubles here being "snowed up," et cetera, the rest will not get here for some time. The want of salt was the great want in food. Its arrival was a great relief. I received company on Christmas and New Year's Day. Having brought wines, et cetera, with us we were obliged to purchase very little, fortunately. Did I tell you of the enormous prices asked for all articles in their stores by the sutlers and the "impudent traders" who are "forced" here with all their merchandise intended for the Salt Lake cities? I had two silver cake baskets with me, as they add so much to the appearance of a table; I thought of something to put in them, and sent to the store (said to be reasonable in its charges as any here) for enough almonds and raisins to fill the two baskets. They cost eight dollars. I had two cakes baked also. Imagine cakes without butter, eggs, milk, or "rising" of any kind, and yet they were tolerable. By cutting them from side to side, and boiling some "fresh raspberries" which I had in a can, with a very little sugar, and spreading them so that they might "soak" all night, I had a tolerable kind of jelly cake. I had quite a good looking table.

—Courtesy Fort Laramie Historical Society

PORK CAKE.

A delightful cake is made by the use of pork, which saves the expense of butter, eggs and milk.

Fat, salt pork, entirely free of lean or rind, chopped so fine as to be almost like lard, 1 pound;

pour boiling water upon it, ½ pint;

raisins seeded and chopped, 1 pound;

citron shaved into shreds, ¼ pound;

sugar, 2 cups;

molasses, 1 cup;

saleratus, 1 teaspoon rubbed fine and put in the molasses.

Mix all these together, and stir in sifted flour to make the consistancy of common cake mixtures, then stir in nutmeg and cloves, finely ground 1 ounce each; be governed about the time of baking it by putting a sliver into it—when nothing adheres it is done. It should bake slowly. (1866)

Mountain man James Clyman kept a journal off and on throughout his life. In the summer of 1844, he joined an emigrant party to Oregon, probably as a guide, and he spent that Christmas camping along the Willamette River in Oregon. In 1845 Christmas Day found him on a bear hunt in California. His entries for December 25 for those years mention the holiday but record no special observance of it.

25 [1844] A Blustering windy rainy night succeded our Christmas and the morning was of the same meterial rain hail and snow with the usual accompaniment a strong South west wind the hills whitened again with snow. . . .

25 December 1845 Chistmas it rained all night the morning thick and foggy with several short Rapid showers. . . .

The famous frontier photographer and artist William Henry Jackson spent Christmas 1866 on a wagon train to California. The party traveled that day the same as usual, but they did have a small celebration in the evening.

Salt Lake Valley *by William Henry Jackson*
—Courtesy Scotts Bluff National Monument

Tues. 25th. Christmas. Got a good start and travelled finely. Roads very good. . . . Walked nearly the entire day. . . . Reached Goshen [Pleasant Grove, Utah] about sunset. . . . Drove through the streets and corralled at the edge of town. Found one store in the place. Was locked up. Roused the wife of the proprietor, and finally obtained what we wished. Bill & I got a dozen of eggs. No wood to be obtained except by buying. Struck a bargain with a fellow for a dollar's worth & he gave us as much dry cedar as five of us could carry. . . . Had a fine time during the evening singing, dancing & general joking. Remained about the fire until near 10 o'clock.

81

AMONG THE FORTY-NINERS headed to California were Mormon groups seeking gold to help fund their new communities. The Flake-Rich Company was a Mormon pack train traveling from Provo, Utah, to the California gold mines from October to December 1849. One of the party, Henry W. Bigler, was "called" to California "to get gold for Father John Smith." Bigler kept a journal during the trip.

Sunday 23d warm and growing wether. I am unwell haveing a cold. Washed my shirt and garment. Some talk of Christmas.

TO ROAST WILD DUCKS OR TEAL.

When the Ducks are ready dressed, put in them a small Onion, Pepper, Salt, and a Spoonful of red Wine; if the Fire be good, they will roast in twenty Minutes; make Gravy of the Necks and Gizzards, a Spoonful of red Wine, half an Anchovy, a Blade or two of Mace, one Onion, and a little Cayenne Pepper; boil it till it is wasted to half a Pint, strain it through a hair Sieve, and pour it on the Ducks—serve them up with Onion Sauce in a Boat; garnish the Dish with Raspings of Bread. (1831)

Mo. 24th I was hunting for Bro. Whittles horse today, in the evening Bro. Pratt came in from hunting, brought in 2 ducks & 1 Curlew for Christmas, a bulock is also drest and Cooks appointed to Cook a Christmas dinner.

Tu. 25th Clear & warm growing wether, the earth is green with grass and wild oats, & had an excellent dinner Considering the materials they had to make it of. plenty of roast beef and potatoes, Baked ducks and plum pooding. as for myself I did not enjoy myself well haveing a pane in my left eye. . . .

WITH NOTHING but a piece of canvas for a home, a broken branch for a tree, and a few pennies' worth of gold dust to buy a Christmas treat, two young brothers created a celebration where others might have seen only despair. Their simple holiday is a profound example of the nurturing and uplifting spirit of Christmas.

FROM BROOKLYN TO CALIFORNIA

We took the overland route to the west, starting early in 1849. It took us nine months to make the trip and, young as I was at the time, the terrible sufferings and privations we endured have never been effaced from my mind.

At Independence, Mo., my father was made captain of a train of 75 immigrants. . . . Our family had one wagon, a prairie schooner . . . and a yoke of oxen. It was slow, difficult traveling and for weeks we plodded on into a world that was a brown, flat plate under an inverted blue cup.

The train broke up as we advanced, and when we had crossed the Rockies and were struggling into the terrors of the great American desert we were alone. Misfortune swept upon us when we had covered part of that hopeless stretch. Our water was nearly gone and our cattle had died. . . . My brother and myself were strong and well able to do our share, but mother and little sister grew weaker.

Day by day we threw away our possessions to enable us to make the distance we must make or perish. . . . Shortly my sister died. I have never been able to identify the spot.

December found us established on our first claim. The nearest settlement was Bidwell's Bar, though that was nothing more than two or three tents, and the nearest town was Marysville, 90 miles away. We had no neighbors and my mother was the only woman for many miles around in that wilderness. With our depleted supplies we were in a bad way. A sheet of canvas stretched on piles served us for a house. It did little but keep the full sweep of the rain from finding us. Furniture we had none, nor beds. We slept on the ground wrapped in our ragged blankets. By day my father, my brother and myself worked at pacer mining on the Upper Feather River.

My mother never recovered from the effects of the trip across the desert. . . . Toward the middle of the month, my father too, fell ill. His trouble was scurvy, due to the wretched food, which was all we could procure. We had managed to get a horse and my brother rode to Marysville where he brought some potatoes at $2.00 a pound and about a gill of vinegar. We scraped the potatoes and soaked the scrapings in vinegar. With this we saved my father's life.

As Christmas approached we two youngsters fell to making plans. Brought up, as all Germans are, to regard Christmas as the great fete of the year, we could not quite forgo observing it, though there was little to rejoice in. We had saved a small quantity of gold dust as our share of the mining operations and we were determined to spend it in celebrating.

Two days before Christmas, my father then being some-what better, my brother and I mounted the horse and started for Marysville, riding foremost by turns. We followed the trail down the river and reached the town worn and tired, but happy for a time in the sound of new voices, the sight of men and dwellings and the thought that we might

This ad for a general store in 1877 Greeley, Colorado, shows the types of supplies available in frontier mining towns.
—From the *Greeley Tribune*, December 19, 1877

CHRISTMAS GIFT

AND

NEW YEAR'S GREETING TO ALL

Eight and one-half lbs A. sugar	$1.00	Sixteen bars White Velvet Soap,	$1.00
Eight lbs granulated sugar,	1.00	Thirteen lbs. Silver Brick Soap	1.00
Nine " light C sugar,	1.00	One pound choice Japanese Tea, formerly $1,	75 cents
Eleven " good dried apples.	1.00	One pound good Japanese tea " 70c	50 cents
Eight " choice " "	1.00	Eight pounds Cranberries	1.00
Eight " choice blackberries	1.00	Good Hams	13 cts
Seven " choice Salt Lake peaches	1.00	Four pounds choice Coffee	1.00
Five " ch ice peeled peaches	1.00	Four and one-half pounds good Coffee	1.00
Five " choice apricots	1.00	Six Cans choice Peaches	1.00
Four and one-half pounds choice plums	1.00	Seven Cans choice Tomatoes	1.00
Eight pounds choice prunes	1.00	Seven Cans " Oysters	1.00
Ten pounds " currants	1.00	Seven Cans Lye	25 cents
Eight pounds " raisins	1.00	One pound assorted Nuts	25 cents
Seventeen pounds Buckwheat Flour	1.00	One Pound good Candies	

And Everything in the same Proportion.

THESE PRICES ARE STRICTLY FOR CASH UNTIL JANUARY 1st.

My entire stock will be sold

AT SUCH EXTREMELY LOW PRICES

That Everybody will be enabled to make

Seventy-five cents go as far as One Dollar at any other Store

A. Z. SALOMON.

purchase some few articles in the store. It took us a long time to make our selection. We had enough for a gift for each one of us.

"What do you see that would make a welcome gift for the father and the mother?" my brother asked me. I looked over the few shelves of goods hopefully. There were small calicos and some colored 'kerchiefs' that I thought mother might like . . . if she would . . . live to wear them. I saw a bright, sharp hunting knife that I wished I might get for my father, but it seemed scarcely the thing to give a sick man. It seemed to me that nothing would be so welcome to them as some delicacy that would break the monotony of the bad food, the soggy flapjacks and salt meat.

"Let us buy something good to eat," I said, and we turned to the provisions. We hesitated over a box of sardines and some smoked herring, until it occurred to us that what we wanted was a still rarer and more tempting dish. Jacob reached over and picked up an object with a glaring label.

"Hermann," he cried. "Look at this. Canned peaches! Could anything be so delicious? Let us take the peaches."

I agreed and we found that the storekeeper would let us have the peaches for the sum we had brought with us. He had but one can and regarded it as the most desirable thing in his stock.

After carefully wrapping up our prize and tying it firmly to Jacob's belt we mounted our horse and started back. When dawn was breaking on Christmas morning we reached our camp by the river.

Our parents lying on their blankets answered our wishes of a "Merry Christmas" as cheerfully as they could. We kissed each other tenderly and talked for many hours of the former happy Christmas days we had spent back in our Brooklyn home. Jacob had brought with him a branch of pine which he had plucked on our homeward journey and he set this up in the earth that formed our floor.

"It's our Christmas tree," he said, and our good mother and father smiled through their tears. We found some bits of ribbon and cloth and all the little trinkets we had retained. With these my brother and I dressed our poor tree and we sat before it, trying to think that it was glorious, all covered with brilliant baubles, and loaded with sweets and packets of good things.

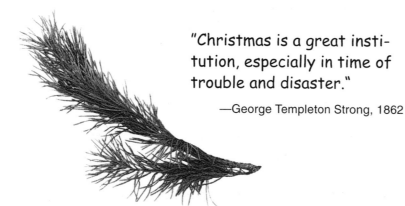

"Christmas is a great institution, especially in time of trouble and disaster."

—George Templeton Strong, 1862

FRIED BISCUITS.
Take a little flour and water and make some dough and roll it thin, cut it into square blocks, then take some beef fat and fry them. (1836)

"What did you get in Marysville?" my father asked. But we only nudged each other mysteriously and would not tell. That was to be the big surprise, and the feast that should make us all believe that we were back in the pleasant land of plenty. We set about preparing the Christmas dinner with great secrecy and care. Jacob fried the flapjacks and made coffee. I mixed flour and water for the biscuits. We had not known salt since our arrival and we used a substitute, which was commonly adopted among the forty-niners, gunpowder. It gave some savor to the food, though I should scarcely recommend it as a condiment.

When everything was in readiness we set out an empty box between the pallets on which our parents lay. This was the table. We had two pails, which served well enough for chairs for Jacob and myself. We brought in the hot meal on tin plates and arranged everything neatly where father and mother could reach without getting up. We both left the tent and ran to where we had hidden the peaches. We opened the can with a knife and Jacob, as the elder, had the honor of carrying it in.

We came in procession, Jacob leading and bearing the peaches like a butler bringing in the wassail bowl, I following. Jacob placed the can on the box with great dignity and looked at father and mother for applause. And then we had our crushing disappointment.

—Courtesy Larry Eick

Neither of them could touch the delicacy. Nor could either taste the meal, which we had arranged with so much pride. We both cried a little, but our mother comforted us and told us that we should eat the share for them.

So we sat down and ate the peaches.

I am afraid that most of the flapjacks and biscuits were wasted.

Our hunger and the rare treat before us made us forget the sorrow of the futile gift and we ate until not even a trace of syrup was left inside the can.

That was Christmas in California in '49. It was a time when we were close to bitterness and pain. . . . Many happy Christmas days I have passed since then, but always there comes a moment, when my children and my grandchildren are about me, when I remember our sad celebration under the canvas roof on the banks of the Upper Feather River.

—The recollections of Hermann Scharmann, from the *San Francisco Call,* December 25, 1909

IN DECEMBER **1852** Myer Newmark, age fourteen, sailed with his mother and five siblings on a clipper ship from New York to San Francisco, where they were to join his father. The family spent Christmas, not unhappily, at sea.

Saturday December 25th

Christmas Day. It is a beautiful day. . . . The sea and the sky are a most beautiful blue, and everything looks happy, merry and cheerful. We all did justice to the dainty dinner set before us, which consisted of roast & Boiled fowl, vegetables, plum pudding and apple sauce, fruits & cider.

—From *Harper's New Monthly Magazine*, July 1874

ENGLISH PLUM PUDDING.

Half a pound of beef suet,
Half a pound of flour,
Eight ounces of raisins,
Eight ounces of currants,
Two ounces of citron,
One nutmeg grated,
Two apples,
Half a pound of sugar,
A wineglass of rum,
Six eggs.

Remove the skin from the suet and chop it very fine, adding the flour until both are thoroughly mixed together; then the raisins seeded, and currants which have been carefully washed and picked. Cut the citron in pieces, have the apples chopped fine, and add sugar, nutmeg, and eggs well beaten. Mix all well together, and then put into a buttered mould, which place in a saucepan which you have filled with water the height of your mould, and simmer gently six hours, then turn your pudding out of the mould and serve, pouring the rum over it and set it on fire. (1886)

IN THE 1870s, Routt County, in northwestern Colorado, just west of the Continental Divide was quite isolated. In December 1916 the *Routt County Sentinel* asked its readers to recount their first Christmas in the area. In this story, four trappers set up camp by the Bear (Elk) River and spent the Christmas of 1874 with a dinner of porcupine stew.

MY FIRST CHRISTMAS IN ROUTT COUNTY
By Tom Iles

I shall begin my story in December of 1874. According to my journal kept in those days, there were then living on the bear river, between the Gore range and the Utah line, the lucky number of just thirteen souls, whose names were as follows: Joe Morgan, keeper of an Indian trading post; Johnny Tow, an old trapper; Albert Smart, founder of the Hayden Colony; Mrs. Smart, his wife; Gordie Smart, brother of Albert; Frank Gonson, employed by the Smarts; Homer Pollock, a prospective settler; Jim Pollock, brother of Homer; George Schlosser and Frank Mann, in partnership with the Pollocks; John Spitzenberger, trapper and guide; John Newton, partner of the writer; and Tom Iles, the writer.

Wednesday Dec 23—Today I packed my new pony and started with Newton, Jim Pollock and George Schlosser on a trapping exposition up the river. We made about four miles, camping for the night at the present location of the Mount Harris coal mines.

Thursday Dec 24—We packed up again and started after having a lively time shooting grouse from the cottonwoods near our camp. We arrived at Elk river about noon, going in to camp about a mile above the mouth of that stream. Set out a few traps for fox and coyotes, then I killed and dressed two nice fat porcupines for our Christmas dinner.

We sat up late that night, talking of our Christmas Eve in comparison with the mirth and joy of years gone by, surrounded by father, mother, brothers and sisters, in eager anticipation of the visit from Santa Claus. We realized, however, that good old Santa would scarcely be able to find us that night.

—From *Harper's New Monthly Magazine*, May 1862

With visions of home and mother fresh in memory, one by one the voices ceased to respond, then I realized that I alone was awake. I had no desire to sleep. I was wondering "Why am I here this cold winter night?" I had left a home of comfort, with kind, loving, and indulgent parents, brothers and sisters. It was not through necessity—it was my voluntary choice. But why? I communed with the stars, and they told me not to ask why. It was the life I felt; that life was irresistible; the life that compelled me—the adventurous spirit of the Pioneer. Gazing long and earnestly at those stars in deepest meditation, slowly my eyelids closed on this, my first Christmas Eve on Bear river, then all was sweet oblivion.

Then–Pop!! went a rifle shot very close to us. Every sleeper was awakened and sprang from his bed with rifle in hand, ready for any emergency.

Pop! Pop! Again and again, we were mystified, till George Schlosser solved it for us. Taking a long stick, he reached over and removed a loaded cartridge belt from the burning log and cast it into the snow. For he had carelessly left his belt on the log the night before; the fire had burned into the log, reaching the belt and exploded three cartridges.

We then noticed the Star in the East and the grey of dawn, as did the Shepherds of old.

We wished one another a "Merry Christmas," just one thousand eight hundred and seventy four years after that memorable morn in Bethlehem when the hosts of Heaven cried out "Glory to God in the Highest; Peace on Earth and good will to men."

After a breakfast of fried grouse, with gravy, hot biscuits baked in a dutch oven, and black coffee, the other three started out to set their traps, leaving me to prepare Christmas dinner.

I got busy as soon as they left, by preparing and cutting up the porcupine I had killed the night before, put it to boil in a camp kettle, and keeping it boiling for four hours. In the meantime, I made a pudding of one part flour, one part suet, and one part raisins, a pinch of salt, and a little baking powder, with water enough to make a stiff batter. I put it into a sack and boiled for two hours. About noon I made the dumplings, but did not put them into the stew till I saw the boys coming. The dumplings were boiled forty minutes. Our dinner was ready soon after they returned.

Thus the following was the menu for the first Christmas dinner in what is now Routt county: Porcupine stew, with dumplings; hot biscuits, with coffee, then our "plum pudding." True we had neither hard sauce nor brandy, but we had a substitute, a thin syrup made of brown sugar, thickened with flour. As I was the cook, I refrain from saying our Christmas dinner was delicious, but that was what the boys said.

Now, my friends I wish to impress upon you that I am making you a great and generous wish when I say: I wish every reader of this may eat his next Christmas dinner with as much relish and as free from care or regrets as did the writer at his first Christmas dinner in Routt county.

Christmas Dinner
Routt County, Colorado, 1874
Porcupine Stew with Dumplings
Hot Biscuits
Coffee
Plum Pudding

GAME STEW WITH DUMPLINGS

For rabbit, beaver, raccoon, porcupine, & c.

Cut meat into pieces and place in a crock with equal parts vinegar and water, 2 sliced onions, 1 teaspoon salt, and mixed spices. The liquor should just cover the meat, which must be turned over once a day for 3 days.

In a large iron kettle fry 6 slices of bacon. Add 1 large tablespoon butter or lard and 2 tablespoons flour. Stir until golden brown. Next add gradually the strained liquor until gravy is sufficiently thinned. Place meat in this and cook slowly for about 2 hours.

Potato dumplings: Boil 6 large potatoes (not too well done). When cool, peel and grate into a bowl, add egg and enough flour to bind the mass, and 1 teaspoon melted butter. Season with salt and pepper. Form dumplings the size of an egg, boiled in salted water. Add to stew. (Late 1800s)

O N December **21, 1902,** the *Anaconda* (Montana) *Standard* ran a description of a prospector's Christmas in 1870s Montana.

Prospectors roughing it in San Juan County, Colorado, 1875; photograph by William Henry Jackson.
—Courtesy National Archives

Saturday 25th This day being Christmas. Snowing Heavy. Employd washing* all day. Got about 44 Dollars this day.

—From the 1853 diary of miner James M. Burr

*Washing means panning for gold.

The prospector who knows when Christmas arrives nearly always makes some provision to celebrate the day. . . . Whether north or south, if an old prospector can get hold of a flag, the star-spangled banner floats from the highest point on the cabin. And, if he cannot secure a real flag, an old red shirt takes its place. . . .

In sections where there are several men located in different cabins, the whole crew, in everyday garb, usually gathers under the roof of the one that has the best layout, and there celebrates the day in a manner as commendable as the exigencies of the occasion will admit. Each one contributes to the feast, and, unless the period of separation from civilization has been a long one, the Christmas dinner is not so bad. The boys just simply have a feast, play cards, if they have any, recall the days when, as youngsters, they waited for Santa, and discuss the possibilities of striking the pay-streak before Christmas comes again. . . .

—From *Christmastime in Montana*, compiled by Dave Walter

Miner's Christmas tree in American City, Colorado
—Courtesy Denver Public Library, Western History Department

MINING CAMP POTATO CAKES

Mash hot potatoes with flour until you have a heavy unleavened dough. Add caraway seeds and roll dough into a large slab from which triangles are cut, the triangles should be four inches across the base. Bake until rich brown. When done split top and add butter. (Undated recipe)

IT WAS VERY COMMON for ladies "back home" to enclose in their letters west some little personal trinket, such as a ribbon, a piece of lace, or some pressed flowers. This tender look at a miner's Christmas appeared in the Christmas 1888 edition of the *Kansas City Journal*.

"Oh I wish that I could be home today. I think we would have a Christmas party. We would have the old gobbler roasted with a score of fat hens, pound cakes, pies, and lots of other good things. But the best of all would be the pleasure of seeing you all. Probably if we live we may be with you next Christmas."

—Gold miner Andrew Hall Gilmore, Placerville, California, 1851, in a letter to his brother in Indiana

THE OLD-TIME CHRISTMAS AT TIMBERLINE
By Will C. Ferril

Denver, Colo., Dec. 20 (1888). . . . Whatever may be the life of the westerner, there are two occasions in the year that recall the old home life—Thanksgiving and Christmas. A feeling of homesickness comes over the old time prospector and cowboy on these two festal days, although perchance all other days of the year may bring to mind none of these tender and happy thoughts of home life. A home sick cowboy; a homesick prospector; yes, nearly always on Thanksgiving and Christmas.

Imagine a point in mid-air about two miles above New York City, and you have an elevation at which over 1,000 miners in Colorado will spend the holiday season. They are shut in by snow and ice; and for months to come they will know as little about what is going on in the busy world as though they were sailors on some vessel frozen up for the winter amid the icebergs of the Arctic regions. Early in the fall, before the snow flies, they are housed in some lofty peaks of the Rocky Mountains, and not until May or June will they again mingle with their fellowmen. With a bountiful supply of food, clothing and medicine, and newspapers they will while away the long winter evenings. . . .

One Christmas I spent up on the mountainside with two or three others. There we had our holiday dinner. It was a wholesome meal, but wanted in those delicacies that a mother or a wife can best prepare.

"I wish we had some flowers for the Christmas table," said one of the boys.

—From *Frank Leslie's Illustrated Newspaper,*
February 19, 1853

98

We all wished the same.

"Get out your old letters," said one.

We all knew what he meant; for many a flower from the old home finds its way in a letter to the boys out West. One found a rose-bud, another a violet, another a daisy, and then another rose was found in a mother's letter. Withered and faded were those tokens from the old homes, but never did the men value flowers more than we did with that withered bouquet.

"Can't someone say grace?" said one of the boys.

No one volunteered.

"The closing lines in my mother's letter," said a boyish fellow, "might do."

"Read them," was the response that came from all.

Heads were bowed around the frugal Christmas board and the young man read.

"God bless you my son, and God bless us all."

I then looked up and saw tears on the cheeks of the weather beaten faces.

—From Will Ferril Collection, Denver Public Library

Not all Christmases in isolated mining camps were lonesome. Pike's Peak prospector William Lesley remembered a holiday party on the Snake River in Colorado in 1877 that was quite a festive gathering.

Christmas at Albert McCargar's

There was going to be a big time at old Albert McCargar's place on Snake river, at the mouth of Slater creek, where Robert McIntosh now has his store, and all of us from the Peak were invited. I was one of the part of about six who accepted, going down with Ed Cody, Dave Miller, Frank Hinman and a couple of others whose names I do not now remember. Hinman later married one of the McCargar girls.

There was four or five feet of snow on the ground, and we started on snowshoes on the night of Dec. 23, making the distance during the night and arriving early for Christmas Eve, when the celebration was to occur. The trip was made in quick time, for we each had a bottle, which made us go faster. . . .

We were then all living at Bugtown, the real name of which was Centennial City, and there were about 75 men in camp, nearly all employed at the big placer, which was backed by J. W. Farwell of Chicago. The store had a stock of $30,000 worth of goods, as it was necessary to lay in supplies in the fall for the work that was to be done in the spring. Everything had been freighted in from Laramie City, through Whiskey park.

Whiskey park got its name at that time. Some parties were there, selling whiskey, and Farwell sent a party out to dump the stuff. They destroyed it, but it was not wasted, for every bottle had a man at its mouth.

```
WHITE, GERRISH & CO.,
    Wholesale and Retail
      DEALERS IN
Provisions, Groceries,
        AND
MINERS OUTFITTING GOODS,
Corner McGaa and F streets,
      D E N V E R .


OUR New Stock has ar    from the States, consist-
ing in part as follows
FLOUR, BACON,
    DRIED FRUIT,
        NAILS, GLASS,
            PUTTY, PAINTS,
                SUGAR, COFFEE,
                    TEA, RICE, CHEESE,
        BOSTON CRACKERS,
CAMP KETTLES, SKILLETS,
BAKE OVENS, PANS, BROOMS,
    PICKS AND PICK HANDLES,
    AXES, SHOVELS, &c.,&c.,
May16th, 1860.    2 tf
```

—From the *Rocky Mountain News*, December 26, 1860

About 30 were at McCargar's for Christmas, and there was a fine time, with a big dinner and a dance, but I never went in for dancing much. Two of the McCargar girls were there, and I can truthfully say they were the most beautiful girls in Routt county so far as I knew, as at that time I hadn't seen any other women in the county. The third Miss McCargar was already gone, she having previously been married to Billy Morgan. . . .

The Christmas celebration at McCargar's broke up when the whiskey gave out, which was probably some time Christmas day, and then a large portion of the crowd went to Dixon for a good time. All of us had plenty of gold dust, which was the money in use in those days, and it surely was a good time we had.

COWBOYS ARE OFTEN among the lonesome at Christmastime. In *Western Yesterdays*, old cowpoke Jack Alder told author Forest Crossen about a Christmas surprise that eased his homesickness.

COWBOY'S CHRISTMAS BOX

I punched cows up in Wyoming most of my life. . . . I remember one Christmas when things looked mighty bleak. . . .

I was up on Pass Creek, in northern Wyoming. I had a new partner, and we hired out to break broncs. It was bitter cold. We'd been out all day, and just gettin' inside that cabin meant a lot, even though it looked gloomier than ever. . . . You see, this was the twenty-fourth of December. Tomorrow was Christmas.

The first thing was a fire. The wood we'd crammed into the old box stoves at opposite corners of the cabin had burned out. The place seemed colder than it was outside. So we began shaving kindling with hands so numb we could hardly hold a knife.

I couldn't help thinking about Christmas. This was the first one I'd ever spent in a lonely camp, a long ways from the gay celebrations of the cow towns. . . .

Now if only I were up in Billings with [my old partner] Hank, a mug of steamin' Tom and Jerry in my hand. The thought of that was so warm and pleasant that I didn't notice that my new partner had lighted the kerosene lamp.

"Jack," he called out.

I whirled around, staring.

"Jack, what's this?"

There in the middle of the floor was a big wooden box. The camp tender, who had made a hurried trip in there that day with the grub and supplies, had left it. There was a tag on it, addressed to us!

"Who's it from, Jack?" he asked.

A Cowboy of the 1880s
—From *Frank Leslie's Illustrated Newspaper*, April 9, 1887

I read the names. From our bosses, in Boston. I never expected anything from them. Why, we hadn't been working for them more'n three weeks. To think they'd remember us.

We pried off that lid in a hurry, began pullin' out things. We was as happy as any two little boys you ever saw. Two Arctic sleepin' bags. We wouldn't be cold any more at night. Thick wool socks, two fine Meerschaum pipes, two pounds of expensive smokin' tobacco, a big fruit cake, candy. Best of all, there was several good books.

"No, these are not the best thing," I told my partner. "The best thing is that our bosses remembered us, two kid bronc twisters out here under the Big Horns." I reached across for my partner's hand. "Merry Christmas Partner."

IN THIS **1917** POEM, artist and writer Charles M. Russell takes a fanciful look at the bachelor Christmas.

Christmas at the Line Camp

Last night I drifted back in dreams

To Childhoods stamping ground

Im in my little bed it seems, the Old folks
    whispering round.

My sox is hung Maws tucked me in

Its Christmas Eave you see

Iv said my prayers blessed all my kin

Im good as good can be

But suddenly Im wakened wide

From out this youthfull dream

By jingling bells thats just outside

Hung on som restless team

Reminded by rumatic shin

And lumbagoed back thats sore

Whiskred face and hair thats thin

I aint no kid no more

An getting my boots I open the door

An Im sum suprised to see

An old time freighter I knowed before

But its years since he called on me

Hes an under sized skinner

Good natured and stout

With a team like himself

All small

Its the same old Cuss

Maw tells me about

Just old Santy Claus raindeers and all

Hes a holding his ribbons like an old timer
would

When he nods his head to me

I wish yound put me right if you could

Im way off the trail says he

I follow the trail of the stork its strange

Me missing his track says he

104

But I'm guessing that bird

Never touched this range

For theres no sign of youngsters I see

You bachulars have a joyfull way

When and wherever your found

Forth of July and Paddy's Day

A Passing the drinks around

But to get the joy that Christmas brings

You must be acquanted with three

A homes but a camp without these things

A Wife, the stork, and me

And then my bunk pall gives me a shake

An growls in a cranky way

Youv got all the bedding

Im cold as a snake

I wonder what day is today

Christmas at the Line Camp, *1917, by Charles M. Russell* —Courtesy C. M. Russell Museum, Great Falls, Montana

Best wishes for your Christmas
Is all you get from me,
'Cause I aint no Santa Claus—
Don't own no Christmas tree.

But if wishes was health and money,
I'd fill your buck-skin poke,
Your doctor would go hungry,
An' you never would be broke.

Another Christmas card, with a shorter poem, from Charlie. —Courtesy Buffalo Bill Historical Center

LIKE MINERS AND COWBOYS, sailors often spent Christmas away from home and in rough company. The following is from the log of Alfred L. Stiles, published in *Log of a Trip around the Horn to San Francisco in 1849:*

Tues 25th *Christmas today and celebrated in diferent ways.
the mate began in his way, by striking the cook under the eye
and making it black and blue. had 2 pigs for dinner & apple
duff. 2 thirds of the passengers drunk besides Capt & mate & 1
or 2 hands. the mate pulled Choate from portland of the
forecastle & struck him severall blows on the head, when
some of the passengers cried out "throw him overboard." as soon
as he heard this he left for his cabin. some sympathy for the
cook and sailor.*

SOMETIMES BEING ON ONE'S OWN can lead to trouble. Texas cowboy Harry Pearson remembered the Christmas his bronc-bustin' buddy Caleb became a desperado.

Caleb, as I said, was quite a swaggerer. He bullied around and men had to take it because they knew he'd never met his equal in fast shooting. Caleb could draw his six shooter in the time it takes to say it, and he never missed so's anybody could tell it. One Christmas Day, him and some more fellows had been gambling all night and day, down on the Green Farm, about five mile South of Marietta, and an argument came up. The man that started the argument, got real bad about it, and jerked his gun out to shoot Caleb. I never saw this because I was just a kid, but I remember all excepting the names of the men that took part. They said that Caleb let him get his gun plum out, then drew and shot him before he could shoot. One shot got him in the heart. Caleb had some sort of a triggerless pistol that shot real fast. I think they called it a "Gun fanner." That meant that his gun didn't have a trigger but was shot by gently hitting the hammer with his hand. Anyway, it shot so fast that this man was killed before he could shoot, and another was shot in the foot.

Caleb had to light out after that, and he became a desparado after that. 'Twas a shame too, because his whole family were good people. I reckon all families has black sheep in them, though.

—From Library of Congress Archives

A FAR WORSE DESPERADO was Harvey Logan, alias Kid Curry, whose 1894 Christmas story was not exactly a vision of sugarplums. I based this on information from *The Wild Bunch* by James Horan.

A CHRISTMAS CURRY CAROL
(A True Story)

Kid Curry was mean, to begin with. There is no doubt whatever about that.

Christmas morning, 1894, Landusky, Montana. Jew Jake's Place was part dry-goods store, part saloon and oddly enough, about to be a part of Christmas history.

This was an odd fellow, Jew Jake! Easy to recognize as he had one leg standing, and the other missing. In the space vacated by the latter leg was propped a Winchester rifle, it was a bit slow going in a three legged race but this volatile leg had silenced at least two troublemakers, which made it a barkeepers best friend. In essence we can say, with clear conscience and easy heart, Jake was not a ladies man nor was he a great dancer. But Harvey Logan (alias Kid Curry) held no interest in women nor dancing that cold Christmas day, so it is at Jake's that we find him, and not in search of canned beans.

The Kid had been doing an exceptional job of wrapping any and all of his Holiday cheer in whiskey. He had been laboring on it most of the day until what ever fragment of goodwill he began with was now completely invisible to any human eye that might be reckless enough to wander in his direction. Kid Curry was in a very black mood and no amount of red or green, nor crystal white could sway him out of it. Black was his, and he wore it like garland! Unfortunately he had a mind to decorate the town.

At some point he grew restless, staring into a glass no longer satisfied him, the need to share was upon him, so out he went to do a little last minute holiday shooting!

In this he showed no prejudice, no one home received more bullets than another! Windows were his favorite! He even

—From *Frank Leslie's Illustrated Newspaper*, January 14, 1882; drawing by Paul Frenzeny

shot the blacksmith sign! He treated all, as equals . . . there were holes everywhere.

Others, who had been in possession of that same special brand of holiday cheer decided they to would join in, after all there was much town left and Kid was only one mean man. It was indeed the charitable thing to do! They proceeded to ventilate the little town until they got bored, or cold or possibly just got thirsty. Then it was back to Jew Jake's for refreshments. Neither the libations nor the bullets worked to fill the blackness Curry held so dear, no matter how regularly or skillfully applied. The void not only remained, but grew in size and hunger, needing tending once again.

Enter into Jew Jake's one Pike Landusky, town father, and a man who should have stayed home.

For months Pike had been looking to deliver a certain caliber Christmas card to Curry, a little note of displeasure for the seduction of his stepdaughter by Lonnie Logan, brother of Harry. Pike and the Kid were sworn blood enemies; murky eyes met as brown teeth clenched, dirty fists swelled. . . . The saloon held its collective breath, ducked under tables and hid their candy canes. Kid struck first, then Pike, and so forth and so on and round about until Pike found himself back to the floor and face to a six-shooter. He did try to reach for his gun, but never had a chance. Six in the face beats one in the coat every time.

Lonnie stole the first wagon he could find, Kid jumped aboard and ere they drove out of sight. . . . He shot what was left of the town to shoot that Christmas night!

One can only imagine that after word of this incident got around, Kid Curry was not invited to a lot of Christmas parties. The same probably held true for Lonnie.

CRIMINALS KEPT the lawmen away from home on the holidays, too. Instead of changing their stockings on Christmas Eve, the sheriffs of Jackson and Clay Counties, Missouri, were ordered to track down Jesse James.

—Courtesy Western Historical Manuscript Collection, Columbia, Mo.

WYATT EARP'S WILD DOVE

Pick ten doves and cut off their wings, feet and head. Remove the entrails and singe off the hair and feathers with a candle. Take a knife and cut the leg and back section away from the breast section. Melt two level tablespoons of beef suet and two of butter in a large frying pan and brown dove pieces well. Take a large pot, cut up a medium cabbage into eighths and place in the pot. Add six large carrots, one level teaspoon of sage leaves, one cup of cooked lima beans and one large onion, diced. Place the browned dove pieces in the pot, add enough water to cover the vegetables and birds about two inches deep. Add the butter and beef suet from the pan. Boil slowly about one hour and one half. Remove the dove and let drain. Add one cup of cooked macaroni to the pot of remaining liquid and serve with buttered bread. (Circa late 1800s)

ONE OF THE MOST POIGNANT Christmases related in this book—nearly as sad as Virginia Reed's experience with the Donner Party—was that of thirteen-year-old Catherine Sager, who spent Christmas of 1847 as a hostage.

Catherine Sager's life was not an easy one. In 1844, at age ten, headed to Oregon with her family in a wagon train, she got her leg crushed under the wheel of the wagon. Forced to ride in the jolting wagon, she lay next to her ailing mother. Later in the journey, her father caught a severe fever and died; her mother's death soon followed.

Whitman Mission by William Henry Jackson —Courtesy Scotts Bluff National Monument

Catherine and her six siblings were taken to live with Marcus and Narcissa Whitman at their mission near Walla Walla, Washington. Three years later, on

November 29, 1847, the local Cayuse Indians, blaming Dr. Whitman for repeated outbreaks of measles, attacked the mission, killing the Whitmans and several others, including Catherine's two brothers. The Indians took forty-seven hostages, Catherine and her sisters among them. One of her sisters died a few days later. Although plans for their release were being negotiated, the hostages spent that Christmas in fear of their lives. Catherine recorded that extraordinary day in her diary.

> Christmas dawned upon us at last. Oh, how unlike any that had ever dawned before! Mrs. Saunders prepared a little treat for the children in her room, but we ate in secret when no Indians were about. . . . We entertained little hope of ever leaving our prison house. We knew that as soon as the news reached the [Willamette] settlement, an army would be sent to our rescue. We also knew that this would be the signal for our death. Our captors had given us to understand that they expected the Americans would send an army to punish them, and their intention to kill us in such a case. It was, therefore, with alarm mingled with joy that we heard of the arrival of three boats at Walla Walla.

Luckily, the Indians did not carry through on their threat. The hostages were freed on December 29. The Sager sisters were sent to Oregon, where they were taken in by separate families.

HAVING REPRESENTED MINERS, cowboys, sailors, and outlaws, we can't leave out loggers in the annals of men alone at Christmas. While logging camps were made up mostly of single men, they did not necessarily suffer a comfortless Yuletide. This description of a lumber camp holiday feast appeared in the *Anaconda* (Montana) *Standard* on December 17, 1898.

THE LONG BOARD OF A LUMBER CAMP COOKHOUSE, CHRISTMAS

There are few city tables that are more heavily laden with good things on Christmas Day than is the long board of the cookhouse at a logging camp. There is a big turkey, of course. More than likely some member of the crew has shot a deer, and the fine, fat saddle of the venison graces the Christmas table. Cranberries have been brought from town, as well as fruit and nuts. There are steaming dishes of vegetables, and there are long rows of pies. There is a big pudding, too, if the cook has been feeling right. The bill of fare is one that would do credit to a big hotel, for these camp cooks are experts and, when they make an effort, the result is sure to be a success. . . .

Outside the door of the cookhouse is suspended a broken circular saw that has been brought up from the mill. The equipment of no logging camp is complete without this. When dinner is ready, the [cook's assistant] pounds away on this saw with a club, and the resulting sound is one that makes a Chinese gong ashamed of itself. It penetrates to the uttermost parts of the forests, and it is sweet music to the hungry toilers in the woods. On Christmas, at dinner time, this tocsin rings out with a more pronounced tone than usual. It discounts in volume and penetrating power any chime of church or cathedral that ever announced the advent of Christmas Day.

—From *Christmastime in Montana*, compiled by Dave Walter

Eating quarters at a lumber camp, circa 1870
—Courtesy University of Wisconsin at La Crosse

MOLASSES PIE. Beat together 5 eggs, add one cup sugar, one cup molasses, butter the size of an egg, and flavor with nutmeg. Mix all ingredients well and pour into two pie pans lined with crusts and bake. (Late 1800s)

RAILROAD WORKERS, too, usually found themselves far from the warmth of home at Christmastime. Like so many others we've seen in this book, they made the best of it. On Christmas of 1882, August A. Anderson, a young man of Swedish descent, was working as a grader on the Northern Pacific Railroad line in eastern Montana. He described his surprisingly jolly holiday in the *Montana Daily Record* (Helena) of December 19, 1903.

—From *Harper's New Monthly Magazine*, June 1869

SWEDISH CHRISTMAS IN A CAVE
Glendive, Montana, 1882

I remember that Christmas of 1882 very well. I don't know that I ever spent a more pleasant Christmas than that one. There was a big crowd of young Swedes in the grading camp [near Glendive] . . . and we decided to have a celebration on the same order that we would have had in the old country.

GLÖGG
(SWEDISH CHRISTMAS TODDY)
In 1 quart water boil 1 cup raisins
and a few other dried fruits. Add 1
stick cinnamon, a few cloves and 20
shelled almonds. Simmer until fruit
is tender. Add a bottle of port wine
and/or brandy. Add sugar and water to taste. Heat through and serve
hot. (Traditional recipe)

Three of us lived in a cave that winter. . . . Early in the winter we had dug a cave in a high bank. We had first cut a doorway and then cut out a room about ten feet square. We had then dug out a fireplace and—with the aid of a large number of powder cans, which strewed the right-of-way—we built a chimney and had as comfortable a home as you could imagine. . . .

Now Christmas Eve in Sweden is the greatest time of all the year, and we Swedes resolved to celebrate in the old-time style. Going to Glendive, we bought five gallons of cognac, and with that we brewed a punch that was simply nectar to the Swedes. The punch was served Christmas Eve in our little cave. The room was so small that the boys, after taking a drink or two, had to leave in order to give the fellows outside a chance. But, by coming in relays that way, the entire camp was served with punch.

We had a very merry time of it that Christmas Eve. We sang the songs of the Old Country and told stories of other days when we had celebrated the festival in the Old Country. As I said, I have never spent a more pleasant Christmas.

—From *Christmastime in Montana*, compiled by Dave Walter

The Stockings Were Hung

Homesteaders and Settlers

EGINNING IN THE MID-1800s, thousands of American families packed up their china, oak dressers, and feather beds and headed west, some in oilcloth-covered wagons, others on foot, pushing handcarts. As the miles wore on, the harsh trail laid claim to the china and the dressers as their weight proved too burdensome and they were abandoned bit by bit at the side of the road.

But one thing did not fall from the wagon, nor was it traded for supplies. Never broken or mislaid, it traveled the full length of the journey and arrived intact at the pioneers' new home. It was just too precious to leave behind: *It was Christmas.*

Family in covered wagon, Nebraska, 1886 —Courtesy National Archives

Family with tree in unidentified Colorado home, circa 1900, asking the age-old question: Shorten the tree or raise the ceiling?
—Courtesy Colorado Historical Society

Often, the home that greeted emigrant families upon their arrival was the same four-by-ten-foot wagon that had transported them there, and it might remain their only shelter through the first winter as they built their new home. Others might make their beds in tents or under lean-tos. Later homes were often only slightly bigger and more comfortable, though more prosperous folks sometimes built houses to rival the most elegant Victorian structures back East. But no matter how meager or how grand, late each December whatever structure was known as home was dressed up and brought to life. Within, families shared stories, songs, prayers, and gifts, perhaps remembering Christmas at the old home even as they created Christmas anew.

Mrs. Custer may have had these pioneer women in mind when she wrote this Christmas message for *Ladies' Home Journal* in 1890.

From the Gallant Custer's Widow

IF INSTEAD of writing a Christmas welcome to the thousands of women to whom this Christmas Journal will go, I could enter the homes myself and talk with you, it would please me far better than using this greeting made formal by pen and paper. Perhaps in the midst of Christmas carols and Christmas cheer there would be no opportunity to take me about your homes and show me what ingenuity, taste and thought you have given to ornamenting and making pleasant the blessed abode for your husband and children.

I might not be permitted, for want of time on your part, to know the history of each gift, which you have planned and thought out late at night, and in the calm of early morning. But still, I dearly wish that I might enter your comfortable homes, and hear of your aims, your blessings and perplexities, your sorrows. In wishing all the good things this world gives may descend on the households to which the Journal goes, I would that it might give me the special privilege to let me enter those thousands of little makeshifts for home throughout our land that the busy women of limited means have set up; the dingy rooms under the eaves, where deft fingers have made such transformations; the little apartments where is ever semi-twilight, where God's beautiful twilight comes in thru the narrow windows—ah, it is to you, brave, but lonely women, if any such read these words, that I wish to send my love, and whatever of courage deep felt words can convey. The widows, the girl bachelors, the solitary old maids, all of you who are so much to me, I envy the printed and pictured sheets of this holiday Journal, the cheer and comfort they carry.

—Elizabeth B. Custer, *Ladies' Home Journal*, December 1890

"Still raining. It has been a sad Christmas for mother. She is homesick, longs for her old home and friends. It's hard for old folks to give up old ties and go so far away to live in a strange land among strange people. Young people can easily form new ties and make new friends and soon conform to circumstances, but it's hard for the old ones to forget. Was invited to a candy pull and had a nice time. Rather a number of young folks camped here. This is a funny looking town anyway. Most of the houses are built of brush. Now that the rains have set in, people are beginning to think of something more substantial. Some have log cabins, others have clapboard like ours."

—From the diary of Sallie Hester, age 14, Fremont, California, December 25, 1849

—Courtesy Colorado Historical Society

123

CHRISTMAS MORNING AT HOME.

—From *The Field and Farm*, 1893

THE man who said "There's nothing sure in the world but death and taxes" might have given a pleasant aspect to this philosophy by noting that Christmas was coming, too, and pretty regular at that.

The rise and progress of Christmas in this country is a very interesting subject of investigation, as showing the diverse character of America's early settlers and the peculiar elements concerned in the development of the features of our present holiday season. The Virginia settlement was cradled in poverty and was too deeply concerned with the problem of existence to celebrate any thing. In New England the life of the Pilgrim Fathers was so hard that statutes were easily enacted forbidding the celebration of Christmas, largely on the ground that the day could not be spared as a time of abstinence from work. A compromise was finally made, however, that only those who worked on that day should have anything to eat during the twenty-four hours.

It was by the Dutch and Germans who settled in New York later that Christmas was first recognized to any notable extent in early times. The Dutch and English brought the Yule log to the Christmas fireside, but it was the Germans, with their old Druidical traditions, who introduced evergreens and planted the first Christmas trees on this continent. Then St. Nicholas, the early Christian patron saint of the young, and Santa Claus, the kindred patron saint among the Dutch, began to be invoked for blessings. Other elements in the population gradually became interested in Yuletide and the Christmas tree, and so the day has grown to its present importance.

The modern Christmas tries a man's reasoning powers to the fullest extent. With him it is a problem just what to give each, and if he makes no mistake he is a wise man indeed. The wisest are those who appreciate the value of good books, and what book is there that is more useful than a work of reference? In the REVISED ENCYCLOPEDIA BRITANNICA the knowledge of the world has been gathered up and its marvel of cheapness makes it possible for every-one to purchase. Try giving a set to your friend and see how he will ap-preciate it.

HERE IS YOUR OPPORTUNITY.

On receipt of only **One Dollar** we will forward to you, charges prepaid, the entire set of 20 volumes, the remaining $9.00 to be paid at the rate of **10 Cents a Day** (to be remitted monthly). A beautiful dime savings bank will be sent with the books, in which the dime may be deposited each day. This edition is printed from new, large type on a fine quality of paper, and is strongly bound in heavy manilla paper covers, which with proper care will last for years. Bear in mind that the entire 20 volumes are delivered to your address, with all charges paid to any part of the United States.

This is a special offer made only to the readers of THE FIELD AND FARM and will remain open for a limited time only.

Cut this out and send to THE FIELD AND FARM.

THIS STORY COMES from *The Trail*, December 1920.

A KENTUCKY CHRISTMAS DINNER IN COLORADO, 1859
By Nancy Fitzhugh Norton

As winter came on apace my father grew somewhat restless, but after we hit upon the idea of having a genuine old Kentucky Christmas dinner at our [Colorado] home he seemed better satisfied. I say "a genuine Kentucky dinner," but that was quite out of the question. A Kentucky Christmas dinner without a turkey was unimaginable. There were reported to be a few wild turkeys in the foothills, but they were hard to find, and of course the domesticated bird was not thought of at the time. Indeed, there were not even chickens. But, barring turkeys, wild game was plentiful and we knew we would have a good feast even without the "bird." At least I knew it, but Father was a little doubtful concerning my culinary qualifications. I told him, however, to bring on his crowd and I would take care of them.

They were an even dozen, and all men. Father was of a sociable disposition and he already had his cronies, all of whom he invited. Not one failed to accept, but all insisted upon contributing to the meal. One went to the foothills for pine boughs for decorations. One undertook to supply a couple of hams of venison; another, dried apples for pie; another the fixings for a cake; still another, a side of bacon, and, last but not least, Tom Prime was to bring a head of cabbage which he had bought from Dave Wall for a dollar during the previous fall and had held it for just such an occasion, as he said he knew this would be—a head of cabbage from the first vegetable patch grown in Colorado. At his own request, our Italian friend was to supply the liquors.

In those days Uncle Dick Wooten was the connecting link between Denver and the Taos Mexican settlements of Northern New Mexico. Taos was old even then, and, according to reports, enjoyed all the most advanced features of Mexican civilization, including a special brand of

Man with antelope, 1890s; Evelyn Cameron photograph
—Courtesy Montana Historical Society, Helena

whisky, which was known—widely known—as "Taos Lightning." This brand had the reputation of giving "more for the money" than any other liquor on the market and was very popular with the Mountain men. My father was used to a very different variety and would have preferred to supply this part of the feast himself; but as his old acquaintance of the Plains insisted, he yielded.

We had a really fine dinner. I made the pies and cakes, but the invited guests did most of the other cooking. No one ever lived who could prepare a piece of venison to better advantage than the old frontiersmen, and they liked nothing better than to show off before a woman in this respect. So the venison was just right, as were the rabbit stew, the pot pie, the boiled cabbage, the potatoes, and, I must say that there

"Rentucky" Christmas Menu
Colorado, 1859

Ham of Venison
Rabbit Stew
Pot Pie
Cabbage, Potatoes
Cake, Dried Apple Pie
Taos Lightning

FRIED CABBAGE.

Slice down a head of cabbage, put it in a stew-pan already prepared with a very little water, butter, salt and pepper; cover and stew about twenty minutes, taking care not to let it burn; beat and strain three eggs, add half cup of good vinegar (beat while pouring in vinegar), then turn mixture on cabbage, stirring briskly all the time; serve immediately. Sour cream may be used instead of eggs and vinegar. To fry fine, place on heated skillet with a table-spoon of butter or beef-drippings, slice, season, cover, stir frequently and fry ten to fifteen minutes, being very careful not to burn it. (1876)

was nothing wrong with the pastries except, of course, that the apples were of the dried variety and the filling rather thin at that. We had only four chairs, so that it was necessary that most of the guests should occupy boxes for seats. However, nobody minded. I was not allowed to leave my seat. The men did the waiting and every one of them insisted upon serving me each time he passed my place. I did not go hungry.

It was a jolly party. Many were the anecdotes that were related and many the songs that were sung. The conversation alternated between discussion of local questions and reminiscences about far distant scenes.

—Courtesy Denver Public Library, Western Heritage Collection

In 1870 Orpha Eliza Baldwin married Alpheus Philetus McNitt and moved to the Colorado Territory. With tender appreciation, Orpha wrote to thank her parents and siblings for Christmas gifts. In spite of a bout of homesickness, she spoke of a very pleasant holiday season with friends in her new frontier home.

January 1, 1871

Dear Family,

Thank you all together and each one separately for the Christmas box you sent us. Everything was just right. The fruitcake was the best I ever ate, and we shared it at our Christmas dinner. Father, your cranberries brought Wisconsin right into our frontier home. We are enjoying the nuts you boys gathered in the woods. How I wish there were more trees out here! After dinner we sat around the fire and cracked the nuts while the men told Indian stories. As old as I am I am almost afraid to go to bed at night. . . .

Carl, I know you raised the hops, which I found in the Christmas box. We cannot get them here, so I have something wonderful to divide with Katie. Now we shall have some proper yeast for our bread. There are many things we can't get here.

Sophie, I wish you could know how glad I am to have the comforter. When people go visiting they usually stay all night, and I have been wondering what I would do for covers. You see, our houses are several miles apart, and our guests come by horse and buggy or wagon. I am glad you pieced the comforter with little squares from all the family dresses. I can just imagine how you looked in each one. It was a great deal of work for you to piece it and get the wool ready to fill it. Be sure to thank the little girls for the holders and pen wipers. I needed both, and I know they would rather play outdoors than sit and sew.

We enjoyed our Christmas. Mrs. Wilson came early and helped me get dinner. She brought cabbage, cooked and ready to warm. I had the corn we dried last summer at

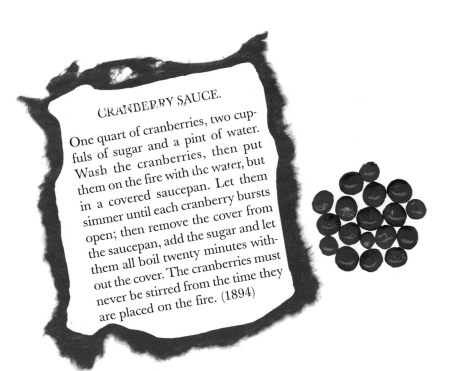

CRANBERRY SAUCE.

One quart of cranberries, two cupfuls of sugar and a pint of water. Wash the cranberries, then put them on the fire with the water, but in a covered saucepan. Let them simmer until each cranberry bursts open; then remove the cover from the saucepan, add the sugar and let them all boil twenty minutes without the cover. The cranberries must never be stirred from the time they are placed on the fire. (1894)

home. Katie brought fried rabbit. My light rolls were good, and your cranberries, fruitcake and nuts made it a feast.

Write to me about your Christmas. I love Alpheus, and I don't let him know that I am homesick for fear he will think I am not happy with him. He hasn't the family ties that I have, and he can't understand. He has no brothers and sisters living, and that makes a difference.

As I wish you a Happy New Year, I look out on a winter scene. The storms of snow and sleet have come. We have enough to eat and plenty of coal, so we are thankful on this New Year's Day.

Alpheus sends his love to you, and so do I.

Orpha

—Reprinted with the kind permission of Emma Alice Hamm

CHRISTMAS GREETING.

FINE CUTLERY
AND
SENSIBLE CHRISTMAS PRESENTS.
A. J. JORDAN.
812 WASHINGTON AVENUE.
ST. LOUIS.

—Northwest Museum of Arts and Culture

CHRISTMAS CARDS are a mid-nineteenth-century invention, an outgrowth of the valentine. Christmas cards caught on in the United States shortly after being introduced in Great Britain. The cards were purchased not just as greetings but also as gifts in their own right, suitable for framing or hanging on the tree as an ornament. Many of the earliest Christmas cards did not look "Christmassy" at all, but showed garden scenes, sailboats, frogs, or robins. By the turn of the century, the sending of Christmas cards was an entrenched American tradition.

—Park County Historical Society

Wishing you a Merry Christmas

—Park County Historical Society

Silvery Chimes how clear is your ring. Oh, let us all in one grand chorous sing. Long live the American Italian girl With her laughing eyes and jet black curl.

A Happy New Year

—Park County Historical Society

—Private collection, Beth Judy

—Park County Historical Society

—Park County Historical Society

—Park County Historical Society

—Northwest Museum of Arts and Culture

—Private collection, Beth Judy

JESSIE BENTON FRÉMONT, wife of explorer John Charles Frémont (whom she called "the Colonel"), first came to California with her two young sons in 1849, when her husband opened a mine there. Her 1890 *Far West Sketches* recounted her experiences. In this excerpt, she describes her preparations for the family's first permanent home in California, which she worked to have ready in time for Christmas. The final result was to be a surprise for her husband.

All my plans were ready and fully thought out in detail. I had the experienced aid of the silent book-keeper, the only one to whom I told my idea—the Colonel was content to accept whatever my surprise should prove to be, only asking a certain limit to be observed, to which the book-keeper and myself gravely answered that the thousands named would be enough, and as soon as he drove away we all went to work. . . .

The silent book-keeper had picked his men, and they were ready; the steady grizzled man from Maine who with his sons had the hauling of wood for the mills—his long gray beard and bunchy clothes making him look like Kriss Kringle as he walked by the oxen of his long team; the capable carpenter directing the placing of all the planks and shingles where they should not break the edges of the drive or hurt the grass; the men who sewed sacks for the ores on hand to make the new carpets and curtains. . . .

The stores in mining towns are curiously supplied with beautiful things and luxuries of all kinds. I had found there fine French wall-papers, fine carpeting and rugs, and rolls of woolen and silk curtain-stuffs. The dining-room was made the workroom where I directed, and cheerful, pleased men helped willingly "to get the Madam's Christmas-box ready."

Indoors and out it was all activity and gayety. I had brought up only one small boy, the eldest, whose positive genius for getting into accidents made it best to keep him near me (and I liked to have him).

Ads for holiday goods

. . . His pride was immense at knowing what not papa, not any of the family, were to know until *le fete de noel*, when he was to say "This is the House that JACK built!" . . .

We made an imposing, irregular, invaluable dining-room in walnut and oak papers and there we set up the Tree. . .

The Tree was the bushy top of a fine long-coned pine. It was another rare joy for the small boy to help choose this and see it cut—see it carefully loaded on to a wood sled and brought into the dining-room to be decorated—to help brush over the long cones with mucilage on which we pressed thin gilt paper, making a cluster of glittering golden cones to each bough. Then it was lifted into place and made firm and secure—a beautiful fragrant glittering tree with the gold star crowning its rich dark green. . . .

We had the most beautiful cakes that could be made. . . . In our village was a thoroughly first-class Vienna baker; the Colonel would not employ men who drank but, knowing good food was necessary to keep the stomach in order, had brought up this man from San Francisco. . . . This baker entered into the Christmas idea with true South German enthusiasm. It would take a paper to itself to describe the beautiful things he made in cakes and in sugar for the Tree. Never had I seen such. They were the best Vienna ideas "regardless of cost"—which Germans never are. The candles sent up were a failure. They had come through the tropics as all freights did then, and were chippy and flaked off. Nor were they large enough for our beautiful Tree. The baker rose to the emergency. He made handsome tapers of beeswax and decorated them artistically with colors and gold leaf, like the decorated blessed wax-lights one buys at cathedral doors abroad. Our Tree was now quite beautiful.

Its fruitage was all ready in the big out-door store-room; cases of candied fruits, boxes of toys and games and picture-books, boxes of colored beads in bunches of strings for our neighbors of the Indian village, pretty brooches and gowns and things for our women who had "come from the States" with us, and gifts for our good Isaac and the few home-people who made our constant life. It was to be a true home-Christmas, not "a party."

While all else was going on the piano had to be tuned. With the family was to come up a very dear friend of mine from New York who was making a short visit to her brother in San Francisco. Her happy temper, her lovely gift of song and sweet ways, made her coming a great Christmas-gift to me. Music was with her a natural expression, but the piano was long unused and wildly out of tune, and the nearest tuner was in Stockton, eighty miles away. . . .

But we found some new strings and the big blacksmith of the mills fastened them on, winding them with a winch—very cautiously—until I said "stop," I tapping along until the sound came right. Manuel, a black man from Virginia, was delighted with this odd exercise of his strength. He also made for me a fine fender of the sieve-iron used to "screen" gold washings, and some stately medival-looking fire-dogs of hammered iron.

The tenth day all was entirely complete and in working order. Fire was lit on the new hearth and no smoking followed; the bricklayer said "it was a good job if it was so hurried."

Everything was now in readiness. All traces of work had been carried off, and smooth order and quiet replaced the busy little crowd of the past ten days. There was a smell of paint, and to say the least an odor of much freshness; but good fires counteracted this, and we kept fragrant cedar pastils burning in each one of the rooms. Everywhere were wreaths of ground-pine, with wild-rose-haws on duty for holly berries, and on our windows was the Christmas Cross. The pretty supper was on the table; its ultracivilized appointments and the sparkling spun-sugar pyramids and frosted-sugar things and bright jellies were concentrated into a picture by the light from a hanging lamp with its fringed crimson silk shade. All our "helping-hands" had exchanged congratulations and good wishes and good-by, over Christmas cake and tea, and now in the quiet of the beautified home the book-keeper showed me its crowning beauty; that everything—and I had gone ahead without counting—had, as we intended, not cost one fifth of the allotted sum. As Secretary of our Treasury this good showing of much profit from small outlay made him serenely content.

It was the triumph of "making the best of things" we had, and using good taste in place of mere spending. And it broadened the circle of local good feeling to have our own neighborhood furnish all supplies; so we were pleased with our work and ourselves. And now impatient to see "the Colonel's" pleasure and his astonishment, for "In such place, 'twas strange to see," a home that was full of comfort and . . . "beautiful exceedingly."

The Christmas-eve closed in dark and misty before our travelers at last arrived. They had been delayed on the mountains by a thick falling

"Back in my memory are the highlights of one Christmas in that lovely old home, of bells and horses, candles and a huge Christmas tree that we children peeked at through always-closing doors, and all the excitement attending a big house full of people, big and little."

—Mrs. Clyde B. Huntley, Oregon settler, mid-1880s

mist which obliged them to great caution, for shelving rocks and deep gorges bordered the winding road. Mounted men with torches, and giving cheery hails, had gone far to meet them, and once down into our valley the blaze of lights from our broad Queen Anne windows made a welcoming beacon.

It was a home-coming of delighted surprises—what a happy clamor it was! And my "surprise" was approved and praised to my heart's content.

My New York friend had no words to express her astonishment and delight—the open piano caught her eye and straightaway her splendid voice filled my hungry ears with triumphant song. But hungry people claimed her for supper: "Bouillon, mayonnaise! game pate! jellies, wedding-cakes, and all Delmonico's!"

The two days' travel across solitary plains with frontier stopping-places closing with the risky mountain crossing in the dark made it, as she said, "a transformation-scene" to come out of the night and the mist into this vision of a New York home—enriched by a frontier welcome. . . .

Near by was a large Indian village, some hundreds settled there. The young women from it came constantly to our house and sat about on the grass chatting together and laughing as they watched our doings with frank curiosity. We were their matinee. Often we stopped at their village on our rides and watched them in turn as we sat on our horses. Their ways all had object and meaning—the sewing of squirrel skins together, the pounding of acorns into meal for bread, the basket weaving, and they were fairly clean and very gay. It was a pleasure to give them beads and such things as they found good to eat or pretty to wear and now we told them—with some Spanish words they understood, and much pantomime—that they must come to see the *fiesta* of the Tree they had watched being cut and carried to the house; that they must bring baskets to carry home *mucho mucho*—spreading our hands, and filling an imaginary basket full of things to eat, and things to wear. They "caught on" and accepted with many laughs of pleasure. . . .

It was hard to induce the young ones to come in to the Tree. Its lights shone out through the broadside of window and we saw them clustered outside, like lunar moths, their white heads bobbing about as they ran around in hushed surprise. At last we got them in, hanging together like bees around the tallest boy, silent, but open-mouthed and staring.

All boys fraternize. Mine began giving to these a lot of Nuremberg pine-wood animals, the first of such things ever seen by them.

"A hog," cried out the big boy as he seized the hyena. His eyes glittered as he hugged the bow-backed beast to his bosom, and no other of the gifts so roused him.

They made off early to their "mam" with a big basket full of toys and sweets, and with many parcels of useful things for her and themselves.

As my youngest boy was but three, it was to him also a first Christmas. . . . When all was ready and the candles lighted he was sent alone into the large quiet room where rose the strange Tree covered with gilded cones and candles and glittering fruits and toys. He was quite silent. With his curly head a little to one side and hands locked behind his back he walked around the strange growth; then going to his special ally he put his hand into his father's and said in his French-English *"Koom see. Kreesmas haze koom!"* . . .

All was as pretty as a picture—and an assurance in widening circles of gentle influences for peace and good-will.

Not all frontier Christmas dinners were entirely successful. In this sweet, funny remembrance, a young pioneer wife prepared a special holiday meal in her new Montana home, with unexpected results.

CHRISTMAS AT THE RANCH AT LAME DEER WITH THE ALDERSONS, MONTANA 1882

We celebrated Christmas in our new home with a party. One of the guests was Josh Sharp, a young lawyer from back east whose brother had a ranch on Tongue River. With Josh came a tall, gawky fellow from New York. This young man had enjoyed every advantage of education and surroundings, but he had no special ease or natural graciousness, and I could not help contrasting him with the shy, friendly, courteous cowboys. Yet later, when we came to know him and he talked, he was so interesting; he had read and traveled, and knew so much that the rest of us didn't know.

Our other guests were Packsaddle Jack and our own boys. They were dressed up for the occasion in their best colored shirts and good trousers, and as always had a clean and attractive appearance. As for the absence of coats, that had long since ceased to trouble me.

I doubt if there was a turkey in Montana that Christmas, but we had oysters! We had persuaded a neighbor, coming from Miles City several days before Christmas, to bring us several cans of these, frozen, and packed in ice as a double precaution. I can make good eggnog and, with Christmas candies to supplement the eggnog, I hoped this dinner would be memorable for them all. I planned to serve it at three. The oysters, I hoped, would make an impression, as they were rarely seen out here on the frontier. For the pièce de résistance we had our own roast beef, that which no better can be found anywhere.

STEWED OYSTERS.

Before cooking oysters, carefully remove all particles of shell. This is not so necessary with the most expensive sorts, but even these sometimes have a treacherous bit of shell in them, which is very disagreeable to encounter. Put one gallon of oysters with their liquor into a granite saucepan, salt and pepper to taste, and three quarters of a pound of very nice butter. Oysters require a quantity of butter if you want them in perfection. Frequently stir them, and when they are thoroughly heated through and begin to cook, stir into them one teacupful of fresh cracker dust, finely pounded. As soon as they are done, which is as soon as they plump out, remove them from the fire. Too much cooking, like too little butter, will ruin an oyster. While cooking stir often from the bottom of the saucepan, otherwise they will burn. (1890)

My table looked very Christmasy with a bowl in the center filled with pine cones and wild rose berries, that grow large and bright and red here. On each side of the bowl were Grandmother's silver candlesticks (for I knew it would be getting candle-lighting time before our dinner was over) and a set of white doilies with border of red edged wheels, and all the silver I owned—even the berry spoon, though there were no berries. The doilies did look pretty on the polished walnut table. I was really proud of myself as I took my seat at the head of the table, with the baking dish of scalloped oysters in front of me and the pretty berry spoon to serve them with. What if my husband did sit on a churn, turned upside down and covered with a rug? What if I sat on a dry goods box, made the right height by my father's copy of Shakespeare, and William Cullen Bryant's "Gems of Prose and Poetry"? The latter book given me by the second of our mail-carrying cowboys, Mr. Miller, when he left Montana. I never knew his background, but he had a most gentlemanly appearance and the book showed evidence of having been much read. Finding it too bulky to carry on horse, he had wanted me to have it.

While my husband carved the beef roast I helped everybody generously to the oysters. I did not notice that after the first exclamation of "think of oysters on a cattle ranch in Montana," nothing was said.

When my husband finished serving and tasted the oysters he said to me, "What's the matter with these oysters?"

I fear some of the guests ate more than was wise just to spare my feelings. I needn't report on how sick some of us were before morning, for the oysters evidently had been tainted before they were frozen. I could have cried of humiliation at my frustrated effort to make this first Christmas a great success. The men were very sympathetic. I think they feared I'd boo-hoo, and kept saying "don't you care" and praising the roast, the pie, and everything else. In spite of the bad oysters, we did have a merry time before the disastrous effects began to appear.

—From *A Bride Goes West* by Nannie Alderson and Helena Huntington Smith

IT WAS OFTEN DIFFICULT for parents in isolated frontier settlements to find gifts and treats to fill their children's Christmas stockings. In an interview for the Spokane *Spokesman-Review,* Frank M. Dalam remembered the challenge of Christmas shopping in Spokane Falls, Washington, in 1883.

This was but a frontier village way back in 1883. There were only a few excuses for stores with stocks limited to bare necessities. . . . The very few stores in existence had made no provision for Christmas, and there was no trinket of any kind that would appeal to children. . . .

We made the round of the whole town, but there was not a toy, not a single doll, not a single book, not a single pound of candy that had not lost its color through contact with flies. . . . No place where anything at all was offered for sale was overlooked, and no closer search was ever made for hidden gold than was made on that particular occasion for some article that would bring joy to the heart of a child. . . .

At last, in a dingy and littered carpenter shop was found a small rocking chair, the entire stock in trade of a small character, which was eagerly pounced upon, but that could go but to one family. . . .

Then a quantity of nuts was found that looked as though they had come across on the Mayflower and a few pounds of stick candy that apparently had been saved from too-intimate relation with flies. . . .

Then the ingenuity of mothers—and what mother is there who does not arise to the occasion when the pleasure of her infants is at stake?—fashioned things out of cloth that answered the purpose of dolls. . . .

[These things and] the entire stock of 10-penny nails of one hardware firm and a claw hammer, [along with] a few handfuls of popcorn . . . were the sum total of our collection. . . .

The things were not very alluring, but we did not propose to let those stockings hang limp and empty Christmas morning, even if we were forced to stuff them with scrap-iron and tin cans.

And when all was said and done and the light broke forth on that Christmas morning of 1883 and those children rushed frantically for their stockings, there was not in all probability a happier family in sparsely settled Eastern Washington.

It touches the heartstrings to look back and think back to that Christmas of so long ago, so many happy ones since that time—and yet few were *more* happy—for our wants were few and there was little difficulty in supplying those wants. . . .

Those were happy days when the greed of gain had not curdled the milk of human kindness. . . .

"Baby's First Christmas"

Hang up the baby's stocking
Be sure you don't forget
The dear little dimpled darling
As ne'er seen a Christmas yet.

—Pioneer Christmas song

143

Making the best of things is a recurrent theme in pioneer stories, especially during Christmastime. For example, these Mormon homesteaders made their own fun, even in the difficult early years of settlement.

The first Christmas [in Ferron, Utah, 1877] was a time of merriment. The women did the best they could to make a feast with their limited provisions. To add some fun to the day, the men and women switched clothes, the wives dressing in their husbands' trousers and the men in their wives' dresses.

—From *Roadside History of Utah* by Cynthia Larsen Bennett

"Although very tired of tent life many of us spent Thanksgiving and Christmas in our canvas houses. I do not remember ever having had happier holiday times. For Christmas we had grizzly bear steak for which we paid $2.50, one cabbage for $1.00 and—oh horrors—some more dried apples! And for a Christmas present the Sacramento river rose very high and flooded the whole town!"

—Catherine Haun, settler, Sacramento, 1849
From *Women's Diaries of the Westward Journey*

DRIED APPLE PIE
Soak 2 cups dried apples in water overnight. Drain off the water and mix apples with 1/2 cup sugar and 1 teaspoon each of allspice and cinnamon. Line a deep buttered dish with paste [pie crust]. Fill it with the apples. Put on another sheet of paste as a lid; close the edges well, and notch them. Bake the pie in a moderate oven, about three-quarters of an hour. (Pioneer recipe)

No 34.

Oklahoma Dugout.

Oklahoma pioneer family in front of their dugout, Christmas Day, 1901 —Courtesy Western History Collections, University of Oklahoma

CHRISTMAS IN A DUGOUT
By Klaudia K. Stoner

On December 18, 1888, an ox-drawn wagon brought the A. M. Nelson family and all their belongings to their new Wyoming home in Weston County. Snow had been falling all day and the travelers were not only damp and chilled but stiff and cramped from sitting so long on the wagon seats. The new home, a dugout in the side of a hill sloping toward the south, looked good after such a journey.

First, they unloaded the big, shining range, set it in place and built a roaring fire. After a warm supper and a good warming of numbed fingers and toes the family went to bed where sleep was almost instant.

The next day was a busy one. They covered the earth floor with 11 thick layers of cat-tail rushes and nailed a bright rag carpet securely over them. The walls were covered with muslin and the furniture and pictures put in place.

With Christmas so near not only much whispering and planning went on but a lot of feverish work on homemade gifts and toys (after little sister was safely asleep).

A few days before Christmas a neighboring cowboy made a cold three-hour ride with some mail, letters and Christmas gifts from relatives and friends "back home." To the children the best things were the real Christmas candy and other "goodies" sent by big brother who was working in Sundance, the nearest town.

In the mail was an invitation from the Brewer family six miles away, to spend Christmas Day with them. The Nelsons anticipated the trip with much excitement and pleasure.

Life on a homestead was very different from most places today as stated in many accounts found in the collections of the Wyoming State Archives, Museums and Historical Department. Sounds were quiet and harmonious—there was not a mechanical sound to be heard. Only the occasional sound of an animal or bird or the wind in the trees broke the silence.

By dawn on Christmas day as their trip began a heavy snow was falling. Mrs. Nelson and the four children snuggled down in the wagon bed piled deep with blankets and comforters. The hot stones and flat-irons kept their feet warm. The father brought out a big umbrella because the snow was wet and the children would surely stick their heads out from under the blankets. Mr. Nelson walked along the wagon, bundled in his heavy wool coat and felt boots.

After the snow stopped falling, the road was easier to see and the father climbed into the wagon. He stood up in front cracking the whip over the backs of the oxen trying to hurry them out of their sober pace. When he met with no success, he seized the umbrella, held it straight out in front of him and suddenly opened it wide. The oxen snorted with surprise and set off at a lumbering gallop, and finally, a dead run with the wagon rattling and bumping along behind them. The dog was barking wildly and all the family screamed with laughter. "What a wonderful ride," they recalled.

The Brewers gave them a warm welcome and they served a bountiful dinner at noon. Roast venison, chicken, wonderful home-made pickles and preserves, delicious buffalo berry jam, pies, cakes and crullers made a feast truly "fit for a king."

The families exchanged carefully made gifts among them-selves—knitted wristlets, mittens made from buckskin Mr. Nelson had tanned that had been embroidered by the mother's skillful fingers; handker-chiefs carefully hem-stitched; old dolls in gorgeous new gowns and a supply of doll bed linen that would rejoice the heart of any doll house wife; doll furniture made from pieces of packing boxes; odd little pretty things made from bits of silk and linen that had been treasured for years on a gown or in a "piece bag." Each gift, no matter how small, had been glorified by the loving care with which it had been planned and fashioned.

Many a Christmas has passed since then, and for the Nelsons that first at the dugout was a memorable one. With the new fallen snow, family and friends, laughter and song, came a promise of greater things and better times to come.

—Courtesy Wyoming State Archives

147

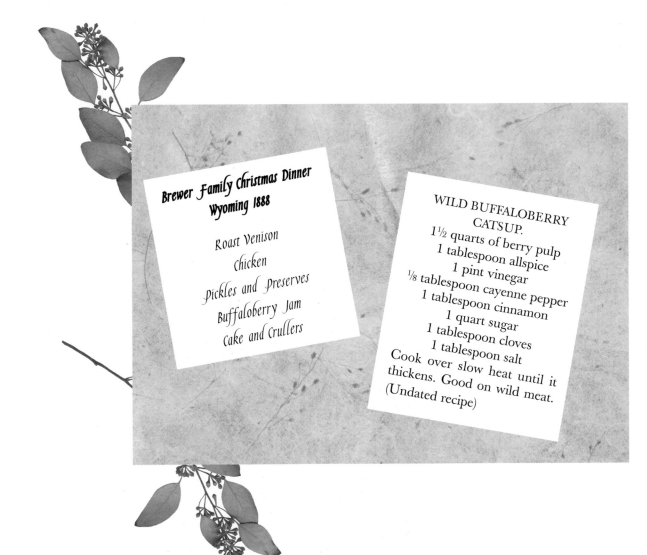

Brewer Family Christmas Dinner
Wyoming 1888

Roast Venison

Chicken

Pickles and Preserves

Buffaloberry Jam

Cake and Crullers

WILD BUFFALOBERRY
CATSUP.
1½ quarts of berry pulp
1 tablespoon allspice
1 pint vinegar
⅛ tablespoon cayenne pepper
1 tablespoon cinnamon
1 quart sugar
1 tablespoon cloves
1 tablespoon salt
Cook over slow heat until it
thickens. Good on wild meat.
(Undated recipe)

"As our staple food was pork, and there were no butchers in town we were rather in a fix and thought our Christmas dinner would suffer, until at last we got hold of some buffalo suet from a hunter returning from the west."

—Percy Ebbutt, Kansas pioneer

**Sod House
Christmas Dinner Menu
Kansas 1875**

Roast Suckling Pig

Wild Ducks

Prairie Fowl

Christmas Pudding

ROAST PIG.

Fill a six weeks pig with a stuffing made of bread and butter moistened with milk and water, and seasoned with pepper, salt and herbs if liked, and sew it up, or tie a string around it; then put it to the fire, dredge it well with a little flour, baste it well with a little butter and hot water (the fire must be hotter at each end than the middle), saving all the gravy that runs from it. When the pig is done enough, stir up the fire; take a coarse cloth, with about a quarter pound of butter in it, rub the pig all over until the crackling is crisp; than take it up. It may be served whole if small, or lay it in a dish, cut off the head, then split the body in two before drawing out the spit; cut off the ears from the head, and lay them at each end, lay the two halves of the body close together in the middle of the dish, split the head and lay at each side with the ears. Take the gravy which has run from the meat, chop the liver, brains, and heart small, and put them into it (boil them before chopping, till tender), and put in a stew-pan with some bits of butter, dredge in flour, and give it one boil, and serve in a gravy-boat. (1876)

149

LIVING IN A PRAIRIE MUD HOME was no excuse for uncivilized living. Most western transplants subscribed to a number of eastern magazines to keep up with news and fashions in the States. *Godey's Lady's Book, The Ladies' Home Journal*, even local newspapers ran scores of pieces advising the housewife on almost every aspect of life, from cleaning the carpets, to visiting the neighbors, to dressing the children, to celebrating Christmas.

Christmas afternoon should be spent in some way in the service of others. We all have something to share; if it is only a loving word or a kindly wish, it may be enough to carry good cheer to some forlorn soul. After dinner, the time is apt to hang a little heavily on the hands that have been so bountifully filled in the morning. The wee ones should have a nap to be ready for the evening, and the older children carry out whatever plan they have formed for the pleasure of others. It may be something for the gratification of their elders, or for the servants of the household, or for some less fortunate children outside their home. Perhaps some loving ministration to the sick or sorrow-stricken, the aged, or lonely.

When this is done it is time to gather round the open fire, or in the warm lamp light, and listen to the Christmas legends and stories. Tea is a secondary consideration after the Christmas dinner. Thin bread and butter and delicate cakes, with milk for the children, will be sufficient. If it can be served informally, so much the better. It seems hard to restrict the children at this festive season, so it is better not to put temptation in their way by having a variety of rich, indigestible dainties. The wise mother will watch that there is no excess. She knows it must be followed the next day by all the symptoms of malaise, that we elders include under the general term of headache, and that the reaction from over-excitement will surely put tempers out of joint, too.

—From *The Ladies' Home Journal*, December 1892

THE LADIES' HOME JOURNAL

CHRISTMAS 1890

Curtis Publishing Company. Philadelphia.

Price 10 Cents.

DECEMBER 1886

CXIII

No. 678

GODEY'S

The MIRROR of FASHION.

X MAS

ISSUE.

LADY'S BOOK

ILLUSTRATED

For the FAMILY CIRCLE.

W. E. STRIKER

PROPRIETOR ● PUBLISHER

1224 & 1226 ARCH STREET.

P.O. Box. H.H. - Phila., Pa.

Entered at the Philadelphia Post Office as second-class matter

Copyright 1886, by W. E. Striker.

The American News Company and all its branches are Agents for the Tr

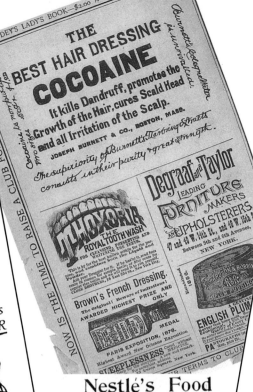

This meditation on the sacredness of the Christmas dinner appeared in *The [Bighorn, Wyoming] Sentinel* in 1884.

THE CHRISTMAS DINNER

CHRISTMAS DAYS and Christmas dinners are essentially of the home. "As sad as a Christmas dinner away from home," is a comparison whose strength has stood the test of endless repetition. The birth of Christ created the first Christmas home. It was only a stable, to be sure, but there was Joseph and Mary and the newborn babe. There are thousands upon thousands of those "elder ones" in the old farmhouses and in the homesteads which stand back from the village street who now with hand-shaded eyes are looking along the road to the four corners or down the tree-guarded walk to the swinging gate for the homecoming of the boys and girls. Grown men and women, with children tugging at their skirts, they may be, but they are boys and girls now and forever to the old couple who await their coming.

Corporations, as it has been said, may have no souls, but something seems to touch them along about Christmas, even though it necessitates a subsequent amount of privation. The keeping of the railroad rates at the normal figure would not turn back one in ten, though the ticket took the pocket money to the last dime. There are few railroad managements, however, that are not now sending broadcast notices under whose business-like statements of mileage rates and round trip ticket prices the man whose heart is at a farmhouse miles away reads this: "You may go home and take Christmas dinner with the old folks and have enough money left to take them a remembrance besides."

Christmas dinner is to be eaten at home; this has come to be regarded as a duty, and it is one of those duties in the fulfillment of which no man or woman nor boy nor girl finds anything but pleasure. The holiday week is a time which is given over by the moderns to a round of merrymaking. It was the custom of their ancestors in Old England and in the continental countries. . . . There are now dancing and gayety at Christmas from East Cape in Puritan New England to the southernmost point of California. But nowhere in all that vast country which comes between these nethermost points of this land can there be found a place where the sacredness of Christmas dinner to the home circle is not maintained, nor where the tie of home life is not strong enough to lead to the homestead the feet of all wanderers that they may pass the threshold in time for mother's Christmas dinner.

THE PREVIOUS ESSAY's sentiments notwithstanding, adult children could not always go back home for "Mother's Christmas dinner," especially when they had moved two thousand miles away. In this December 29, 1891, letter, Montana settler Elizabeth Chester Fisk, wife of newspaperman Robert E. Fisk and mother of six, described her frontier Christmas for her parents back in Connecticut, adding wistfully how she wished they could have shared it.

Our children passed [the day] pleasantly as could have been expected. We had twenty at dinner including the baby, and twenty-five for the tree. Auntie Mae and all the family were up, and the Anderson's, Grace and her family, and eight of us. . . .

We sat down at four o'clock at two tables. . . . As soon as the Andersons came we lit the tree using electric lights. The effect was good and we had no candles to watch and no wax drippings to clear from the carpet or gifts. We had many little and pretty things upon the tree as there were so many to be remembered. . . .

I wish you could have seen the little ones. They are beautiful children and were so happy. Grace's baby had his mouth in a round O all the time till he grew sleepy and tired. . . . How I wish you could have been here in person and enjoyed it with us. . . .

—From *Lizzie: The Letters of Elizabeth Chester Fisk, 1864–1893*, edited by Rex C. Myers

Most small frontier towns did not have permanent churches or resident clergymen. These communities were served by circuit riders—priests and ministers traveling by wagon or horseback to visit isolated settlements and homesteads. The Rev. Cyrus Brady was one such traveling minister. The December 1899 edition of *The Ladies' Home Journal* ran the tender and poignant story of a Christmas he spent with an impoverished homestead family in Wyoming.

WHAT CHRISTMAS MEANS IN THE FAR WEST
By the Rev. Cyrus Townsend Brady
(Author of "For Love of Country," "For the Freedom of the Sea," etc.)

One Christmas Day I left my family at one o'clock in the morning. Christmas salutations were exchanged at that very sleepy hour, and I took the fast express to a certain station whence I could drive up country to a little farm church in which there had never been a Christmas service. It was a bitter cold morning, deep snow on the ground, and a furious north wind raging. The climate is variable, indeed, out West; I have spent Christmas Days in which it rained all day, and of all of the days of the year on which to have it rain Christmas is the worst. . . .

I hired a good sleigh and two horses and drove to my destination. The church was a little old brick building standing right out on the prairie. There was a smouldering fire in a miserable worn-out stove, which hardly raised the temperature of the room a degree, although it filled the room with smoke. The wind had free entrance through the ill-fitting window and door frames, and a little pile of snow formed on the altar during the service. I think there were twelve people who had braved the fury of the storm. There was not an evergreen within a hundred miles of the place, and the only decoration was a sage brush. To wear vestments was impossible, and I conducted the service in a buffalo overcoat and a fur cap and gloves, as I have often done. It was short, and the sermon was shorter.

After service I went to dinner at the nearest farmhouse. Such a Christmas dinner it was! There was no turkey, and they did not even have a Chicken. The menu was cornbread, ham and potatoes—and few potatoes at that. There were two children in the family—a girl of six and a boy of five. They were glad enough to get the ham—their usual bill-of-fare was composed of potatoes and cornbread, and sometimes cornbread alone. My wife had put up a lunch for me, fearing I might not be able to get anything to eat, in which there was a small mince-pie turnover, and my children had slipped a small box of candy in my bag as a Christmas gift. I produced the turnover, which by common consent was divided between the children. Such a glistening of eyes and smacking of small lips you never saw!

"This pie makes it seem like Christmas after all," said the little girl with her mouth full.

"Yes," said the boy ditto, "that an' the ham."

"We didn't have any Christmas this year," continued the small maiden. "Last year mother made us some potato men." (That is, little animal and semi-human figures made out of potatoes and matches, with buttons for eyes—these go into many stockings of the poor out West.)

"But this year," interrupted the boy, "potatoes was so scarce that we couldn't have 'em. Mother says that next year, perhaps, we will have some real Christmas."

They were so brave about it that my heart went out to them. Children and no Christmas gifts! Only the chill bare room, the wretched, meagre meal. I ransacked my brain. Finally something occurred to me.

MINCEMEAT FOR PIE

Four pounds of lean boiled beef, chopped fine, twice as much of chopped green tart apples
1 pound of chopped suet
3 pounds of raisins, seeded
2 pounds of currants, picked over, washed and dried
1/2 pound citron, cut up fine
1 pound of brown sugar
1 quart cooking molasses
2 quarts sweet cider
1 pint of boiled cider
1 tablespoon salt
1 tablespoon black pepper
1 tablespoon mace
1 tablespoon allspice and 4 tablespoons cinnamon
2 grated nutmegs
1 tablespoon cloves
Mix throughly and warm on the range until heated through.
Remove from the fire and when nearly cool stir in a pint of good brandy, and a pint of Madera wine.
Put in a crock, cover it tightly, and set in a cold place where it will not freeze, but keep perfectly cold.
Will keep all winter. (Late 1800s)

After dinner I excused myself and hurried back to the church. There were two baskets there which we used for the collection, old but rather pretty. I selected the best one. Fortunately I had in my grip a very pretty little "house-wife" which contained a pair of scissors, a thimble, needles, thread, a tiny pincushion, an emery bag, buttons, etc.—I am , like most ex-sailors, something of a "needle-man" myself. I emptied the contents into the collection basket and garnished the dull little affair with the bright ribbon ties ripped off the "housewife," and went back to the house.

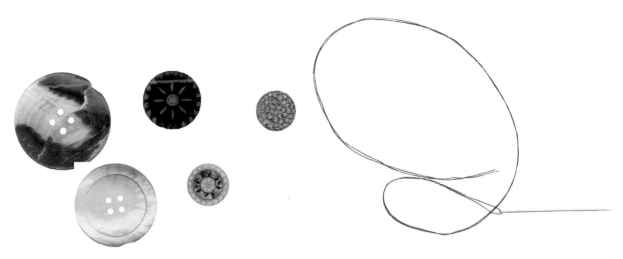

To the boy I gave my penknife, which happened to be nearly new, and to the girl the church basket with the sewing things for a work-basket. The joy of those children was one of the finest things I have ever witnessed; the face of the little girl was positively filled with awe as she lifted the pretty and useful articles from the "housewife" one by one, and when I added the small box of candy that my children had provided for me they looked at me with the feelings of reverence, almost as a visible incarnation of Santa Claus. They were the cheapest and, I can truly say, most effective Christmas presents it was ever my pleasure to bestow. I hope to be forgiven for putting the church furniture to such secular use.

THIS STORY IS BASED on information from John E. Baur's *Christmas on the American Frontier, 1800–1900.*

A NEBRASKA CHRISTMAS, 1865

The year had been a kind one to the Block family. Their crops had been good and bountiful, leaving plenty of stores for the winter. The country was at peace, and after a great deal of labor, by all appearances the farm was to be a success. Being so blessed, Mr. Block was resolved that they should keep Christmas in the manner they had been accustomed to "back home," so he left the comforts of his small sod house and set out on his three-day walk to Omaha to buy the ingredients for his family's celebration.

Upon reaching his destination he purchased gifts for his family, a few holiday treats for the dinner table, and a twenty-five-pound bag of wheat flour to replace the usual cornmeal. He then turned around and began the hundred-mile journey home with fifty pounds of Christmas on his back. The end of the second day found him only thirty miles outside of Omaha, for the weight of his sack required him to rest often.

The next day was Christmas Eve, and he walked as fast as he could in spite of the distance that lay before him and the unlikelihood he would reach home in time for the holiday that had placed him on this Nebraska road. It was about dusk when he happened upon a covered wagon with two lean horses standing beside it. Glancing about, he found a woman gathering firewood and inquired about her situation, for it was odd to see a wagon traveling the plains alone.

She explained how her husband, who now lay in the back of the wagon, was badly injured during the building of their home. Not only was he not healing, but becoming worse, and their farm, which lay just twenty-five miles west of Block's own, was failing as well. She was headed to Omaha in hopes of his recovery and her finding work enough to get them through the winter.

Martin Block kept the holiday spirit in his heart as well as on his back.

Midday Christmas, the wagon rolled up to the Block farm. He had indeed arrived in time, bearing gifts, food, and the fineries of the season, along with another family, who remained with them until spring, when the husband was able to plow again, and with seed borrowed from Block planted a successful crop.

STUFFED HAM.

A home-cured ham, nothing less elegant will do for a Christmas dinner, and it should be two years old. Lay it to soak over night in a boiler full of cold water. When ready to cook it, cut off the hock neatly just above the joint. Scrape and wash it carefully and trim off all of the outer edges, giving it a pretty shape. Weigh it and allow . . . a quarter of an hour for every pound. Put it in a boiler, cover well with cold water and boil slowly and steadily until done. As the water around the ham boils away add more, so that it is always well covered. When a fork stuck to the bone comes out readily, it is done. Now take it up and carefully peel off the skin.

Have ready a stuffing made of one teacupful of bread-crumbs just moistened with fresh milk, six grains of allspice and six cloves pounded fine, a pinch of cayenne pepper, a teaspoonful each of finely rubbed-up thyme, savory and marjoram, one teaspoonful of celery seed pounded fine, one large tablespoonful of butter, and one raw egg, mixed together.

With a sharp-pointed knife make incisions all over the ham about two inches apart. Turn the knife about to make the incision hold as much as possible, then fill each place full. Rub the ham all over with the well-beaten yolk of an egg. Sift lightly over that fine cracker-dust and set in the oven to bake slowly for one hour. (1890)

Booth Family Christmas Dinner Menu
Denver, Colorado, 1885
Stewed Oysters
Boned Turkey
Stuffed Ham
Mashed Potatoes, Turnips, Beets, Fried Celery
Gelatin with Fruits and Nuts, Candied Sweet Potatoes
Plum Pudding, Baked Lemon Pudding
Fruit Cake
Nuts
Candied Oranges
Coffee

GRACE JOHNSTON CLEMENSON grew up in a log cabin in northern Minnesota in the early twentieth century. Most of the stories in our book occurred earlier, but places like Minnesota were still "the frontier" even in the 1920s. This is an excerpt from Mrs. Clemenson's book *Grandmother's Stories*.

CHRISTMAS IN THE LOG CABIN

Christmas was the bright spot in the dark and dreary winters. The excitement and mystery of it all cannot be described. The mystery was in the form of Santa Claus with his eight reindeer galloping through the air. Old Santa himself came slipping silently down the chimney. How could he find our house tucked away in this frozen, out-of-the-way spot in the great big world? This was another mystery to me.

We began our preparation for . . . Christmas. First, there was the baking and the candy making. Then the house was cleaned and scrubbed spotless. On Christmas Eve day we all dressed in our warm outdoor clothes, for this was the day to go hunting for our Christmas tree. We all got into the sled. With horses pulling, we rode through the snow, and into the woods. After a long ride and careful searching, we finally found just the right tree. At home, daddy set the tree up in a corner of our living room. We all helped put on the decorations. Then we got out our homemade gifts which we had wrapped and carefully hidden away. When the gifts were in place, we were ready for our supper. Mother had a kettle of bean soup cooking all afternoon, and we smelled fresh corn bread coming from the oven. We were hungry now, and ate heartily.

After the meal was over and the kitchen was tidied up, we went into the living room and sat around the tree. Daddy lit the candles. We opened our gifts to one another. After our gift exchange was over and the excitement died down, daddy told us that it was time to hang up our stockings and go to bed. On a small table near the tree we left cookies and milk for Santa Claus. Now we were hurried off to bed. We waited for sleep that did not come. I listened to strange noises around the tree,

Unidentified North Dakota homestead and family
—State Historical Society of North Dakota

and thought that Santa must surely be there. I closed my eyes tight. In a minute I was asleep. Suddenly I was awakened by a shout. "Merry Christmas! Santa Claus has been here!" At last the great day had arrived. I got up in a daze and looked around. I glanced at the little table. Yes, the cookies and milk were gone. Santa never failed us. Best of all, he came with an abundance of the best. He left dolls, tea sets, books, blocks, drums, sleds, nuts, candy, apples, and best of all, an orange in the tip of every stocking. I discovered as I grew up that my daddy's well-to-do relatives in St. Louis and Minneapolis were Santa's most active helpers.

Another Christmas stands out in my mind. That was the year of the Christmas tree fire. Uncle John and Aunt Laura and their five children, Wanda, Ruth, Sheila, Maxine and Alice, who was the baby, came for Christmas. They came many miles in a covered sleigh, a two-days' journey from their home in Gonvick. The brought their gifts and a paper Santa Claus. How well I remember the excitement on Christmas Eve Day. Daddy and Uncle John said that we must all get dressed in our outdoor clothes for we were going to the woods to hunt for a Christmas tree. We all went, Wanda, Ruth, Sheila, Maxine, Vern, Crystal and Me. I remember that Grandpa Champ also decided to ride along. We had quite a sleigh load. I wondered where we would put the tree.

BEAN SOUP.

Put two quarts of dried white beans into soak the night before you make the soup, which should be put on as early in the day as possible.

Take five pounds of the lean of fresh beef—the course pieces will do. Cut them up, and put them into your soup pot with the bones belonging to them, and a pound of bacon cut very small. Season the meat with pepper only, and pour on it six quarts of water. As soon as it boils take off the scum, and put in the beans (having first drained them) and a head of celery cut small, or a table-spoonful of pounded celery-seed. Boil it slowly until the meat is done to shreds, and the beans all dissolved. Take out the bones with a fork before you send it to table.
(1851)

"We used to get thick catalogues from Montgomery Wards, they started up the year I was born [1872] and there were a few families that my folks always neighbored with, not many, and in the fall they all put in a big order together and it came in a big box about Christmas time."

—Remembrance of Mrs. Fred Brooks, settler, North Platte, Nebraska

We found a small nicely shaped little spruce. Everyone agreed that it was just the right one. The rest of the day was spent setting up the tree and putting on the decorations. Mother and Aunt Laura put on the tinsel, popcorn strings and icicles. Each child was given an ornament to put in place. Mine was a gold star made of card board with a string attached. I hung it carefully on a lower branch.

Last of all the candles were fastened on. They were tiny wax candles set into a holder which was snapped onto the branches. The paper santa clause was hung on the wall beside the tree. Gifts were arranged under the tree. Now we were ready for the lighting of the candles.

We all sat down on the floor, admiring the tree and watching daddy as he lit the candles. One by one they began to shine, emitting a soft glow to the room. Suddenly the paper santa clause came down. It fell against a lighted candle. Everything began to burn. The blaze spread fast. Uncle John and daddy jumped up and doused the tree with pails of water which they kept on hand in one corner of the room. We received many soggy gifts. I do not remember any dampened spirits.

—Courtesy Wyoming State Archives

One can see where attention to detail can mean so much—is it not the addition of the sliced lemons that makes this dish so enticing?

CALF'S HEAD SOUP.

Lay one large calf's head well cleaned and washed, and four pig's feet, in bottom of a large pot, and cover with a gallon of water; boil three hours, or until flesh will slip from bones; take out head, leaving feet to be boiled steadily while the meat is cut from the head; select with care enough of the fatty portions in the top of the head and cheeks to fill a tea-cup, and set aside to cool; remove brains into saucer, and also set aside; chop the rest of the meat with the tongue very fine, season with salt, pepper, powdered marjoram and thyme, a tea-spoon of cloves, one of mace, half as much allspice and grated nutmeg. When the flesh falls from the bones of the feet, take out the bones, leaving the gelatinous meat; boil all together slowly, without removing the cover, for two hours more, take the soup from the fire and set it away until the next day. An hour before dinner set the stock over the fire, and when it boils strain carefully and drop in the reserved meat. Have these all ready as well as the force-meat balls, to prepare which rub the yolks of five hard-boiled eggs to a paste in a wedgewood mortar, or in a bowl with the back of a silver spoon, adding gradually the brains to moisten them, also a little butter and salt. Mix with these, two eggs beaten very light, flour the hands and make this paste into balls about the size of a pigeon's egg; throw them into the soup five minutes before taking it from the fire; stir in a large table-spoon browned flour rubbed smooth in a little cold water, and finish the seasoning by the addition of a glass and a half of sherry or Madeira wine, and the juice of a lemon. It should not boil more than half an hour on the second day. Serve with sliced lemons. (1876)

A simpler, yet more revolting pioneer recipe:

BLOOD PUDDING

Catch the fresh blood from a cow or sheep in a bucket containing a few tablespoons of salt. Stir well. Remove the stomach and clean well. Add pepper and fat, and pour the blood in. Tie the stomach shut and boil for one to two hours. Allow to cool, then slice. {Undated recipe}

Need something to wash it down with?

TURNIP-WINE.

Take a good many turnips, pare, slice, and put them in a cider-press, and press out all the juice very well. To every gallon of juice have three pounds of lump-sugar, have a vessel ready, just big enough to hold the juice, put your sugar into a vessel, and also to every gallon of juice half a pint of brandy. Pour in the juice, and lay something over the bung for a week to see if it works. If it does, you must not bung it down until it has done working; then stop it close for three months, and draw it off in another vessel. When it is fine, bottle it off. (1805)

A Glorious Time Is Assured

Community Celebrations

URING THE EARLY YEARS of western migration, the first few Christmases for many settlers, especially women, were tinged with loneliness. But as the miles began to close up between isolated stage stations, ranches, and mining camps, they grew into settlements, and settlements grew into towns. When a town, large or small, came together to celebrate Christmas, that's when magic could happen: a beautifully decorated tree could materialize, along with impossible gifts—one for each person. A dance hall could transform into a church. Folks might dance without sleeping for two days and nights. Competing newspapers might shake hands and take a vacation. An outlaw might preside over an elegant feast. Adults might believe in Santa Claus.

The writings in this section illustrate at least two phases of community building. In the early stage, everyone in a community knew one another. Celebrations were informal—a party at so-and-so's house, a gathering around a brimming barrel of spirits. Larger parties, which the whole settlement might attend, required a bit more planning, to allow enough time to get the word out and to order adequate food and drink. At this stage in a community, different types of people coexisted on more or less equal footing—homesteading families, business owners, bachelor miners, even outlaws. Organized charity was unnecessary; if someone was in need at Christmas, neighbors chipped in to play Santa.

As a town's population grew, things took on a different tone. Refinements and rules began to appear. Society began to separate into classes, and like groups splintered off to celebrate among themselves. Compared with earlier frontier gatherings, fabulous entertainments were now available: fireworks, ice skating, and elaborate church services. Social welfare was still addressed, but in a more organized and less personal way.

But it little mattered whether a place was a cluster of canvas tents or a municipality of two-story homes, when a western community gathered together to celebrate Christmas, they were in a sense celebrating life.

A crowd of children await Santa Claus in downtown Bozeman, Montana, on Christmas Day, circa 1896.
—Courtesy Gallatin County Historical Society

MERRY CHRISTMAS

The Christmas Ball which the Big Horn People are giving on Christmas Eve at Sackett & Skinner's Hall will be an occasion of great jollification and we are sure all who attend will enjoy a Merry Christmas.

The ball to be given on Christmas Eve in Sackett & Skinner's Hall is given for the benefit of all inclined to attend and no other invitation other than public notice has been or will be sent out. Everyone is invited and will be cordially received. A glorious time is assured.

—*The Sentinel*, December 20, 1884

—From the *Daily Argus,* Fargo, North Dakota, December 22, 1883

—From the *Daily Oregonian*, December 18, 1882

170

Santa Cruz Mission
—From *In and Out of the Old Missions of California* by George Wharton James, 1907

AMERICANS BEGAN to populate California in significant numbers around the 1840s. Before that, Spanish Franciscans established many missions throughout the future state to convert the local Indians. This recollection of Christmas at an early California mission was printed in the *San Francisco Call,* December 1899.

BEFORE THE GRINGO CAME
By José Ramon Pico

Christmas in California before the Americans came was a season when all the grown people had as much fun as the children do now. And the children had so much fun that they never got over it and ever after loved play and presents more than work and hard bargaining.

There was no business in the country then but the raising of cattle. All summer long the cows fed over the oat-covered hills in the mornings and mowed away the clover into their four stomachs during the afternoons, as they stood beneath the sisal groves.

By November each one was as fat as it could get and yet manage to walk. The vaqueros and *Los Indios* came many days' journey across the San Joaquin Valley, driving big herds of cattle to be killed for hides and tallow. There were no roads and the only way to get the products to market was to drive the animals themselves.

For six weeks then there was plenty of work. All day long green hides were being hung over poles and dry hides were being packed away. Suet by the ton was dumped into the smoking cauldrons and far into the night the sweating Indians worked ladling out melted tallow with big wooden dippers into bags made of rawhide. . . .

In killing so many cattle there was more meat than could be eaten or sold, and the choicest parts of the beef were cut into long strips, dipped in a strong boiling brine full of hot red peppers, and then hung over rawhide lines to dry in the sun, making a very appetizing and nutritious food known as *carne seca,* which is used during the rest of the year for preparing the delicious enchiladas and chili con carne.

Soon after the first of December the last hide would be piled under the roof, the last scoop full of tallow ladled into its bag and the sacks and sacks of carne seca stowed away with the chilies and frijoles in the attic.

Then commenced the preparations for the *Fiesta del Cristo, La Noche Buena.*

Chickens by the dozens were boiled and for days the Indians worked pounding parched corn in stone mortars; the rich meal was rolled around the tender chicken, and the whole was then wrapped with chilies in corn husks to be steamed. These, packed away in jars, would keep until wanted by reason of the quantity of red pepper in the seasoning.

All this time the Indians had been eating, eating, day and night; the Mahalas [Indian women] made bread of acorns, laurel nuts and horse chestnuts; baked beans and meats. . . .

Mucha fiesta! There never had been such plenty until the padres came.

TAMALES

1 pound dried corn husks
6 cups masa harina (corn flour)
1/2 cup lard
2 teaspoons salt
5 pounds chicken, beef, or pork, seasoned, cooked, and chopped

Soak husks in water until soft. Cream lard and mix with masa. Add water or stock to form soft dough. Spread thin layer of dough onto husk. Spread heaping spoonful of meat over dough. Roll up carefully. Wrap another husk around the tamale and tie the ends. Steam for about an hour. (Traditional recipe)

Native Californians
—From *Harper's New Monthly Magazine*, October 1868

By Christmas there would sometimes be three hundred Indians at the mission of Santa Clara, and many whole families of our relatives and rancheros who lived adjacent would come. . . . We made presents, though there was no Santa Claus then.

To the Indians we gave young beeves to kill for fresh meat and also red blankets and handkerchiefs. To the padre at the mission we gave such things as . . . *carne seca,* peppers, sweet potatoes and sacks of beans to supply their kitchen, and big bundles of dry hides for them to use in making chairs and furniture and also for use in fastening the timbers of the buildings. Everything was then fastened with rawhide, as we had no nails. . . .

On *La Noche Buena* at our hacienda there were always many families beside our own. My uncle, Pio Pico, was twice the Governor of California, and my father was one of the Justices who correspond to our Chief Justice of the Supreme Court—Judge of the Court of the Primera Instancia. . . .

One Christmas Eve, I remember best, there was a full moon. Over all the ground there was a glittering frost, just enough to whiten everything, yet not enough to even nip the orange trees which at this season of the year hang full of fruit and blossom both. . . .

We had much music—guitars of the Mexican and Spanish type, made with twelve strings of wire, and mandolins. After supper there was dancing in the patio, coffee and *cigaritos* on the veranda, and singing everywhere. Someone said it was a beautiful night for a horseback ride over the valley to the Mission Santa Clara. The horses in the corral were soon saddled. There were twenty-five or thirty of us young men and women. Our horses were the best of the big herds that were attached to every rancho. . . . The saddles, bridles and spurs were heavily covered with silver bullion ornaments, as in those times we put silver on our horses instead of on our dining room tables; for Spaniards . . . live on horseback, and they eat but to live, instead of living to eat.

Riding out of the patio gate it was like a scene from the time of the Moors in Spain. As our horses snorted in the cold air they spun the rollers in their bits, making music that only the Spanish horse knows.

Our course led us through the beautiful *alameda,* where the moonlight streamed through the branches that laced overhead and continued in perspective to the vanishing point.

Coming to the Mission Santa Clara, there was a ruddy light as of a burning building, that turned out to be the Indian encampment, holding one of their ceremonious dances that always precedes business, pleasure or war. We always saw to it that the Indians had plenty to eat, for there was no easier way to keep them in subjection than by making presents of food, and at Christmas time we had the better reason of wishing to show them the substantial benefits of Christianity.

At all of the fires were Indians cooking and eating. After they had eaten for a time they began to steal away and hide in the darkness, except for a few of the oldest men and women, who stayed to replenish the fire. Suddenly loud yells split the air, and from behind trees on the flat and rocks on the hill Indians came running in as though to murder and scalp those about the fire. Then from the other side came the war cry, and other Indians rushed to defend the elders. After that was a sort of sham battle, all laughing, wrestling and rolling on the ground till tired and ready to eat again.

When the Indians were through with their play the padres came slowly from the Mission, the Indians formed in line after them and marched away to the night mass, to listen to the simple story of the Child in the manger and to gaze upon the Old Testament scenes shown in pictures on the walls. . . .

So the allegory of the evening showed how the Indians had thought only of war, how they had sought their enemies and pursued them, and how at last they had come to church. . . . Back to the hacienda again faster than we came, to where the oranges leaned over the dark fountain pool. Then into the patio, where fragrant coffee from Mexico, tortillas and *tamales de las gallinas* were served steaming hot from the big fireplace in the kitchen. Though we danced until morning, there was not a sleepy eye in the house. When daylight came we went to our rooms or took siestas in the hammocks under the verandas and were ready for *almuerzo* [lunch] when the bell rang.

And so for a week our Christmas lasted.

H ENRY WARNER wrote his recollection of Denver's first Christmas for the *Denver Times* in December 1900.

DENVER'S FIRST CHRISTMAS (1858)

The sun had hardly risen when Santa Claus made his appearance. [But this Santa was] an ordinary frontiersman who had fought Indians and scouted and hunted across the vast and fertile plains. He carried a rifle and was smooth shaven. [It was Dick Wooten.]

He had a couple of wagons laden with frontier merchandise, chiefly in barrels. Wooten put up a tent beside his wagon, rolled his stock inside, then rolled a barrel onto a log platform, smashed in the top with an axe and invited

DENVER'S FIRST CHRISTMAS CELEBRATION

Tapping the barrel and having a high old time.

—Courtesy Denver Public Library, Western History Department

the on lookers to "pitch in and he'p y'rselves!" In honor of Christmas.

[In the barrel] was what in those days we termed "Taos Lightning." It came from Taos, N.M., and was warranted to kill at 40 yards. . . . None felt obliged to resist temptation. Convenient wagon wheels were soon being used as crutches by those who had allowed themselves to gather in the influence. . . . Men lying flat on their backs because of physical inability to stand, held out their hands for more.

Menu
Denver's First Christmas, 1858

Oyster Soup, Ox Tail Soup

Salmon Trout, with Oyster Sauce

Boiled Corn Beef, Buffalo Tongue, Mutton, Pork, Ham, Beef Tongue, Elk Tongue

Roast Venison a la Mode, Smothered Buffalo, Antelope, Beef, Mutton, Pork

Grizzly Bear a la Mode, Elk, Mountain Sheep, Mountain Pig, Mountain Pheasant,

Mountain Rabbit, Turkey, Duck, Sage Hen, Prairie Chicken

Black Mountain Squirrel, Prairie Dog, Snipe, Mountain Rat, White Swan, Quail, Sand Hill Crane

Baked Potatoes, Boiled Potatoes, Rice, Baked Beans, Boiled Beans, Baked Beets

Fried Squash, Stewed Pumpkin

Mince Pie, Current Pie, Apple Pie, Rice Pie, Peach Pie, Mountain Cranberry Pie,

Tapioca Pudding, Bread Pudding, Rice Pudding

Brazil Nuts, Almonds, Hazelnuts, Filberts, Pecans, Wild Currants, Raisins,

Prickly Pear, Dried Mountain Plum

Wines & Spirits:

Hockheimer, Madeira, Champagne, Golden Sherry, Cherry Bounce, Hock, Monongahela Whiskey,

Claret, Brandy, Scotch Whiskey, Jamaica Rum, Bourbon Whiskey, Taos Lightning

OYSTER SOUP.

Take two quarts of fine oysters, strain the liquor and if there is not liquor sufficient to make your soup, put as much water, one onion, two blade of mace, boil, have ready a piece of butter say from a quarter to half a pound, with flour sufficient to thicken, rub them up together. Season with pepper and salt to your taste. When just ready to dish throw in at least half a pint of rich cream, then give one more boil, fend up to table. The oysters will be plump and the soup very nice. (1801)

PRAIRIE DOG.

Build a large fire. Gut the prairie dog and salt the cavity and close with sticks. Singe hair off dog. Dig hole under fire about 6 feet deep. Put the dog in the hole and cover it with dirt, then build up the fire on top. After 4 to 6 hours dig up dog. (Undated recipe)

BREAD PUDDING.

One quart sweet milk, quart bread crumbs, four eggs, four tablespoons sugar; soak bread in half the milk until soft; mash fine, add the rest of milk, the well beaten eggs and sugar, and a tea-cup raisins; bake one hour, serve warm. (1876)

A LA MODE VENISON.

Cut deep incisions all over the venison, and then fill them with the following stuffing: One teacupful of finely-crumbled bread, one teacupful of finely-minced fat pork, one teaspoonful of sugar, one of salt, one of mixed spices, finely pounded—mace, allspice and cloves—one teaspoonful of celery seed, one gill of chopped-up celery, one gill of butter and one raw egg, salt and pepper to taste, and one silver-skinned onion the size of an nutmeg; mince fine and mix all well together. Stuff the venison, rub over the outside with soft butter, dredge well with flour, and put in a pan with a pint of water and tablespoonful of butter.

Do not have the oven too hot, but cook slowly for the first hour, basting and dredging frequently. After an hour increase the heat and let it brown more rapidly. If it is an ordinary sized leg of venison two hours and a half will be required to cook it. As soon as blood ceases to run when it is pierced, it is done, and should be removed from the oven and kept warm until sent to the table. Serve with currant or guava jelly. (1890)

One by one the pioneers went down and out, and when the sun crept into bed that night, there were forms stretched out in deep slumber over the prairie. . . .

Nobody ever has forgotten that Christmas. . . . the first Christmas in Denver. Before night, the generous distributor of whisky was known as "Uncle Dick" and the name has stayed with him. . . . He opened up a place of business the next day, and before the New Year of 1859 started he was the leading merchant of the Rocky Mountain region.

The high honor of having the first Christmas tree in Denver goes to a woman known as Countess Katrina Marat, wife of the camp barber, who decorated her tree with hand-dipped candles and gingerbread children, animals, and stars.

The great feast was followed by hearty toasts and the singing of songs, which included, "The Star-Spangled Banner," "A Hit at the Times," "Rosalie, the Prairie Flower," "Home of My Boyhood," and "The Mountain Boy's Call."

D ENVER'S SECOND Christmas was even more memorable than its first. This article appeared in western newspapers in 1924.

THE FAMOUS TURKEY WAR
By Will C. Ferril

Denver, Dec. 23. It was Christmas time in 1859 and the boys all wanted to celebrate the day with turkey dinners. Turkeys were scarce in those days and a fine-looking old gobbler had hardly one chance in a thousand to survive the holiday season.

There were roughs and toughs here then in large numbers, who attempted to run things in their own way, and there arose what will ever be known as the "famous turkey war of '59."

It came about this way.

At that time there were two towns at the mouth of Cherry creek, Denver and Auraria, the latter being the larger of the two and the combined population aggregating about 2,000 people. Those being the early days in the Rocky mountain country, there were only about 200 women here. Lawlessness was getting the upper hand and it was a mooted question for a while as to whether the toughs or the respectable element would gain the ascendancy. The turkey war brought things to a focus. It was not a friendly war between buyers as to who should obtain turkeys by bidding the highest prices, but it was a war with pistols and rifles.

Both sides were heavily armed and meant business. The toughs and the roughs stole the turkeys and that did mean war. The better element was thoroughly aroused and excited, and every man had his gun ready for business. The roughs saw what a row they had stirred up and they, too, armed for battle.

It seems that the day before Christmas, a ranchman drove into Auraria with a wagon load of fine wild turkeys, knowing that they would command a handsome price in the Christmas market. But he little thought what a row he was about stirring up. On what was then known as Ferry street, there was a long row of saloons and gambling dives, and in front of these the ranchman halted with his turkeys. A large crowd immediately collected around the wagon, for everybody wanted turkey for his Christmas dinner. He began to negotiate for the sale of his turkeys, when the bummer element having collected in the saloons suddenly sneaked forth and ere anyone was aware of what had occurred, had stolen every turkey out of the ranchman's wagon.

Auraria and Denver soon became all excited. Not only was the question of a fine Christmas dinner involved, but that of whether the bummers should further rule the pioneer twin cities. The respectable element had put up with a good deal, but the stealing of that wagon load of fine turkeys brought matters to a climax. A citizen's meeting was called. Speeches were made. Everybody was indignant at the lawless element. The citizen's meeting appointed a committee to investigate this heinous outrage, which proceeded at once to business. A large number of witnesses were examined, and from the testimony adduced, it was shown that Thomas Clem, William Todd, alias Chuck-a-Luck, William Harvey, William Karl, alias Buckskin Bill, and others were guilty of stealing the turkeys. The report of the committee created still greater

Saloon "courthouse" in Colorado mining town;
drawing by Alfred Mitchell
—From *Frank Leslie's Illustrated Newspaper*, November 27, 1886

excitement. The citizens continued arming themselves, and the bummers began marshaling their forces either for defense or attack, as the circumstances might best indicate. The bummers became bolder toward evening, and paraded Auraria and Denver, all heavily armed.

They were noisy and boisterous, and the crack, crack of their pistols and rifles was heard as they fired into the air. Peaceable citizens were stopped on the streets, and with six-shooters flashed in their faces, were threatened. The outlook continued to be more desperate, but in the meantime the quiet arming of the citizens went on. About 9 o'clock that night, W. H. Middaugh, father of Asa Middaugh, now residing at Del Norte, Col., was fired at while standing in front of the Vasquez house in Ferry street. This shot was fired by a man named McCarty, and just grazing Middaugh's head, passed through the door. Middaugh had been one of the most important witnesses against the turkey thieves, and, hence the cause of the attack on him. This but added to the excitement which had already become intense. A few moments later, after Middaugh entered the hotel, he was fired at a second time by a man named George Harvey, who, like McCarty, missed his aim.

At that time there was a military organization here known as the "Jefferson Rangers," and a messenger was at once dispatched to their armory where they were drilling, and informed of the serious condition of affairs. The rangers immediately filed into line and marched toward the scenes of disturbance, but the bummers had left before they arrived. But as the rough element had threatened to burn the town, the rangers patrolled the streets. In the meantime, McCarty, who had fired the first shot at Middaugh, had been killed by Tom Pollock, a son-in-law of Colonel Chivington. . . . McCarty had drawn a Bowie knife on Pollock, and the latter killed him with a blow from the butt end of his rifle. Immediately after McCarty's death, Harvey met Pollock and drew his revolver, but the click, click of revolvers and rifles warned Harvey that it was not wise for him to proceed further in his murderous intentions, and he hurried away. No further disturbances occurred that night.

Later a meeting of the citizens was held and resolutions adopted that Karl, Todd and Harvey must leave the town in five hours or be hanged. Most of the thieves accepted these terms. . . .

The town now quieted down, but the rangers and citizens kept a close watch for several days. Thus ended the "turkey war" in Denver, which is one of the most remarkable Christmases on record.

—Courtesy Denver Public Library, Will Ferril Collection

TO ROAST A TURKEY.

Make a force-meat of grated bread-crumbs, minced suet, sweet marjoram, grated lemon-peel, nutmeg, pepper, salt, and beaten yolk of egg. You may add some grated cold ham. Light some writing paper, and singe the hairs from the skin of the turkey. Reserve the neck, liver, and gizzard for the gravy. Stuff the craw of the turkey with the force-meat. Dredge it with flour, and roast it before a clear brisk fire, basting it with cold lard. Towards the last, set the turkey nearer to the fire, dredge it again very lightly with flour, and baste it with butter. It will require, according to its size, from two to three hours roasting.

Make the gravy of the giblets cut in pieces, seasoned, and stewed for two hours in a very little water; thicken it with a spoonful of browned flour, and stir into it the gravy from the dripping-pan, having first skimmed off the fat. (1851)

From the *San Francisco Chronicle*, December 12, 1888

TURKEYS, PIGEONS AND BROKEN BLUE ROCKS.

Successes With Rifle and Smooth-Bore by Kearns, Baker, Wheeler and Cole.

The second day of George Bird's pigeon and turkey tournament was about as untoward as the first, thanks to the very ungenial altitude of Jupiter Pluvius. Active work on the ground was not commenced much before noon, and even then all the boys who took their chances in the various shoots were clad as if for a day in the marshes or tules.

Between 10 o'clock and noon some dozen and a half of turkeys had been satisfactorily disposed of, all being fair specimens of the Christmas bird, and giving good evidence of plethoric feeding. All kinds of rifles were employed, but the invariable distance was 250 yards. The prime turkey winner was Mr. Kearns, who also made his mark on Sunday.

After giving Andrews and Jones a hard half-hour's work getting the water out of the trench, a blue-rock shoot was opened on a subscription of $2 50 each by seven shooters, the money to be divided into two prizes of $10 and $7 50. Cole made a clean score and took first money, the rest of the pot becoming the property of Fred Baker, with one saucer short of the decade. Wheeler, who is something of a terror on live birds, came out at the short end, with 4 only.

In the next shoot, also at ten blue rocks, Baker swept the deck with a clean score, and Captain Wheeler came next with 8. Only three participated, and Baker claimed the single pool, amounting to $7 50.

The third shot, at five pairs of blue rocks, was won by Wheeler, who again corraled the pool, Donovan being second. Appended are the scores:

First pigeon shoot; 10 blue rocks; 18 yards rise; $2 50 entrance; 7 subscribers; money divided, $10 and $7 50.

```
Wheeler.............0 1 0 0 0 1 0 0 1 1— 4
Card...............1 0 1 1 0 1 1 1 0 1— 7
Cole...............1 1 1 1 1 1 1 1 1 1—10
Baker..............1 0 1 1 1 1 1 1 1 1— 9
Donovan............0 1 1 0 1 0 0 1 1 1— 6
Smith..............1 0 1 1 0 0 1 1 0 1— 6
Harper.............1 1 0 0 1 1 1 1 0 1— 7
```

Second shoot; 10 blue rocks; $2 50 entrance; 3 subscribers; single pool:

```
Wheeler............0 1 0 1 1 1 1 1 1 1— 8
Baker..............1 1 1 1 1 1 1 1 1 1—10
Smith..............1 0 0 0 0 1 1 0 1 0— 4
```

Third shoot; 5 pairs double blue rocks; 15 yards rise; $2 50 each; 3 subscribers; single pool:

```
Wheeler.......11 11 11 11 11—10
Baker.........01 10 00 01 10— 4
Donovan.......10 11 11 11 11— 9
```

Before the afternoon was over Captain Wheeler's quondam opponent, Holtz, put in an appearance on the ground, and it took very little "blarney" to get up a match between them at a dozen live birds each. The old salt got away with his old-time opponent by a score of 10 to 8, the winner starting off with the lead and maintaining it to the end. Their match was for $25 a side, and governed by Hurlingham rules:

```
Wheeler......1 1 2 1 0 1 1 2 0 1 2 1—10
Holtz........1 2 0 1 1 0 2 1 1 0 0 2— 8
```

A large Oakland gathering is expected at the Point to-day, when both "birds," live and blue rock, and turkeys will be on the sporting bill of fare.

184

"The giving of gifts was not like it is now because we simply could not buy them . . . . We would have a church service, and a community tree. At this community tree we would each get some candy and the presents from our friends. We girls always struck pretty heavy pay dirt. Each swain would remember us in some way. They had to fashion their presents by hand, but we practically furnished our rooms by these presents."

—Mrs. Neil Niven, settler, Granite, Oregon

An Oregon Christmas, 1855
By William V. Wells

Now, in Oregon, where people reside ten miles apart, and call a man a neighbor who lives half a days journey away, it is not so easy to make up a fashionable party, for sundry reasons, as fifth Avenue, or any other of the "close settlements" of New York. If a hop is to take place, weeks must be given to prepare in; the "store clothes" taken out, aired and brushed, old bonnets furbished up, horses driven in from distant pasture, and saddles made ready. Then the nearest settlement must be applied to for a proper amount of whisky and sugar, raisins and flour. But on the occasion above alluded to (Christmas), great efforts were made to have matters go off with éclat. Deacon L—, residing on the ocean beach, about twenty miles to the southward of Coo's Bay, and known as the most liberal, warmhearted old gentleman of Southern Oregon, had appropriated, some time in advance, the right to give the Christmas ball. It was to last two days and two nights. Oceans of whisky, hills of venison and beef, no end of pies and "sech like." The ladies of Coo's County were to be there, and a fiddler from the distant point of Port Orford itself engaged. To this feast did all hands look forward with secret longing and hope. . . .

LEBENBAUM BRO'S.

GROCERS,

215 and 217 Sutter St., and Polk St., Cor. California.

LARGEST ESTABLISHMENT.

HOLIDAY ATTRACTIONS!

Rare Vintages of Our Importation of Genuine Brands of

French Clarets, Sauternes, Burgundies, Madeiras, Sherries and Port Wines, Champagnes.

Renowned brands of Old Whiskies, Cognacs, Jamaica Rum, Arrac and Cordials.

French Fruit Glace, Wiesbaden Preserves, Fancy Raisins, Nuts, La Favre's Plum Pudding and Sauce, Shrimp Salad, and Lemon Syrup for Punches.

Imported Fancy Cheeses, Boneless Goose Breasts, and a large variety of other Holiday Condiments.

OUR COFFÉE AND TEAS STAND UNRIVALED

☞ SEND FOR OUR CATALOGUE AND PRICES ☜

—From the *San Francisco Chronicle*, December 12, 1888

Party in Butte, Montana, 1897
—Courtesy World Museum of Mining, Butte, Montana

And on Christmas eve the ball commenced. There were gay roystering blades from Port Orford, gallants from Coo's Bay, select men and distinguished individuals from all over the country, and belles from every where. Such a recherché affair had not occurred since the settlement of the Territory. For two nights and days festivities continued; and after all the dancing, riding, drinking, singing, and laughing—and all this without sleeping, and with determination to "never give up"—there were buxom forms and brilliant eyes that dared us to another breakdown!

—From *Harper's New Monthly Magazine*, October 1856

CHRISTMAS DAY, 1865, IN VIRGINIA CITY, MONTANA
By Father Francis Xavier Kuppins

Christmas day, 1865, was a memorable day in Virginia City in the Territory of Montana. The events that happened there on that great Holy Day were narrated hundreds of times, and in the most distant settlement of the Territory, and they lingered along in the minds of men. I have heard them scores of times, in many and various forms, and with unimportant alterations, but always leaving the main events standing out prominently.

Virginia City at that time was a prosperous settlement, the center of various mining camps in the district. It was a wild place, hardly to be called civilized. Communication with the States was slow, with most goods imported by ox train from Ogden or Salt Lake. The stage had only recently been established, but at prohibitive prices. There was, as yet, no telegraph. The medium of commerce was gold dust or nuggets, weighed in small apothecary scales, or guessed at by a two-finger or a three-finger pinch. Metal coin or paper currency were seldom seen. Although population of the district was estimated to be about 10,000, there were hardly any families in the place; all were individual men of every nation, and tongue. Some fifteen or twenty married couples was all that the place could boast of; children were never seen. There were some refined persons, but they were mixed and lost in the crowd. The refining influence of women to leaven the manners of the people was absent. The Vigilance Committee had been organized the year before, had in three weeks executed over twenty persons and was now at the height of its power. They assumed to themselves the office, not of protecting life or property, but of dealing out swift and summary punishment to any transgressor.

The town had been elected Capital of the Territory, in place of Bannack, whose star had set when a few of its richest claims were exhausted. General Thomas Francis Meagher, appointed Acting Governor,

Christmas day 1865 was a memorable day in Virginia City in the territory of Montana. The events that happened there on that Great Holy Day were narrated hundreds of times, and in the most distant settlements of the territory; & they lingered long in the minds of the Catholics. I have heard them scores of times, in many and various forms, and with many & unimportant alterations, but always leaving the main events standing out very prominently.

Virginia City at that time was a very prosperous centre settlement of various mining Camps in the district. It was a wild place and could hardly bee called Civilized. Communication with the states was very slow; most of the goods were imported by oxtrain from Ogden or Salt Lake. The Stage had only recently been established but at prohibitive prices. There was as yet no telegraph. The medium of Commerce was gold, dust or nuggets, which was weighed in small apothecary scales, or guessed at by a two finger or a three finger pinch. Metal Coin or paper Currency were never seen. The population of the district was estimated to be about 10.000. There were hardly any families in the place; all were individual men, of every Nation, and tongue, some 15 or 20 married Couples was all that the place could boast of; Children were never seen. There were refined persons, but they were (mixed) and lost in the crowd. The refining influence of woman

Father Kuppins's original handwriting —Courtesy Midwest Jesuit Archives

had arrived in the Territory during the preceding summer and taken up residence in the Capital. The legislature was to meet in a couple of weeks for the first time in this new Capital, and many law-makers were already at the place before Christmas. Many miners were idle on account of the frost; and the approaching holiday season brought together an unprecedented numerous population. Every hotel, lodging house and cabin was crowded to its utmost capacity.

A priest, on mission in those days, besides vestments, altar stone, and chapel, also carried provisions and blankets; all his travels were on horseback, and few journeys were undertaken during which he was not obliged to camp out a few nights. When lodging was obtained it most generally was only a shelter under a stranger's roof, and a place to spread your blankets on the floor. There was no mail from the Indian Country where the priest lived and no notice could be sent of an intended visit.

In 1865 Father Giorda arrived in Virginia City a few days before Christmas, and took up his lodging at the cabin of a pious Catholic miner. He, in company of that worthy man, spent all evening and all next day in trying to secure a place that might serve for a Chapel on that great Holy day. Any hall, dining room, large store, or large room would have been gladly accepted, or rented at any price, for a place of worship; but none could be secured, not even for a few hours before breakfast hour; no, not even a couple of hours in the forenoon during the quiet hours of business from nine to eleven o'clock could any room or hall be secured. Late that night exhausted, footsore and more heartsore after the fruitless search, the Father and his companion retired to rest hoping and praying better success in the morning. What prayers and reflections were on that night, considering the many points of similarity to a like occurrence in Judea, is a subject of reflection.

Late that evening, in a place where the youth and the sporting fraternity of the town amused themselves at cards or dice, someone mentioned that a Catholic priest was in town and had been trying all day to find a place for holding service on Christmas day and had not succeeded. This was too much for the hearers. The old faith, though it had lately shown few signs of life, now burst from the embers in a fair blaze. A firm resolve took possession of many; a place must be found for the Christmas celebration; that was the verdict, and without definite plans they dispersed, determined to find ways and means in the morning.

The leader of the crowd was not a man of procrastination principles. We will call him Mr. Hugh O'Neill. He wore the champion's belt, and had posted a standing challenge to any aspirant ready to try issue in the ring according to the rules of the Marquis of Queensberry. Though late, Hugh O'Neill went to see General Meagher, the Governor, who was well known. Both were of one nation, country, both of one religion, and it did not take long to form a plan of action. It would be a shame, a burning and everlasting shame, if the Catholic religion could obtain no place for worship on Christmas day; and that in the Capital of Montana, and the Governor there. Both men were equally indignant. Shortly afterwards the proprietor of the theatre, the largest place in town, had his sleep interrupted and was compelled to listen to business propositions. A large amount of gold would be paid for the rent of the theatre for two weeks. This and other equally eloquent arguments brought consent and all dates and engagements were cancelled. The actors were easily persuaded that a two weeks' rest during the Holiday season would give them a good rest—so necessary for their health.

In the morning a committee of two waited on Father Giorda, with a most pressing request that he come at once to the theatre and meet the Governor and Hugh O'Neill. The Father, overjoyed at all the news, did not know how to express his thanks in words, but we may be sure that the angels recorded his aspirations. Some few alterations in the arrangement of screens and seats were suggested, and then General Meagher by his supreme authority claimed Father Giorda as his guest, and all rights of individuals or promises of priest were declared void and null. Himself

Spreading the word; drawing by R.F. Zogbaum
—From *Harper's Weekly*, December 24, 1887

with two assistants would see to his comfort and entertainment. Hugh O'Neill took charge of the alterations of the theatre.

In a little while carpenters, decorators, helpers of every kind, friends of O'Neill, turned the theatre into a veritable bee hive. His quiet suggestions are looked upon as orders; loads of evergreens disappear in a few minutes and are seen in garlands, emblems or festoons. An immense cross is planted in front of the door to proclaim to the world the interior change. A large cross over the door and also one to surmount the roof proclaims that it is a place of worship. There is nothing subdued, or simple in manner in those decorations; like the camp, they are bold, profuse and aggressive. The interior decorations were equally profuse. All pictures or signs of a distracting nature are removed or covered under the evergreen wreaths and religious emblems of crosses, crowns, hearts, etc. An altar, communion railing, and confessional have been constructed, all decent and serviceable. Hugh O'Neill directs and manages the whole transformation of the theatre into a church.

All day the news around town, and in the neighboring camps was very unusual and almost unprecedented. Numerous messengers on splendid mounts brought the glad tidings that the theatre had been rented, that there would be Christmas service for Catholics, that the priest was the guest of Governor Meagher. All items of interest, and the fruitless search for a hall, were told hundreds of times, and every Catholic was earnestly invited to be present. Messengers succeeded messengers; some sent directly by the Governor, some by O'Neill. Many volunteered and no Catholic was overlooked. From Summit and Central, Dobietown, Nevada, the whole length of Alder Gulch, and Stinking Water Creek, the commotion drew the attention of the whole population. There never had been such stir the year before, at the discovery of gold in Last Chance Gulch. There had been a great stampede, but the preparations, now, appeared more stirring.

It was well known that there was friction between the Governor and the Vigilance Committee, no one knew to what extent, or when a storm would burst loose. At the time of the organization of the Vigilance Committee, and their first executions, there had also been seen an unusual number of persons bringing messages to their friend; but now there were joyful tidings, nothing secret or hidden. And the response to the repeated invitations, that had been lukewarm and faint-hearted from some in the morning, became warm, fervent and determined by evening.

Towards the close of the day General Meagher came to see what progress had been made in the work at the theatre. Congratulating Hugh O'Neill over his Splendid work, he was interrupted by the proprietor who had also come to see and who expressed himself in no uncertain words; in his opinion his theatre had been utterly ruined for further business, by those exterior and interior emblems and decorations. The General and lieutenant had never hesitated in difficulty before, and now in answer to his complaint asked him to set his price on the building. It was accepted and the earnest money to make the bargain binding was paid on the spot. These men were not hampered by regulations of canon law, consultations, and delays in decisions of Bishops; they did not think it was necessary to speak to the priest about it. They knew their neighbors would all endorse the act, and that the angels would applaud.

The news that the theatre was bought for a church was the crowning event of that day, and was heralded everywhere; and then the further news that there was to be midnight Mass, and that a church choir was organized, and that it would be midnight high Mass, and that all were expected to help pay for the theatre was fresh news to be thoroughly circulated. On the morning of Christmas Eve, Hugh O'Neill was at his self-imposed task. The decorations needed a few finishing touches, the altar a little extra decoration, the candles to be placed in proper and symmetrical form. The seats required a little more orderly arrangement. The holy water font at the door was not neglected, and visitors who came by the score out of curiosity, or from a motive to make sure that all reports were genuine, were reminded by the sexton that no loud remarks or distracting behavior was tolerated. They were politely requested to kneel down, say some prayer, and stay a while to rest their souls.

All day long a good number of persons were in the church, raising their hearts to heaven, not distracted by the stream of visitors. All formed a firm resolution to be generous on Christmas day. The priest was free from the ordinary distracting cares of preparing the altar and church. He could give his whole mind to prayers and devotions, and spend all afternoon and night in the Confessional, till it was time for midnight Mass. Long before the appointed hour the church was crowded to its utmost. Many unable to gain admittance resigned themselves to the inclemency of the weather, and knelt at the door.

As the hour approached the choir intoned the Adeste Fideles O'Neill lit the candles, assisted the priest in vesting, and by his devout reverential manner, edified all.

Father Giorda preached a consoling sermon. After the gospel and sermon, General Meagher prepared to take up the collection among the congregation. It has often been mentioned that he had a large white delft plate. This had been found among the latest invoices of goods in the territory. (Up to that time a tin plate had been the orthodox receptacle for the offerings of the faithful.) On this delft plate were two spoons, a teaspoon and a tablespoon, with which the members might, with ease, transfer the shining gold dust from their buckskin purse to the plate. There was no announcement about the collection, the priest knew nothing about it. Every member of the congregation was thoroughly alive to the occasion. No member so devout that he failed to see the General or the plate.

The number and devotion of the worshippers, the earnestness in their prayers and all their actions, and especially the numbers of communions, attracted the attention of all. The whole atmosphere seemed to breathe a spirit of piety such as never had been experienced in Virginia City.

After Mass, General Meagher requested all to remain in their seats a few moments, and in words as only he could command, presented the offering. In the name of the whole community, of every claim in this mountain district, in the name of every person present and in his own name, he presented this house to God, that his infant Son might find a dwelling place amongst them and that His minister might take care of it. He offered to God and to religion the largest and most suitable house in town. Would to God, it were made of marble. This house henceforth is the House of God, a Catholic church, we give it and here is the price, in God's noblest metal, gold pure as it was washed from the earth yesterday; pure, it has not yet seen the smelting pot to receive its capacity of alloy; no Caesar or potentate has as yet set his image or superscription on it; it is Virgin gold and has not been contaminated by any traffic or commerce; it never will be spent in a better cause; as God has given it in abundance without measure, so they return it to God, without weight, but plenty to secure the house, free without debt, as an abiding place to God forever. It would never be said of them that there was no place for Christ. So he hoped the priest would make this place his permanent residence and the sogarth aroon would ever have amongst them *"Cead mille failthe."*

The priest tried to express his thanks, but was overcome to tears. Hugh O'Neill, his strong attendant, supported the frail form, and, guiding his faltering steps, led him away, that Christmas day of 1865 in the rough, uncouth, wicked frontier mining camp of Virginia City, Montana—tempered and tamed by the spirit of Christ's birth!

—Courtesy Midwest Jesuit Archives

CHURCH CHRISTMAS EVENTS

DECORATING A CHURCH ALTAR.

By Eben E. Rexford.

PALMS and other potted plants are usually used in the Christmas decoration of the church; but a much finer effect can be secured by grouping these at points *away from* the altar, and decorating that with vines or evergreens. If holly is procurable, it can be massed about the altar, and arranged along the chancel-rail in a carelessly artistic way, and be made much more effective than any potted plants, as the latter always have a more or less formal air about them in spite of all efforts to avoid it. If you have tall palms place them in the background. If both holly or evergreens and flowering plants are used, do not combine them, but keep the flowers to one side. The two do not harmonize. One "kills" the other, to make use of the term which artists use to express inharmonious combinations of colors. In this case, it is not so much a clash of color as it is of individuality. Holly berries and leaves require nothing in the shape of flowers to bring out their beauty, but show to the best advantage by themselves, or when used with evergreens. In wreathing the chancel-rails, fasten the sprays to a rope or cord with fine wire or string, and do not attempt any regularity in size or shape of festoons when you come to put the wreathing in place. Aim to produce an unstudied effect. A charming effect is produced by sprinkling the leaves of holly or evergreen with mucilage, and sifting powdered mica over them. This will glisten in the evening like frost. If the supply of holly berries is limited, crystallized grasses can be worked in effectively. There are varieties of shrubs growing in swampy places, which bear scarlet fruit which makes a very satisfactory substitute for the holly. If holly leaves are not procurable, go to the florist, or some person having a private green-house or conservatory, and borrow an old plant of English ivy. Throw the vines over the altar, letting the ends of the branches trail on the floor at sides and front. Among the dark green foliage—which should be washed before using to bring out its glossy beauty—fasten the berries gathered in the swamp, and use grasses among them, if you choose. Some of the berries can be dipped in mucilage and dusted with mica, and combined with the scarlet clusters. The frosty white and glowing scarlet harmonize well and contrast strongly, and heighten the effect of each other. The rich green of the ivy will throw out the colors most effectively. In some respects I prefer the ivy to holly as its long branches are much easier to arrange satisfactorily. Simply throw them over the altar and they seem to almost arrange themselves. A pure white cross can be placed on the altar with sprays of ivy winding about it and trailing over its arms. If thought preferable, a cross or star made entirely of berries either in their natural color or frosted, can be placed in front of the altar, against a background of ivy or evergreens. In this case I would not use clusters of berries at other points of the altar decoration, but confine the effect to the designs into which they are worked.

Exterior of Zion Lutheran Church, with congregation
—Courtesy Buffalo Bill Historical Center

Interior of Zion Lutheran Church, Germania (Emblem), Wyoming, decorated for Christmas, 1900 —Courtesy Park County Historical Society

—From *Ladies' Home Journal*, 1890

St. Mary's Church, Aspen, Colorado, 1885
—Courtesy Denver Public Library, Western History Department

Grace Church, Colorado Springs, 1870s
—Courtesy Denver Public Library, Western History Department

THE M. E. CHURCH

According to the announcement, there was indeed a splendid time afforded the children of the Methodist Sunday School on Christmas Eve. By seven o'clock the house was well filled and very soon it was crowded to overflowing. Judge J. M. North, the superintendent of the Sabbath school, presided.

A concert of little over half an hour introduced the exercises which was in every way appropriate and well rendered. Then followed the distribution of the cornucopias full of good things for the children which had been prepared by the Supt. for each member of the school, and the presents that had been placed on the tree by parents and friends. This of course was amusing and exciting to the children and interesting to all.

The performance as a whole, we must pronounce a fine success, and Judge North and his assistants deserve great credit. The concert was elevating and purifying, and brought to mind the great gift of God to the world 1877 years ago when Jesus was born in Bethlehem.

—From *Boulder County News*, December 1877

PRESBYTERIAN CHURCH

The Presbyterians seem to have adopted as their motto Monday evening "Beauty in Simplicity," and carried it throughout their celebration. The trimming of the church was not at all elaborate. The festoons upon the walls, and over the door; two neatly arranged mottoes at the upper end of the room "Unto you is born this day a Savior," and "Thanks be unto God for his unspeakable gift." The programme was in harmony with the rest, brief and simple. The exercises were opened with the Mendelssohn's Christmas Hymn by the choir. This was followed by prayer, reading of scriptures and a short address by the Pastor. The last item upon the program was distribution of gifts; and here the utmost system and order prevailed; and a striking absence of confusion was noticeable. Each scholar received from the school a uniform gift. The look of perfect contentment and satisfaction which beamed from the faces of the little ones proclaimed their hearty concurrence in the vote for uniformity of gifts. Assuming as our basis that which we regard as the true one, that the main object of such a celebration is the gratification of *the children*; we should not hesitate to pronounce that given by the Presbyterian church a complete success. If, on the other hand, we start out with the idea that a Christmas tree is for display, without special regard to the little folks well—well, then, this may have been a failure, we leave others to judge.

—From the *Boulder County News,*
December 1877

Dastardly Outrage—On Christmas Eve, while the Sunday school children were enjoying their festival, and some hundreds of spectators present a rock was thrown through the window of the hall at Major J. S. Fillmore. It missed its mark, but struck Mrs. Stock on the neck, inflicting a severe bruise. What could have prompted the attack upon Mr. F., we are at a loss to guess.

—From the *Rocky Mountain News,* December 28, 1861

The colored people of the A.M.E. church will have a Christmas dinner in the Fisk block this afternoon at half past one o'clock and in the evening. A festival will be held and a Christmas tree put on exhibition. These will be joyous occasions.

—From the *Daily Sun* (Cheyenne,
Wyom.), December 24, 1877

VALMONT, COLORADO, 1876

The people of Valmont and vicinity unite in having a Christmas Tree, in the Presbyterian Church, on Monday evening, where Santa Claus may make his calls. We speak for many when we say we hope no gentleman will be so rude as to attend such a gathering and befoul the floor with his filthy tobacco juice. All children, ladies and gentlemen are cordially invited.

—From the *Boulder County News,* December 1876

I n 1870 THE EDITOR of *The Atlantic Monthly* offered the popular author Brett Harte a $10,000 contract for a years' worth of his writing. The contract was fulfilled with five poems and four stories, of which "How Santa Claus Came to Simpson's Bar" was one. This is a slightly condensed version:

How Santa Claus Came to Simpson's Bar
By Brett Harte

It had been raining in the valley of the Sacramento. The North Fork had overflowed its banks, and Rattlesnake Creek was impassable. The few boulders that had marked the summer ford at Crossing were obliterated by a vast sheet of water stretching to the hills. The upstage was stopped at Granger's; the last mail had been abandoned in the tules, the rider swimming for his life. "An area," the *Sierra Avalanche,* with pensive local pride, "as large as the Massachusetts is now under water." . . .

Further on, cut off and inaccessible, rained upon and bedraggled, smitten by high winds and threatened by high water, Simpson's Bar, on the eve of Christmas Day, 1862 clung like a swallow's nest to the rocky entablature and splintered capitals of Table Mountain, and shook in the blast.

As night shut down on the settlement, a few lights gleamed through the mist from the windows of cabins on either side of the highway, now crossed and gullied by lawless streams and swept by marauding winds. Happily most of the population were gathered at Thompson's store, clustered around a red-hot stove, at which they silently spat in some accepted sense of social communion that perhaps rendered conversation unnecessary. Indeed, most methods of diversion had long since been exhausted on Simpson's Bar; high water had suspended the regular occupations on the gulch and on the river, and a consequent lack of money and whiskey had taken the zest from most illegitimate recreation. Even Mr. Hamlin was fain to leave the Bar with fifty dollars in his

—From *Harper's New Monthly Magazine*, October 1874

pocket—the only amount actually realized of the large sums won by him in the successful exercise of his arduous profession. "Ef I was asked," he remarked somewhat later—"ef I was asked to pint out a purty little village where a retired sport as didn't care for money could exercise hisself, frequent and lively, I'd say Simpson's Bar; but for a young man with a large family depending on his exertions, it don't pay." As Mr. Hamlin's family consisted mainly of female adults, this remark is quoted rather to show the breadth of his humor than the exact extent of his responsibilities.

Howbeit, the unconscious objects of this satire sat that evening in the listless apathy begotten of idleness and lack of excitement. Even the sudden splashing of hoofs before the door did not arouse them. Dick Bullen alone paused in the act of scraping out his pipe, and lifted his head, but no other one of the group indicated any interest in, or recognition of, the man who entered.

It was a figure familiar enough to the company, and known in Simpson's Bar as "The Old Man." A man of perhaps fifty years; grizzled and scant of hair, but still fresh and youthful of complexion. A face full of ready but not very powerful sympathy, with a chameleon like aptitude for taking on the shade and color of contiguous moods and feelings. He had evidently just left some hilarious companions, and did not at first notice the gravity of the group, but clapped the shoulder of the nearest man jocularly, and threw himself into a vacant chair.

"Jest heard the best thing out, boys! Ye know Smiley, over yar—Jim Smiley—funniest man in the Bar? Well, Jim was jest telling the richest yarn about . . ."

"Smiley's a fool," interrupted a gloomy voice.

"A particular skunk," added another in sepulchral accents.

A silence followed these positive statements. The Old Man glanced quickly around the group. Then his face slowly changed. "That's so," he said reflectively, after a pause, "certainly a sort of a skunk and suthin' of a fool. In course." He was silent for a moment, as in painful contemplation of the unsavoriness and folly of the unpopular Smiley. "Dismal weather, ain't it?" he added, now fully embarked on the current of prevailing sentiment. "Mighty rough papers on the boys, and no show for money this season. And tomorrow's Christmas."

There was a movement among the men at this announcement, but whether of satisfaction or disgust was not plain. "Yes," continued the Old Man in the lugubrious tone he had within the last few moments unconsciously adopted—"yes, Christmas, and tonight's Christmas Eve. Ye see, boys, I kinder thought—that is, I sorter had an idee, jest passin' like, you know—that maybe ye'd all like to come over to my house tonight and have a sort of tear round. But I suppose, now, you wouldn't?

Don't feel like it, maybe?" he added with anxious sympathy, peering into the faces of his companions.

"Well, I don't know," responded Tom Flynn with some cheerfulness. "P'r'aps we may. But how about your wife, Old Man? What does she say to it?"

The Old Man hesitated. His conjugal experience had not been a happy one, and the fact was known to Simpson's Bar. His first wife, a delicate, pretty little woman, had suffered keenly and secretly from the jealous suspicions of her husband, until one day he invited the whole Bar to his house to expose her infidelity. On arriving, the party found the shy, petite creature quietly engaged in her household duties, and retired abashed and discomfited. But the sensitive woman did not easily recover from the shock of this extraordinary outrage. It was with difficulty she regained her equanimity sufficiently to release her lover from the closet in which he was concealed, and escape with him. She left a boy of three years to comfort her bereaved husband. The Old Man's present wife had been his cook. She was large, loyal, and aggressive.

Before he could reply, Joe Dimmick suggested with great directness that it was the "Old Man's house," and that, invoking the Divine Power, if the case were his own, he would invite whom he pleased, even if in so doing he imperiled his salvation. The Powers of Evil, he further remarked, should contend against him vainly. All this delivered with a terseness and vigor lost in this necessary translation. "In course. Certainly. Thet's it," said the Old Man with a sympathetic frown. "Thar's no trouble about thet. It's my own house, built every stick on it myself. Don't you be afeard o' her, boys. She may cut up a trifle rough—ez wimmin do—but she'll come round." Secretly the Old Man trusted to the exaltation of liquor and the power of courageous example to sustain him in such an emergency.

As yet, Dick Bullen, the oracle and leader of Simpson's Bar, had not spoken. He now took his pipe from his lips. "Old Man, how's that yer Johnny gettin' on? Seems to me he didn't look so peart last time I seed him on the bluff heavin' rocks at Chinamen. Didn't seem to take much interest in it. Thar was a gang of 'em by yar yesterday—drownded out up the river—and I kinder thought o' Johnny, and how he'd miss 'em! Maybe now, we'd be in the way ef he wus sick?" The father, evidently touched not only by this pathetic picture of Johnny's deprivation, but by the considerate delicacy of the speaker, hastened to assure him that Johnny was better, and that a "little fun might 'liven him up."

Whereupon Dick arose, shook himself, and saying, "I'm ready. Lead the way, Old Man: here goes," himself led the way with a leap, a characteristic howl, and darted out into the night. As he passed through the outer room he caught up a blazing brand from the hearth. The action was repeated by the rest of the party, closely following and elbowing each other, and before the astonished proprietor of Thompson's grocery was aware of the intention of his guests, the room was deserted.

The night was pitchy dark. In the first gust of wind their temporary torches were extinguished, and only the red brands dancing and flitting in the gloom like drunken will-o'-the-wisps indicated their whereabouts. Their way led up Pine Tree Canyon, at the head of which a broad, low, bark-thatched cabin burrowed in the mountainside. It was the home of the Old Man, and the entrance to the tunnel in which he worked when he worked at all. Here the crowd paused for a moment, out of delicate deference to their host, who came up panting in the rear.

"Prahaps ye'd better hold on a second out yer, whilst I go in and see that things is all right," said the Old Man, with an indifference he was far from feeling. The suggestion was graciously accepted, the door opened and closed on the host, and the crowd, leaning their backs against the wall and cowering under the eaves, waited and listened.

For a few moments there was no sound but the dripping of water from the eaves and the stir and rustle of wrestling boughs above them. Then the men became uneasy, and whispered suggestion and suspicion passed from the one to the other. "Reckon she's caved in his head the first lick!" "Decoyed him inter the tunnel and barred him up, likely." "Got him down and sittin' on him." "Prob'ly biling suthin' to heave on us: stand clear the door, boys!" For just then the latch clicked, the door slowly opened, and a voice said, "Come in out o' the wet."

The voice was neither that of the Old Man nor of his wife. It was the voice of a small boy, its weak treble broken by that preternatural hoarseness which only vagabondage and the habit of premature self-assertion can give. It was the face of a small boy that looked up at theirs—a face that might have been pretty, and even refined, but that it was darkened by evil knowledge from within, and dirt and hard experience from without. He had a blanket around his shoulders, and had evidently just risen from his bed. "Come in," he repeated, "and don't make no noise. The Old Man's in there talking to mar," he continued, pointing to an adjacent room which seemed to be a kitchen, from which the Old Man's voice came in deprecating accents. "Let me be," he added querulously to Dick Bullen, who had caught him up, blanket and all, and was affecting to toss him into the fire, "let go o' me, you d—d old fool, d'ye hear?"

Thus adjured, Dick Bullen lowered Johnny to the ground with a smothered laugh, while the men, entering quietly, ranged themselves around a long table of rough boards which occupied the center of the room. Johnny then gravely proceeded to a cupboard and brought out several articles, which he deposited on the table. "Thar's whiskey. And crackers. And red herons. And cheese." He took a bite of the latter on his way to the table. "And sugar." He scooped up a mouthful en route with a small and very dirty hand. "And terbacker. Thar's dried appils too on the shelf, but I don't admire 'em. Appils is swellin'. Thar," he concluded, "now wade in, and don't be afeard. I don't mind the old woman. She don't b'long to me. S'long."

He had stepped to the threshold of a small room, scarcely larger than a closet, partitioned off from the main apartment, and holding in its dim recess a small bed. He stood there a moment looking at the company, his bare feet peeping from the blanket, and nodded.

"Hello, Johnny! You ain't goin' to turn in again, are ye?" said Dick.

"Yes, I are," responded Johnny decidedly.

"Why, wot's up, old fellow?"

"I'm sick."

"How sick?"

"I've got a fevier. And childblains. And roomatiz," returned Johnny, and vanished within. After a moment's pause, he added in the dark, apparently from under the bedclothes, "And biles!" There was an embarrassing silence. The men looked at each other and at the fire. Even with the appetizing banquet before them, it seemed as if they might again fall into the despondency of Thompson's grocery, when the voice of the Old Man, incautiously lifted, came deprecatingly from the kitchen.

"Certainly! Thet's so. In course they is. A gang o' lazy, drunken loafers, and that ar Dick Bullen's the ornariest of all. Didn't hev no more sabe than to come round yar with sickness in the house and no provision. Thet's what I said: 'Bullen,' sez I, 'it's crazy drunk you are, or a fool,' sez I, 'to think o' such a thing.' 'Staples,' I sez, 'be you a man, Staples, and 'spect to raise h-ll under my roof and invalids lyin' round?' But they would come—they would. Thet's wot you must 'spect o' such trash as lays round the Bar."

A burst of laughter from the men followed this unfortunate exposure. Whether it was overheard in the kitchen, or whether the Old Man's irate companion had just then exhausted all other modes of expressing her contemptuous indignation, I cannot say, but a back door was suddenly slammed with great violence. A moment later and the Old Man reappeared, haply unconscious of the cause of the late hilarious outburst, and smiled blandly.

"The old woman thought she'd jest run over to Mrs. MacFadden's for a sociable call," he explained with jaunty indifference, as he took a seat at the board.

Oddly enough it needed this untoward incident to relieve the embarrassment that was beginning to be felt by the party, and their natural audacity returned with their host. I do not propose to record the convivialities of that evening. The inquisitive reader will accept the statement that the conversation was characterized by the same intellectual exaltation, the same cautious reverence, the same fastidious delicacy, the same rhetorical precision, and the same logical and coherent discourse somewhat later in the evening, which distinguish similar gatherings of the masculine sex in more civilized localities and under more favorable auspices. No glasses were broken in the absence of any; no liquor was uselessly spilt on the floor or table in the scarcity of that article.

It was nearly midnight when the festivities were interrupted. "Hush," said Dick Bullen, holding up his hand. It was the querulous voice of Johnny from his adjacent closet: "0 dad!"

The Old Man arose hurriedly and disappeared in the closet. Presently he reappeared. "His rheumatiz is coming on agin bad," he explained, "and he wants rubbin'." He lifted the demijohn of whiskey from the table and shook it. It was empty. Dick Bullen put down his tin cup with an embarrassed laugh. So did the others. The Old Man examined their contents and said hopefully, "I reckon that's enough; he don't need much. You hold on all o' you for a spell, and I'll be back"; and vanished in the closet with an old flannel shirt and the whiskey. The door closed but imperfectly, and the following dialogue was distinctly audible: "Now, sonny, whar does she ache worst?"

"Sometimes over yar and sometimes under yer; but it's most powerful from yer to yer. Rub yer, dad."

A silence seemed to indicate a brisk rubbing. Then Johnny:

"Hevin' a good time out yer, dad?"

"Yes, sonny."

"Tomorrer's Chrismiss ain't it?"

"Yes, sonny. How does she feel now?"

"Better. Rub a little furder down. Wot's Chrismiss, anyway? Wot's it all about?"

"Oh, it's a day."

This exhaustive definition was apparently satisfactory, for there was a silent interval of rubbing.

Presently Johnny again:

"Mar sez that everywhere else but yer everybody gives things to every-body Chrismiss, and then she jist waded inter you. She sez thar's a man they call Sandy Claws, not a white man, you know, but a kind o' Chine-min, comes down the chimbley night afore Chrismiss and gives things to chillern—boys like me. Puts 'em in their butes! Thet's what she tried to play upon me. Easy now, pop, whar are you rubbin' to—thet's a mile from the place. She jest made that up, didn't she, jest to aggrewate me and you? Don't rub thar. . . . Why, dad!"

In the great quiet that seemed to have fallen upon the house the sigh of the near pines and the drip of leaves without was very distinct. Johnny's voice, too, was lowered as he went on, "Don't you take on now, for I'm gettin' all right fast. . . . But it's mighty cur'o's about Chrismiss—ain't it? Why do they call it Chrismiss?"

Perhaps from some instinctive deference to the overhearing of his guests, or from some vague sense of incongruity, the Old Man's reply was so low as to be inaudible beyond the room.

"Yes," said Johnny, with some slight abatement of interest, "I've heard o' him before. Thar, that'll do, dad. I don't ache near so bad as I did. Now wrap me tight in this yer blanket. So. Now," he added in a muffled whisper, "sit down yer by me till I go asleep." To assure himself of obedience, he disengaged one hand from the blanket, and grasping his father's sleeve, again composed himself to rest.

For some moments the Old Man waited patiently. Then the un-wonted stillness of the house excited his curiosity, and without moving from the bed he cautiously opened the door with his disengaged hand, and looked into the main room. To his infinite surprise it was dark and deserted. But even then a smoldering log on the hearth broke, and by the upspringing blaze he saw the figure of Dick Bullen sitting by the dying embers.

"Hello!"

Dick started, rose, and came somewhat unsteadily toward him. "Whar's the boys?" said the Old Man.

"Gone up the canyon on a little pasear. They're coming back for me in a minit. I'm waitin' round for 'em. What are you starin' at, Old Man?" he added, with a forced laugh; "do you think I'm drunk?"

The Old Man might have been pardoned the supposition, for Dick's eyes were humid and his face flushed. He loitered and lounged back to the chimney, yawned, shook himself, buttoned up his coat, and laughed.

"Liquor ain't so plenty as that, Old Man. Now don't you get up," he continued, as the Old Man made a movement to release his sleeve from Johnny's hand. "Don't you mind manners. Sit jest whar you be; I'm goin' in a jiffy. Thar, that's them now."

There was a low tap at the door. Dick Bullen opened it quickly, nodded "good night" to his host, and disappeared. The Old Man would have followed him but for the hand that still unconsciously grasped his sleeve. He could have easily disengaged it: it was small, weak, and emaciated. But perhaps because it was small, weak, and emaciated he changed his mind, and drawing his chair closer to the bed, rested his head upon it. In this defenseless attitude the potency of his earlier potations surprised him. The room flickered and faded before his eyes, reappeared, faded again, went out, and left him—asleep.

Meantime Dick Bullen, closing the door, confronted his companions. "Are you ready?" said Staples. "Ready," said Dick; "what's the time?" "Past twelve," was the reply; "can you make it?—it's nigh on fifty miles, the round trip hither and yon." "I reckon," returned Dick shortly. "Whar's the mare?" "Bill and Jack's holdin' her at the crossin'." "Let 'em hold on a minit longer," said Dick.

He turned and re-entered the house softly. By the light of the guttering candle and dying fire he saw that the door of the little room was open. He stepped toward it on tiptoe and looked in. . . . Everything was quiet. With a sudden resolution he parted his huge mustaches with both hands and stooped over the sleeping boy. But even as he did so a mischievous blast, lying in wait, swooped down the chimney, rekindled the hearth, and lit up the room with a shameless glow from which Dick fled in bashful terror.

His companions were already waiting for him at the crossing. Two of them were struggling in the darkness with some strange misshapen bulk, which as Dick came nearer took the semblance of a great yellow horse.

It was the mare. She was not a pretty picture. From her Roman nose to her rising haunches, from her arched spine hidden by the stiff machillas of a Mexican saddle, to her thick, straight bony legs, there was not a line of equine grace. In her half-blind but wholly vicious white eyes, in her protruding underlip, in her monstrous color, there was nothing but ugliness and vice.

"Now then," said Staples, "stand cl'ar of her heels, boys, and up with you. Don't miss your first holt of her mane, and mind ye get your off stirrup quick. Ready!"

There was a leap, a scrambling struggle, a bound, a wild retreat of the crowd, a circle of flying hoofs, two springless leaps that jarred the earth, a rapid play and jingle of spurs, a plunge, and then the voice of Dick somewhere in the darkness. "All right!"

"Don't take the lower road back onless you're hard pushed for time! Don't hold her in downhill! We'll be at the ford at five. G'lang! Hoopa! Mula! GO!"

A splash, a spark struck from the ledge in the road, a clatter in the rocky cut beyond, and Dick was gone. . . .

It was one o'clock, and yet he had only gained Rattlesnake Hill. For in that time Jovita had rehearsed to him all her imperfections and practiced all her vices. Thrice had she stumbled. Twice had she thrown up her Roman nose in a straight line with the reins, and resisting bit and spur, struck out madly across country. Twice had she reared,

—Sketches by Jerome H. Smith and Charles M. Russell, from *Frank Leslie's Illustrated Newspaper*, May 18, 1889

and rearing, fallen backward; and twice had the agile Dick, unharmed, regained his seat before she found her vicious legs again. And a mile beyond them, at the foot of a long hill, was Rattlesnake Creek. Dick knew that here was the crucial test of his ability to perform his enterprise, set his teeth grimly, put his knees well into her flanks, and changed his defensive tactics to brisk aggression. Bullied and maddened, Jovita began the descent of the hill. Here the artful Richard pretended to hold her in with ostentatious objurgation and well-feigned cries of alarm. It is unnecessary to add that Jovita instantly ran away. Nor need I state the time made in the descent; it is written in the chronicles of Simpson's Bar. Enough that in another moment, as it seemed to Dick, she was splashing on the over-flowed banks of Rattlesnake Creek. As Dick expected, the momentum she had acquired carried her beyond the point of balking, and holding her well together for a mighty leap, they dashed into the middle of the swiftly flowing current. A few moments of kicking, wading, and swimming, and Dick drew a long breath on the opposite bank.

The road from Rattlesnake Creek to Red Mountain was tolerably level. Either the plunge in Rattlesnake Creek had dampened her baleful fire, or the art which led to it had shown her the superior wickedness of her rider, for Jovita no longer wasted her surplus energy in wanton conceits. Once she bucked, but it was from force of habit; once she shied, but it was from a new, freshly painted meetinghouse at the crossing of the county road. Hollows, ditches, gravelly deposits, patches of freshly springing grasses, flew from beneath her rattling hoofs. She began to smell unpleasantly, once or twice she coughed slightly, but there was no abatement of her strength or speed. By two o'clock he had passed Red Mountain and begun the descent to the plain. Ten minutes later the driver of the fast Pioneer coach was overtaken and passed by a "man on a pinto hoss"—an event sufficiently notable for remark. At half-past two Dick rose in his stirrups with a great shout. Stars were glittering through the rifted clouds, and beyond him, out of the plain, rose two spires, a flagstaff, and a straggling line of black objects. Dick jingled his spurs and swung his riata, Jovita bounded forward, and in another moment they swept into Tuttleville, and drew up before the wooden piazza of "The Hotel of All Nations."

What transpired that night at Tuttleville is not strictly a part of this record. Briefly I may state, however, that after Jovita had been handed over to a sleepy ostler, whom she at once kicked into unpleasant consciousness, Dick sallied out with the barkeeper for a tour of the sleeping town. Lights still gleamed from a few saloons and gambling houses; but avoiding these, they stopped before several closed shops, and by persistent tapping and judicious outcry roused the proprietors from their beds, and made them unbar the doors of their magazines and expose their wares. Sometimes they were met by curses, but oftener by interest and some concern in their needs, and the interview was invariably concluded by a drink. It was three o'clock before this pleasantry was given over, and with a small waterproof bag of India rubber strapped on his shoulders, Dick returned to the hotel. . . . And then he sprang to the saddle and dashed down the lonely street and out into the lonelier plain, where presently the lights, the black line of houses, the spires, and the flagstaff sank into the earth behind him again and were lost in the distance. . . .

Suddenly Jovita shied with a bound that would have unseated a less practiced rider. Hanging to her rein was a figure that had leaped from the bank, and at the same time from the road before her arose a shadowy horse and rider.

"Throw up your hands," commanded the second apparition, with an oath.

Dick felt the mare tremble, quiver, and apparently sink under him. He knew what it meant and was prepared.

"Stand aside, Jack Simpson. I know you, you d—d thief! Let me pass, or—"

He did not finish the sentence. Jovita rose straight in the air with a terrific bound, throwing the figure from her bit with a single shake of her vicious head, and charged with deadly malevolence down on the impediment before her. An oath, a pistol shot, horse and highwayman rolled over in the road, and the next moment Jovita was a hundred yards away. But the good right arm of her rider, shattered by a bullet, dropped helplessly at his side.

Without slacking his speed he shifted the reins to his left hand. But a few moments later he was obliged to halt and tighten th saddle girths that had slipped in the onset. This in his crippled condition took some time. He had no fear of pursuit, but looking up he saw that the eastern stars were already paling, and that the distant peaks had lost their ghostly whiteness and now stood out blackly against a lighter sky. Day was upon him. Then completely absorbed in a single idea, he forgot the pain of his wound, and mounting again dashed on toward Rattlesnake Creek. But now Jovita's breath came broken by gasps, Dick reeled in his saddle, and brighter and brighter grew the sky.

Ride, Richard; run, Jovita; linger, O day!

For the last few rods there was a roaring in his ears. Was it exhaustion from loss of blood, or what? He was dazed and giddy as he swept down the hill, and did not recognize his surroundings. Had he taken the wrong road, or was this Rattlesnake Creek?

It was. But the brawling creek he had swum a few hours before had risen, more than doubled its volume, and now rolled a swift and resistless river between him and Rattlesnake Hill. For the first time that night Richard's heart sank within him. The river, the mountain, the quickening east, swam before his eyes. He shut them to recover his self-control. In that brief interval, by some fantastic mental process, the little room at Simpson's Bar and the figures of the sleeping father and son rose upon him: He opened his eyes wildly, cast off his coat, pistol, boots, and saddle, bound his precious pack tightly to his shoulders, grasped the bare flanks of Jovita with his bared knees, and with a shout dashed into the yellow water. A cry rose from the opposite bank as the head of a man and horse struggled for a few moments against the battling current, and then were swept away amidst uprooted trees and whirling driftwood.

The Old Man started and woke. The fire on the hearth was dead, the candle in the outer room flickering in its socket, and somebody was rapping at the door. He opened it, but fell back with a cry before the dripping, half-naked figure that reeled against the doorpost.

"Dick?"

"Hush! Is he awake yet?"

"No. But Dick   "

"Dry up, you old fool! Get me some whiskey, quick." The Old Man flew and returned with an empty bottle! Dick would have sworn, but his strength was not equal to the occasion. He staggered, caught at the handle of the door, and motioned to the Old Man.

"Thar's suthin' in my pack yer for Johnny. Take it off. I can't."

The Old Man unstrapped the pack, and laid it before the exhausted man.

"Open it, quick."

He did so with trembling fingers. It contained only a few poor toys—cheap and barbaric enough, goodness knows, but bright with paint and tinsel. One of them was broken; another, I fear, was irretrievably ruined by water, and on the third ah me! there was a cruel spot.

"It don't look like much, that's a fact," said Dick ruefully. "But it's the best we could do. . . . Take 'em, Old Man, and put 'em in his stocking, and tell him—tell him, you know—hold me, Old Man—" The Old Man caught at his sinking figure. "Tell him," said Dick, with a weak little laugh—"tell him Sandy Claus has come."

And even so, bedraggled, ragged, unshaven and unshorn, with one arm hanging helplessly at his side, Santa Claus came to Simpson's Bar and fell fainting on the first threshold. The Christmas dawn came slowly after, touching the remoter peaks with the rosy warmth of ineffable love. And it looked so tenderly on Simpson's Bar that the whole mountain, as if caught in a generous action, blushed to the skies.

OUTSIDERS OFTEN SEE things that escape the resident's notice. Rose Kingsley came to America from England in the fall of 1871. On December 20 she and her brother, Maurice, traveled to Denver—by then a good-size city—and spent Christmas Mile High–style. She described her experience in a letter home.

Denver, 1866, by Theodore R. Davis
—From *Harper's Weekly*, January 27, 1866

As Christmas comes but once a year, and it is many a long day since we spent it together, we determined to give ourselves a treat. So on the 20th of December M [aurice] shut up his books and papers; I wound up my affairs . . . and at 12:30 we were . . . en route for a week in Denver. When we crossed the Divide the difference in climate showed strangely. . . . Northward, the country is covered with a solid cake of frozen snow, two to twelve inches deep. . . .

Denver looks wintry enough, under six inches to a foot of snow; but it is full of life and bustle. The toy-shops are gay with preparations for Christmas trees; the candy stores are filled with the most attractive sweetmeats; the furriers display beaver coats, and mink, ermine and sables, to tempt the cold passer-by; and in the butchers shops hang, beside the ordinary beef and mutton, buffalo, black-tailed deer, antelope, Rocky Mountain sheep, quails, partridges, and prairie-chicken.

The streets are full of sleighs, each horse with its collar of bells; and all the little boys have manufactured or bought little sleds, which they tie to the back of any passing cart or carriage; and get whisked along the street until some sharp turn or unusual roughness from the road upsets them. . . .

We found plenty of old friends up here, and have made many more since we came. In the frank unconventional state of society which exists in the west, friendships are made much more

Wright & Mongan Meat Market, Cannon City, Colorado, 1893
—Courtesy Denver Public Library, Western History Department

easily than even in the eastern states, or still more in our English society; and, if one wants to have, as the Americans express it, a "good time," one must expand a little out of one's insularity, and meet the hearty good will shown one with adequate response. . . .

On Friday evening, after two hours skating at the rink, we went out for a sleigh drive, the first I have ever had; and most delightful it was. We were muffled up in blankets and buffalo robes and all our furs. The thermometer was two degrees below zero; the moon as clear as day; and, with a capital pair of horses, we flew over the smooth sparkling snow, our sleigh bells jingling in the frosty air. When we got home, about 11 p.m. M[aurice] looked just like Santa Claus, with his moustache and hair all snowy white from his frozen breath.

Christmas Day was bright, and even hot in the sun; and we had to pick our way to church through the rivers of melted snow. The Episcopal church looks rather like a wooden coach-house outside; but inside it is very nice, and was prettily decorated. The excellent Bishop of Colorado, Dr. Randall, is still in the East, getting together a number of clergy to come out to the Territory;

Two Montanans bundled up in a sleigh, 1913
—Courtesy Wilma Foote, from *Echo of Crosscuts and Rails* by Joan M. Draszt

Christmas circa 1890
—Courtesy Wyoming State Archives

CHRISTMAS TREE CELEBRATION

There will be a grand Christmas tree ball and raffle given by the Vorwaerta Turn Verein at their hall, corner Tenth and Larimer street, West Denver on Saturday and Sunday Evenings December 25 and 26. Admissients.

—*Denver Times*, December 24, 1880

or we should have had the pleasure of hearing our Christmas sermon from him. But even his absence mattered little to anyone who had no chance of getting to church for two months; the dear familiar service alone was quite enough to satisfy one. The singing, by an amateur quartet choir, of two ladies and two gentlemen, was very good, but florid.

I was asked to eat my Christmas dinner at Colonel M—'s, where Miss J— boarded; and, simply because I was her friend, everyone in the house made me welcome. Dinner of the ortho-dox turkey and mince-pie over, we were summoned to the Christmas tree in the parlour, which was decorated, in place of our holly berries, with strings of raw cranberries and snowy popcorn, pretty to look at, and nice to eat.

There are several children in the house; and I hardly know whether they or their . . . nurses were most delighted. One little girl, who had charge of Mrs. M—'s lovely baby, was nearly

—From the *Denver Times*, December 8, 1899

crazy, as every one in the house had put something on the tree for her; and when a large brown paper parcel was given her, down went the poor baby on the floor, as she tore the parcel open and found a pair of new boots inside. I shall never forget the child's ecstasy . . . [smiling] from ear to ear.

The evening passed with games and amusement, and constant refreshments in the shape of candy and hickory-nuts; and suddenly our host turned round to me and said, "Now I'll sing something for you"; and began the first verse of "God save the Queen." It sent a thrill over me, hearing it a thousand miles west of the Mississippi for the first time since leaving England. And then I was made to sing it all through; for though the tune is familiar enough in America, no one present knew the right words. It was a pleasant ending to a pleasant evening.

—From *Christmas and New Year's in Colorado*

LIKE DENVER, Cheyenne, Wyoming, was a well-established town by the 1870s. This editorial rumination on Christmas is from the *Daily Sun*, December 25, 1877.

In considering this day, whose mind does not revert back to the years of their childhood when on Christmas eve they felt joyful and happy in anticipation of what Santa Claus would bring them? How reluctantly they went to bed, resolved to keep awake until he came, but at last dropped off to sleep disturbed only by pleasant visions of stockings full of candy, toys, dolls, etc. Thus it was last night with millions of little ones. This morning how early they awakened to examine what had been left for them. How joyous the shout "Merry Christmas" which bursts from their lips as they rush to their parents bed-room to show the gifts each little stocking holds. Such is Christmas to childhood and we trust there is not a hearthstone in Cheyenne this morning where children are but will be the scene of merry mirthfulness. . . .

Christmas with all its joys and glories is upon us. It is seen in the busy throng, in the confectionary establishments, the jewelry stores, the large and fashionable dry goods stores—everywhere. We find its approach heralded in the humble home of the poor man as well as in the edifice of the banker. The millionaire with his coffers of gold cannot say, "Christmas is for *me* alone," but *all,* rich and

The Daily Sun [Cheyenne, Wyoming], December 21, 1877

Yesterday morning about 10 o'clock Charles F. Shaw wanted to make a raise of a few dollars to spend during the Holidays. Having no money and being too lazy to work, he concluded the best way to raise the wind would be to steal an overcoat and sell it. Just as he was putting his resolution into execution at the Revolution store on the corner of Eddy and Sixteenth streets, Henry Harrington stepped out and nabbed him. The coat, worth about $20.00 was hung out as a sign, not as a temptation to thieves. Henry took his man to the cooler, and later in the day the light-fingered gent was tried before Caliph Fisher and sentenced to serve three months in the county jail. Harrington was at first tempted to kill the fellow and turn the corpse over to Coroner Goldacker, and then reason resumed its sway, and he didn't do anything of the sort.

222

poor, black and white, high and low, have a common interest in this day, one of the holiest and happiest of the year. Youth and age alike wear a pleasant smile on their countenances. The old walk upright once more, the young are blithesome and gay. The very air is rife with the odor of candies, plum puddings and pies. To our nasal appendages comes the savory odor of roast turkeys, geese and ganders. Many is the unfortunate gobbler who will today gobble his last gobble to satisfy the gobbling propensity of humanity.

If there is a family known by any one as too poor to be joyful, visit them and leave *something,* be it ever so little, to make their hearts glad.

PIONEER SCHOOLTEACHER Leoti L. West remembered the Christmas of 1884 in Walla Walla, Washington, in her book *The Wide Northwest:*

Schoolhouse tree, n.d.
—K. Ross Toole Archives, University of Montana, Missoula

That winter we had decided to have a great union Christmas tree for all the Sunday schools of the city at Small's opera house. It seated comfortably 1200 people. Committees were appointed. Literally tons of Christmas presents of candy, nuts, toys and all the other things which go with such festive occasions were brought to the building. At 6 o'clock, the work was completed and all went to their homes for supper, excepting a man and his wife who were left as caretakers.

A half hour later, the roof, because of the weight of accumulated snow and ice, collapsed, and the room was filled with debris. Fortunately, the people were near the beautiful trees fully laden with the presents, and so no one was injured. Had the accident occurred an hour later, many people would have been wiped out of existence.

I have never before or since experienced a period when all hearts were filled with such a spirit of thankfulness as then. I am one of those who believe that the great "I am," who controls the destinies of the human family, protects each individual born into the world until such time as his work is accomplished. . . .

The presents were reclaimed from the wrecked building on Christmas day. Everybody was happy.

HERE IS ANOTHER colorful small-town Christmas vividly remembered, from the *Spokesman-Review*, December 27, 1964, by Edith L. Boyd:

Try to picture the small town of Spokane Falls in the winter of 1884–85 . . . a cluster of low buildings on the level land between the river and the Northern Pacific Railroad tracks, perhaps four to six blocks of scattered shops and businesses . . . a sprinkling of houses spraying out to the surrounding trees and up to the foot of the south hill. . . .

Christmas is a magic word to children no matter where they may be when it becomes a reality. To me the first Christmas time in Spokane Falls was glamorous with the sunlight on abundant new-fallen snow sparkling over wide spaces. Where I had lived before in Portland, Ore., the sparse snow in city streets was not lovely or inviting and soon disappeared. Here everyone enjoyed it, children revelled in it with, as always, snow-ball fights, forts, snow men and coasting [sledding]. All this was new to me and I entered into it heartily, even to making angels by lying down in the snow and swinging my arms around to shape the wings. It all was such fun! . . .

Coasting was the general out-door sport, no matter if one were young or old. . . . On long bob-sleds holding five or six, or small sleds with one belly-flopper they sped the swift way down, shouting and laughing. When the trudging back became an effort, the coasters gathered around the fires that lighted every slide and ate scorched popcorn. Someone would start a song and as the sound spread, other groups joined and the hills vibrated with lively music.

Then there were sleigh rides in a big wagon bed on runners, where one sat on sweet hay and sang and sang, rivaling bells on the horses. Also, one could ride in trim, elegant cutters, wrapped in fur robes, with lively horses trotting smartly, gay bells jingling. . . .

In all our churches the Christmas observance was typical, a time of mystery and joyous excitement. At All Saints Church on First & Jefferson

Streets, where I belonged, we followed the general pattern. The rector, Mr. C. C. Burnett, brought a not-too-big fir tree and branches of fir and cedar from his ranch away out on the Little Spokane and asked help in decorating the chapel. We gathered in the cold little room and made wreaths and garlands to hang on the bare walls until they looked festive.

All Saints was then only a mission church and had no money for spending, so all gifts and trimmings were donated by the parents. We girls of the Sunday School went to the home of our teacher and strung popcorn and cranberries and made little boot-shaped bags of colored tarleton to be filled with candy and hung on the tree. The little candles that lighted that tree glowed and flickered with a beauty no electric bulbs can equal now-a-days. Lest a candle fall or lean over and start a blaze, a young man stood guard with snuffers and a bowl of water, but never was there a bit of trouble.

This was Christmas Eve at All Saints; a beautiful time with the singing of carols and the reading of the wonderful story that never is old.

Children with sleds in Butte, Montana, n.d.
—Courtesy World Museum of Mining, Butte, Montana

M ISSIONS WERE SMALL towns unto themselves. The following letter is from *The American Missionary* magazine, March 1889:

CHRISTMAS AT FORT YATES, DAKOTA

Our readers will be glad to welcome Miss Josephine E. Barnaby to her new field of work, and to a place in the pages of the *Missionary*. She is of the Omaha tribe, was a student at Hampton, then spent some time in a training school for nurses in New Haven, Connecticut, and is now the assistant of Miss Collins at the Grand River Station.

My Dear Friends:

We have been so busy getting ready for Christmas that we have had no time to write to our friends. Miss Collins told the Indians on Sunday last that we were going to have a tree and wanted all the Indians to come, the real old ones as well as the young men and women. She told them of how our Savior was born on Christmas day, how the people came and gave him gifts, and we, in remembering his birthday, would give them little gifts. . . .

Yesterday morning, while Miss Collins pinned the names on to the presents, I went up to the school-house, and by the help of two native teachers planted the tree in a cracker-box and put the little colored candles on. In the afternoon, we took the presents up and hung them on the tree; we put up a curtain to hide the tree, and then in the evening put out several Japanese lanterns on the corners of the house and over the door, and rang the bell; while the bell was ringing, you could see the Indians coming from all parts of the village. It was a pretty sight. The ground was covered with snow, it was just between the light and dark, and a few bright stars were shining through the clouds. The room is not very large, so Miss Collins proposed that they should stand. It was well they did, for they were packed tightly together, the men and boys on one side, the women and girls on the other. After all came, we sang Joy to the World, in Dakota, with several other hymns; they all sang very loud. Then Wakanna told them about Christ's birthday, then we lighted the little

Apache children with Christmas tree, 1898, Fort Sill, Oklahoma Territory
—U.S. Army Field Artillery and Fort Sill Museum

candles and took the curtain away, and you can imagine there were some wide-open eyes and big, smiling faces.

There were over two hundred, and each one received something. . . . After they had their gifts, we passed refreshments; we then had the fireworks; the red light was wonderful to them the first they had ever seen. They went home seeming very happy. We want to thank our friends who were so kind as to send us those pretty things for the Christmas tree.

I myself have never before spent such a happy Christmas, because previously all my kind friends have always tried to make me happy, and this time I worked hard to make some one else happy, and I find that is the best kind of happiness.

Truly your Indian Friend,
Josephine E. Barnaby

228

BY THE LAST decades of the nineteenth century, the West had not just towns but cities from Texas to Washington. As populations grew, events became more formalized, and charity became a team effort. After a fire in 1889 turned the young community of Spokane into a tent city, the students at the high school organized a Christmas charity effort. This look back appeared in the *Spokesman-Review* (Spokane, Washington) on December 24, 1916.

David Bemiss . . . the first superintendent of schools, was full of pride at the graduation of that class of 1891. Mr. Bemiss it was who . . . suggested the taking up of a collection of gifts to be distributed to the needy. Goodness knows, after that terrible fire of 1889 there was plenty of need everywhere.

For the Christmas of 1889 they called their holiday charity the "Apple and Potato" collection, as at first they brought only apples and potatoes to be given to the hungry. The high school did not have any Christmas convocation, but in the grade schools, as has been the plan from time immemorial and probably will be ad infinitum, the children celebrated Christmas by speaking pieces and singing songs appropriate to the glad season.

Mrs. J. Grier Long can remember [1889] when she was only 10 years old and her family had just moved to the little city. . . . Mrs. Long in those old days belonged to a club of eight of the young girls who called themselves the "Circle of Eight." This club planned collections and worked hard to see that everybody who needed things was remembered at Yule time.

"There was a great deal of suffering and want right after the fire," said Mrs. Long, "we owned the second plastered house in town; William Heaton's folks had the first one and most of the folks lived in tents. . . ."

The Circle of Eight greatly enjoyed their work and in the summertime they took flowers to the sick, or special poor families whom the different members of the club looked after, and in the winter time they

If there be any person or family in this community too poor to buy Christmas presents for their young children, I would like them to call on me personally for aid. All communications of this nature considered strictly confidential. Also, if there be persons in this community in need of provisions, who are unable to purchase them, I would like to know of them.

—A. Z. Salomon

From the *Greeley Tribune*, December 19, 1877

When we say that sales at one of our toy stores on Saturday reached $500, and two of our confectionary stores nearly the same aggregate, it may be surmised that Santa Claus remembered the children. We are glad too that some of our good citizens remembered the poor, leaving this family a load of coal, and that one a supply of food, and another one gifts of clothing, accompanied here and there with a greenback and words of good cheer. Young and old, rich and poor, we believe that it was a Merry Christmas with the most of us.

—From the *Colorado Tribune*, December 28, 1870

pasted scrapbooks for the orphans and treasured every picture that ever appeared in the town for these quaint volumes, so that every child in the institution sooner or later had a scrapbook.

The girls divided off the town into eight districts, the most prominent of which were the Poverty Flat and Hangman Creek districts, and they kept track of their pet poor families and their needs so that at Christmas time they would be useful and welcome. The girls cut the tops of the tiny trees and made tiny Chinese dolls out of peanuts, just hundreds of them. . . .

The girls also made quantities of clothing themselves for the younger children of these families, and their mothers helped them to cut and fit some of their own castoff garments for these poor children. Note that they did not merely fling a pile of trunk-smelly, dilapidated old clothes into baskets and leave them hit or miss as is the method followed largely by the progressive and busy present day generation. The circle also made little Tarleton bags and filled them with candy and traveled about the country with their gifts in their fathers' buggies.

"Really," said Mrs. Long, "I believe I covered the needy families of my district more effectively in that old buggy in those days than I cover the cases of people whom I try to help in my automobile today."

BY THE **1890s,** Brown's Hole, Utah, in a valley between the Cold Spring Mountains and the Diamond Mountain area, had attracted cattle and sheep ranchers as well as a few prospectors and homesteaders. Because the nearest sheriff was ninety miles away, the place also attracted outlaws, including the notorious "Wild Bunch." The residents of the Hole were rather fond of the outlaws, and the feeling was mutual. In 1895, to show their appreciation for past kindnesses, Butch, Sundance, and company hosted a six-hour Thanksgiving dinner for the town.

The Wild Bunch, December 1900. (Left to right, standing) Bill Carver, Harvey Logan ("Kid Curry"). (Sitting) Harry Longabaugh ("Sundance Kid"), Ben Kilpatrick, George Parker ("Butch Cassidy")
—Courtesy University of Oklahoma Libraries, Western History Collections

One might find it hard to believe that such a remote town could furnish the fixings for the party's hearty menu, but the Brown's Hole general store was surprisingly well stocked.

Blue Point Oysters
Roast Turkey with Chestnut Dressing and Giblet Gravy
Cranberries
Mashed Potatoes, Candied Sweet Potatoes, Creamed Peas
Celery, Olives, Pickled Walnuts, Sweet Pickles, Fresh Tomatoes
Hot Rolls, Sweet Butter
Roquefort Cheese
Coffee with Whipped Cream
Pumpkin Pie, Plum Pudding with Brandy Sauce
Mints, Salted Nuts

CANDIED SWEET-POTATOES.

Steam the sweet potatoes until perfectly done, and peel them. Have ready two teacupfuls of sugar boiled into a syrup, with one and a half teacupful of water. It should be like the syrup of preserves. When removed from the fire, but still warm, stir into it a very heaping tablespoonful of nice butter.

Slice the potatoes into a baking-pan that will hold them without being quite full. Pour over them the syrup, put extra bits of butter about on top of them, and set them in the stove to bake. Now and then tilt the pan and dip up and pour over the potatoes some of the syrup. Do not let the top get dry. Bake rather slowly for about an hour and a half. Serve in the pan in which it is baked and send to the table hot. (1890)

Ann Bassett attended the historic get-together and remembered Butch this way:

Poor Butch, he could perform such minor jobs as robbing banks and holding up pay trains without the flicker of an eyelash, but serving coffee at a grand party that was something else. The blood curdling job almost floored him, he became panicky and showed that his nerve was completely shot to bits. . . . This just shows how etiquette can put fear into a brave man's heart.

—From *John Jarvie of Brown's Park* by William L. Tennent

BUFFALO BILL CODY is probably best remembered for his role in glamorizing the American West with his Wild West shows. But he performed another role, which played before a much smaller audience. For many years during the late 1800s and early 1900s, Cody, one of the nation's foremost entertainers, played Santa Claus for children. In this undated poem, D. H. Winget immortalizes Cody's soft side.

Buffalo Bill dressed as Santa Claus, with children at the San Bonito, New Mexico, mining camp, 1911
—Courtesy Buffalo Bill Historical Center

Buffalo Bill as Santa Claus: A True Story Told in Verse

By D. H. Winget (DeWitt Harris)

'Twas Christmas on the border
Before the days of Railroads,
When many a horse thief swung,
When men, to seek their fortunes,
Took their lives into their hands,
And dug and washed for gold dust
In those far off golden sands.

It was rough I tell you partner,
Out in those mining camps,
With none but rough, big bearded men,
Whose memory on me stamps,
The fact, that 'neath the woolen shirt,
There beat big hearts and true,
And tender as a woman's,
And honest, through and through.

The games were not as gentle,
As tennis and croquet,
'Twas fashion to play poker there
And bags of dust the pay.
A mile or so from our gulch,
A washerwoman lived,
Whose little children ate and wore
From what she scraped and saved.

This Christmas night I tell about,
One of the boys was out;
He saw the washerwoman's light,

And turned him right about.
Straight for the lighted cabin —
For he was looking 'round
For a young gang of thieves and outlaws
The cabin's light he found.

With tiger tread he hastened,
"I've found them in their den,"
Thought he, "and now I'll listen,
I think I've got my man."
With hand upon his pistol
He neared the cabin door,
And listened to the voices
Then could not wait for more.

And this is what the brave scout heard
Out on the border wilds:
"Oh Ma! Tomorrow's Christmas!"
The sweet voice was a child's.
"And will good Santa Claus come down
And bring us toys and skates,
And pretty dolls and candies too,
Like he used to in the States?"

"God grant he may," the mother sighed,
"But I am not so sure,
That Santa Claus will be so kind —
Now that we are so poor.
But go to bed my darlings,

And say your evening prayer;
Remember God is in the West
As well as 'way back there."

The scout went to the window
Through which the bright light shone
He saw her kiss the children,
"God bless you both, my own."
"God danged if I can stand it";
The scout brushed away a tear
To which his eyes a stranger
Had been for many a year.

The children went to bed then,
And left their mother there,
And overcome with bitter grief,
She knelt in earnest prayer;
"Oh God," she said and weeping,
"Remove this bitter cup;
How can I bear to cross them,
They've hung their stockings up.

I've not a slice of bacon
Or crust of bread to eat,
When they awake for breakfast,
Nor nothing good nor sweet.
Thy will be done oh Father
But if it be thy will,
Oh let me get some clothes and wood
To ward off cold and chill."

'Twas too much for the hardy scout;
He turned to move away,
But heard the children's voices,
And to hear what they would say.
He neared their bedroom window,
And while he waited there
He listened to their lisping
As they raised their voice in prayer.

"Oh God bless our dear mama,
Who works so hard all day,
And buys good things for us to eat,
When the miners come and pay,
And God you know she loves you,
And don't like folks what swears,
And makes her little children
Kneel down and say dere prayers.

And God, if 'taint much trouble,
I'll ask some more, because
You see to-night is Christmas,
And please send Santa Claus
To put fings in our stockings,
We hung dem up out there;
Susie's by the chimney,
And mine is on the chair.

Now God please don't dis'point us,
Just send whatever suits;
Send Sis a pair of nice warm shoes
And me a pair of boots.

And God please send a blanket,
This cover's awful thin,
And big cracks all through the house
They let the cold in.

Now God I'll say good night to you
Because I'se awful cold,
And if I ask for too much things
You'll think I'se getting bold.
But if you please, before you go,
I'll ask you—this is all—
If it ain't too expensive
Send my poor ma a shawl."

"You bet your life He will my boy,"
The scout said soft and low—
Then turned away with silent tread,
Then to the camp did go.
"Wake up you fellers, one and all
And ante up with me,
I'll show you how to gamble
In a way you'll like to see."

"Now what's excited Buffalo Bill
I wonder?" shouted one;
"Just listen," said the border scout,
"While through my talk I run."
And then he told the story through,
The facts set plain and clear;
And many a rough old miner's hand
Arose and brushed a tear.

"Now here's a twenty-dollar piece,
Who'll ante up with me
To make the little children
Go wild and dance with glee?"
The poker tables bore rich fruit—
The stacks of gold heaped high;
"I'll go you one and raise you two."
"I'll stay with you or die."

Bill took his hat and passed it 'round,
"Be lively, boys, because
Before the sun is up, you know,
We'll all be Santa Claus."
The boys all chipped in coin and dust
Like men who business meant,
And then from out that gambling den
To another one they went.

And told the story o'er again—
The same results all 'round—
And others joined the merry throng,
And "Chink" the gold did sound.
They went the rounds of all saloons
And gambling dens in camp,
With big, rough, honest, manly hearts
And torches for a lamp.

It warn't no scrimping crowd, you bet,
The money poured like rain;
The rough old miners stood not back,
Nor were their efforts vain.

The money came, the men increased,
Then went they to the store
To buy the things the children wished,
Warm clothes and food and more

Than had been thought or asked for
By the children while at prayer,
Or the mother in her fondest wish
For her little darlings there;
And many a miner rough choked up
At the thought of cruel fates,
For some had wives and loved ones
Away back in the States.

They heaped a pile of everything
The border store contained
For the widow and her children
Until nothing else remained
For them to do, but get it there
To the widow's lonely home —
Then was their night's work finished,
And then abroad they'd roam.

And there were lots of rough fellows
(For I was in the crowd)
And each man gathered up a load,

Though no one spoke aloud,
And then led by Cody
To the widow's lonely hut,
Across the gulch, beyond the hill,
We took the shortest cut.

Then quiet every miner
Deposited his load
Before the little cabin door,
Then gathered in the road;
And in that pile was everything
The widow could desire;
And of pure virgin gold a sack
Still made the pile rise higher.

And to the sack they tied a note
Which bade the widow cheer,
And said: "Accept this Christmas gift
From One who's always near,
For God has heard your children,
And this is here because
It was your darlings' earnest prayer,
And God sent Santa Claus."

"Who'll stand guard till day break?"
"Buffalo Bill," said Cy,

"And with his trusty rifle
He'll guard the gift or die."
A man all clad in buckskin
Stepped out and said "I will."
The miners knew the gift was safe —
The man was Buffalo Bill.

On the bright Christmas morning
She opened wide the door,
And an avalanche of Christmas
Came tumbling to the floor.
The children heard the rumble
Of the gift, and without pause,
They came in from the bedroom
And shouted "Santa Claus!"

The widow knelt down beside them,
Despite their childish prank;
With streaming eyes and fuller heart
Returned to God her thanks,
And stealthy through the bushes
There moved off one so still.
"God bless you little Cubs," said he,
Then vanished Buffalo Bill.

—Courtesy Buffalo Bill
Historical Center

236

IN 1896 SOME VERY CLEVER speculators decided to name their little Wyoming hamlet Cody to honor the great western icon Buffalo Bill Cody and to attract his scores of fans to the town. It worked. Today the Irma Hotel still stands as physical proof of Cody's immortality in the area. Cody opened the hotel in 1902 and named it for his youngest daughter. The Irma was once hailed as the most impressive hotel between St. Louis and the Pacific Coast. In 1905 it served up a Wild West Christmas dinner reflective of its owner's flamboyant style.

Buffalo Bill (next to coach) in front of the Irma Hotel, 1894 —Courtesy Park County Historical Society

Roman Punch.—Grate the yellow rinds of four lemons and two oranges upon two pounds of loaf-sugar. Squeeze on the juice of the lemons and oranges; cover it, and let it stand till the next day. Add a bottle of champagne, and the whites of eight eggs beaten to a froth.

Front of menu for the Irma's 1905 Christmas dinner
—Courtesy Buffalo Bill Historical Center

Irma Hotel Christmas Dinner 1905
Cheese Straws, Caviar Canapés
Green Turtle Soup, Consommé Imperial
Celery in Branches, Pin Money Pickles, Pearl Onions
Shrimps a la Mandin Cases
Stuffed Young Pig, Robert Sauce
Baked Apples, Roast Domestic Duck
Fine Herbs Cress Jelly, Waldorf Salad
Choice Baked Potatoes, Asparagus Tips on Toast
Sweet Potato Cutlets, Maple Syrup
Roast Prime Rib of Beef, Glace Pan Sauce
Roast Young Turkey Stuffed, Cranberry Jelly
Hot Mince Pie, Pumpkin Pie
Fruitcake, Cream Cheese, Salted Wafers
Champagne Punch
Coffee, Cocoa, Milk, Tea

Buffalo Bill's home Christmas tree reflected his unusual personality.
—Courtesy Buffalo Bill Historical Center

Christmas card from European tour of combined Barnum & Bailey and Buffalo Bill's Wild West shows, 1903
—Courtesy Buffalo Bill Historical Center

EVERY BOUGH LADEN WITH GOOD WISHES

FROM THE
BARNUM & BAILEY STAFF
WITH
BUFFALO BILL'S WILD WEST.
8. BEACONSFIELD TERRACE LONDON W.

1903.

1904.

Cody sent this photograph of himself and an unidentified girl (probably his daughter) to his sister Julia as a Christmas card in 1894. —Courtesy Buffalo Bill Historical Center

Old-Time Christmas Fun

AMERICA'S CHRISTMAS traditions of the nineteenth century—in both the East and the West—were ladled from the great melting pot of cultures. In Europe, holiday celebrations included decorations, feasts, music, perfomances, gift giving, games, and special rituals. Of these customs, many were adopted in the United States. For instance, the English traditionally played games at Christmas. Some of them—such as blindman's buff, charades, and hide-and-seek—came with Anglo immigrants to America, though here we rarely limited our game playing to Christmastime. Another British holiday favorite was the telling of ghost stories, an idea that did not begin or end with Dickens. Americans of German, French, Spanish, Dutch, Scandinavian, and many other heritages also contributed to our nation's holiday traditions and lore.

"Of Christmas in the New World we need not speak at all, since its customs, for the most part, have been transplanted from the Old."

The Nation, 1883

Montana children trying out a new Christmas present, perhaps, in this undated photograph
—Courtesy K. Ross Toole Archives, University of Montana, Missoula

Probably the most famous Christmas song written in the 1800s was "Silent Night," penned in Austria in 1818, but many others were composed in America during the century. "It Came Upon a Midnight Clear" (1849), "We Three Kings" (1854), "O Little Town of Bethlehem" (1865), and "Away in a Manger" (sometime before 1885) were among the most enduring. Of the secular Christmastime tunes of the day, "Jingle Bells," written in 1856, is undoubtedly the best known.

Sweets such as candy, cookies, and cakes were a Christmas tradition in nearly every Christian culture, as was singing. Many Christmas carols sung in America were European songs from the 1600s or earlier, including "Deck the Halls," "Hark, the Herald Angels Sing," "Oh Come, All Ye Faithful," and "The Twelve Days of Christmas." By the end of the nineteenth century, Americans had composed a number of new carols, many of which we still sing today. In this chapter, we will examine the main elements of American frontier Christmas celebrations, along with ideas for you and your family to create your own old-time Christmas fun, including games, crafts, and candy recipes.

DECK THE HALLS

AS AN OBVIOUS WAY of creating a festive atmosphere, decorations have been part of the Christmas celebration for centuries. Any plant offering color in winter, such as holly, was naturally utilized. The ultimate Christmas decoration, the Christmas tree, came to America relatively recently, in the mid-1800s. Until then, celebrants got by with wreaths and garland, bells and candles, and other seasonal adornments. On the frontier, in addition to evergreen boughs and berries, decorations were cleverly devised from pictures clipped out of magazines, old buttons, bits of lace and ribbon, painted nuts, strings of apples or berries, and paper chains. Through mail-order catalogs, glass ornaments and embroidered table linens could be had.

"In that very first year there were no florists or green houses and we depended wholly on the wild growing things for decorations. . . . In winter were fir and cedar boughs and pine cones for Christmas wreaths and garlands. We found and cherished the wild kinnikinic with its shiny green leaves and scarlet berries that made lovely table decorations. In the late fall, my mother gathered dried clusters of small white blossoms, everlasting flowers, she called them, and added them to the green and red kinnikinic to make a real Christmas beauty in our house. I do not see the spreading mats of the kinnikinic at the edge of the woods around the land any more and I miss it."

—Edith L. Boyd remembrance from the *Spokesman-Review* [Spokane, Washington], December 27, 1964

THE CHRISTMAS WREATH
By Isabel A. Mallon

Who would think that there needed to be a plea for the Christmas wreath! And yet, from over the country the Gradgrinds of civilization are objecting to its glossy, green leaves and its bright, red berries, and saying that it is nothing but a bit of sentimentality, is it, my masters? A bit of gentle, kind memorial; so is every remembrance of a birthday or a joyful wedding. So it is a bit of sickly sentimentality when you do not think it worthwhile to put a little bunch of flowers on the grave of the baby who, two years ago, screamed with delight at the sight of the Christmas tree glittering with its gay lights and funny fruit. We want a little more of sentimentality in this world and a little less realism. The Christmas wreath, the star of Bethlehem hung in your window and mine, tells the outsiders that we believe that the Christ has come, and that we wish good-will to men. In many a home it is the only token of Christmas, and the bit of green, telling, as it does, of a belief in the present and a hope for the future, is something too precious to be cast aside. Say, mother, that it is your boy or mine, far off in some city alone on Christmas Eve; say that he has done that which is wrong and has fled from the sight of all who knew him. Say that he has been wandering around wondering what they are all doing at home,

---

WHITE GINGERBREAD.

Three pounds and a half of sifted flour
Two pounds and a quarter of brown sugar
Ten eggs
A pound and a half of butter
A large tea-cup of ginger
A large tea-cup of milk: sour, if you have it
Two small tea-spoonfuls of saleratus or pearl-ash

Stir together the butter and sugar. Beat the eggs till very light, and then stir them into the butter and sugar alternately with the flour, a little at a time. Then stir in gradually the ginger. Warm the milk (which ought to be sour) and while warm, dissolve in it the saleratus. Stir it (while foaming) into the mixture, and then stir the whole very hard. You may add, at last, a tea-spoonful of oil of lemon. Butter some square baking pans. Put in the mixture, as thick as you please, and bake it in a moderate oven. When cold, cut it into squares. See that the oven is hottest at top, when you bake the cake.
It will keep much longer than molasses-gingerbread and is very nice. (Undated recipe)

thinking of the time when he helped fix Christmas' wreaths, and now there seems no home, no God, nothing for him. He passes by his neighbor's window, and the bright light from across the street shows him the green wreath and the red star just as it was last year. It is in somebody else's window, to be sure, but then he knows that though the world is so big, though the people are so many, there are yet those who put up the sign of joy and gladness that gives him, a stranger within the gates, a thought of a new life and a willingness to go ahead with all his might, that he may go back, not unlike the prodigal, to the old home and be welcomed with joy and honor. That's what the wreath in the window does. It whispers in every berry, in every green sprig, of hope and encouragement, and it tells again and again that the angels are proclaiming afresh, "Glory to God in the highest, and on earth peace and good-will to men."

—From *Ladies' Home Journal*, 1892

ICED APPLES

Pare and core one dozen large apples, fill with sugar and a little butter and nutmeg. Bake until nearly done, let cool, and remove to another plate, if it can be done without breaking them, (if not, pour off juice). Ice tops and sides with cake-icing, and brown lightly; serve with cream. (1876)

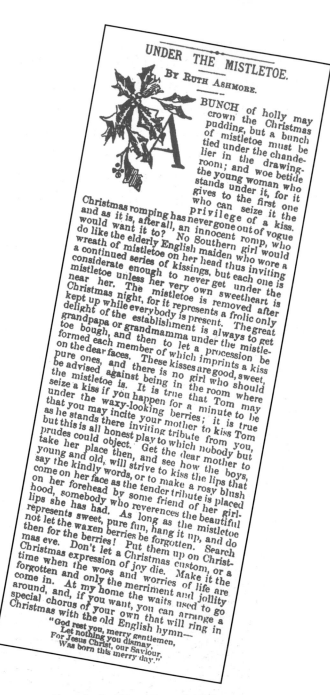

UNDER THE MISTLETOE.

By Ruth Ashmore.

A BUNCH of holly may crown the Christmas pudding, but a bunch of mistletoe must be tied under the chandelier in the drawing-room; and woe betide the young woman who stands under it, for it gives to the first one who can seize it the privilege of a kiss. Christmas romping has never gone out of vogue and as it is, after all, an innocent romp, who would want it to? No Southern girl would do like the elderly English maiden who wore a wreath of mistletoe on her head thus inviting a continued series of kissings, but each one is considerate enough to never get under the mistletoe unless her very own sweetheart is near her. The mistletoe is removed after Christmas night, for it represents a frolic only kept up while everybody is present. The great delight of the establishment is always to get grandpapa or grandmamma under the mistletoe bough, and then to let a procession be formed each member of which imprints a kiss on the dear faces. These kisses are good, sweet, pure ones, and there is no girl who should be advised against being in the room where the mistletoe is. It is true that Tom may seize a kiss if you happen for a minute to be under the waxy-looking berries; it is true that you may incite your mother to kiss Tom as he stands there inviting tribute from you, but this is all honest play to which nobody but prudes could object. Get the dear mother to take her place then, and see how the boys, young and old, will strive to kiss the lips that say the kindly words, or to make a rosy blush come on her face as the tender tribute is placed on her forehead by some friend of her girl-hood, somebody who reverences the beautiful lips she has had. As long as the mistletoe represents sweet, pure fun, hang it up, and do not let the waxen berries be forgotten. Search then for the berries! Put them up on Christmas eve. Don't let a Christmas custom, or a Christmas expression of joy die. Make it the time when the woes and worries of life are forgotten and only the merriment and jollity come in. At my home the waits used to go around, and, if you want, you can arrange a special chorus of your own that will ring in Christmas with the old English hymn—

"God rest you, merry gentlemen,
Let nothing you dismay,
For Jesus Christ, our Saviour,
Was born this merry day."

—From *Ladies' Home Journal*, 1890

FROM THE LATE 1800s to the 1940s, there was a children's journal entitled *St. Nicholas,* which was available by mail to children living out West and elsewhere. These volumes with their brilliant red covers were anxiously awaited by children living in sometimes isolated places. Issued twice yearly, the journal was about 500 pages in length and offered stories, poetry, contests, games, and crafts. Many a prairie parent must have been thankful for such a constructive outlet for their children's "cabin fever." The following is one activity from the 1908 edition of *St. Nicholas:*

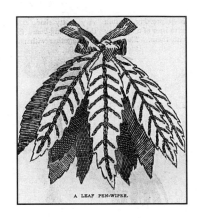

A LEAF PEN-WIPER.

A Leaf Pen-Wiper

Your pattern for this must be a beech-leaf—a long one—or you may trace the shape from this illustration. Outline the shape, and from the model thus secured cut six leaves in flannel—two green, two brown, two red, or red, white, and blue, or any combination you like. Snip the edge of each leaf into very thin points, and chain stitch veins upon it with gold colored floss. Attach these leaves together by the upper ends, arranging under them three triply pointed leaves of black broadcloth or silk to receive the ink, and finish the top with a small bow of ribbon.

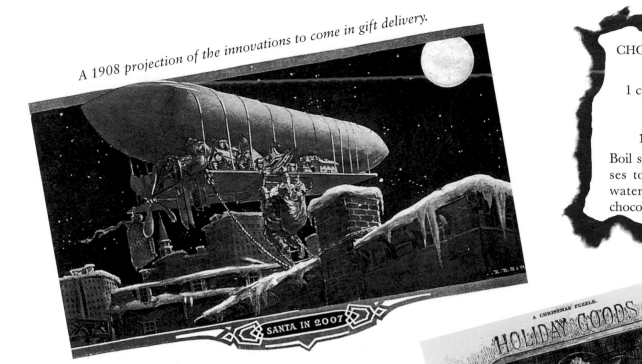

A 1908 projection of the innovations to come in gift delivery.

SANTA IN 2007

CHOCOLATE CARMELS

1 cup sugar
1 cup melted chocolate
1 cup milk
1 cup molasses
1 tablespoon flour

Boil sugar, flour and molasses together until crisp in water, then add milk and chocolate and boil. (1897)

JUMBLES

One pound flour, one of sugar, half pound of butter, three eggs, a little cinnamon. Mix first the flour and sugar and let them dry a little. Beat the eggs, then mix the butter and eggs together—then mix them all and knead them well, roll the dough small and long. Form them like a hoop. Dip them in pounded sugar, bake them on paper. (1839)

A CHRISTMAS PUZZLE.

HOLIDAY GOODS

Other magazines besides *St. Nicholas* also offered fun Yuletide ideas. Instructions for this pinecone "Old Father Christmas" appeared in *Godey's Lady's Book* in 1868.

536   GODEY'S LADY'S BOOK AND MAGAZINE.

OLD FATHER CHRISTMAS.

MANY of our subscribers will be happy to copy the well-known figure on our illustration

the head with a fur cap. The doll has, moreover, a basket of blue card-board on the back, filled with confectionery and small toys; on

for their young darlings, and thus make Merry Christmas still merrier. This doll is principally composed of five fir-cones. Two of them form the arms, two the legs, one the body. The boots, which are cut out of wood, are fastened upon a board, and are pointed off at the top. These points, two inches long, are inserted into the fir-cones which form the legs, after holes have been bored into the latter. The arms and legs are fastened on the body with gum and wire. The hands are made of papier-maché, and are gummed on the arms. The head is also of papier-maché, the hair and beard of flax. The doll has a waistband of moss to hide the wire. The neck and shoulders are covered with a black crochet comforter,

the other shoulder a net filled with nuts and apples; in one hand a miniature Christmas tree; in the other a nutcracker and birch-rod.

CROCHET BORDER.

OLD FATHER CHRISTMAS

Many of our subscribers will be happy to copy the well-known figure on our illustration for their young darlings, and thus make Merry Christmas still merrier. This doll is principally composed of five fir-cones. Two of them form the arms, two the legs, one the body. The boots, which are cut out of wood, are fastened upon a board, and are pointed off at the top. These points, two inches long, are inserted into the fir-cones which form the legs, after holes have been bored into the latter. The arms and legs are fastened on the body with gum and wire. The hands are made of papier-maché, and are gummed on the arms. The head is also of papier-maché, the hair and beard of flax. The doll has a waistband of moss to hide the wire. The neck and shoulders are covered with a black crochet comforter, the head with a fur cap. The doll has, moreover, a basket of blue card-board on the back, filled with confectionery and small toys; on the other shoulder a net filled with nuts and apples; in one hand a miniature Christmas tree; in the other a nutcracker and birch-rod.

THE HOLIDAY.

"THE CHRISTMAS BELLS ARE RINGING"

Words and Music by A. H. Miles

How clear their sound when sweetly
They grace the Sabbath day,
Inviting those who meetly
Unite to praise and pray;
Oh, let us heed their ringing,
And joyfully repair
To God's own Temple, singing
Glad hymns of praise and prayer.

How glad their sound when brightly
They swell the marriage lay,
When hearts are beating lightly
And everything is gay;
Oh, may their tuneful greeting
Lead us in thought, at least,
To yonder joyful meeting
At the great marriage feast.

And may their music ever
Remind us, as they ring,
Of songs that falter never
Where angel voices sing;
And may our songs ascending
Sound where their music swells,
In joyous anthems blending
With angels' songs and bells.

This song appeared in a children's magazine called
The Holiday, *December 27, 1890.*

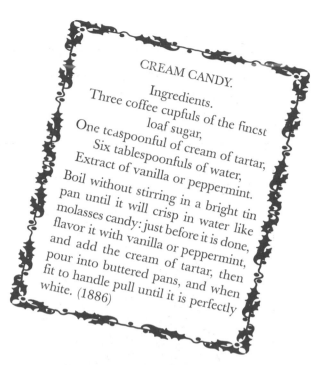

CREAM CANDY.

Ingredients.
Three coffee cupfuls of the finest
loaf sugar,
One teaspoonful of cream of tartar,
Six tablespoonfuls of water,
Extract of vanilla or peppermint.
Boil without stirring in a bright tin
pan until it will crisp in water like
molasses candy: just before it is done,
flavor it with vanilla or peppermint,
and add the cream of tartar, then
pour into buttered pans, and when
fit to handle pull until it is perfectly
white. (1886)

HERE COMES SANTA CLAUS

DIFFERENT CULTURES AT different times have fashioned their own versions of the great midwinter gift bearer. The American Santa Claus is essentially a descendant of the Dutch St. Nicholas (*Sinter Klaas*). Born in approximately A.D. 270 in what is now Turkey, this orphan of a wealthy family devoted himself to helping the less fortunate and ultimately served as the bishop of Myra. St. Nicholas became the patron saint of children, sailors, and pawnbrokers, to name a few. He arrived on American shores with the first wave of Dutch settlers in 1624. They had already invoked his protection during their voyage across the sea; their ship's figurehead was a carving of him. In gratitude, perhaps, or to ensure his continued help, building a statue to Nicholas was among the first things the newcomers did.

In America, Sinter Klaas quickly began to evolve into Santa Claus. His physical appearance went through various metamorphoses. In the nineteenth century, the stroke of a pen—of two pens, really—changed the image of Santa Claus from bishop to elf. One of these pens belonged to Clement Moore, author of the poem "A Visit from St. Nicholas," first published in 1829. Moore included many of the newer, developing conceptions of Santa in his poem—most notably, the jolly man's sleigh and eight reindeer. The second pen belonged to cartoonist Thomas Nast, who in 1866 added Santa's workshop, a register of good and bad children, and an ice palace at the North Pole.

In Dutch tradition, St. Nick leaves gifts in stockings—a reference to a legend in which the saint dropped bags of gold down a chimney to provide dowries for three impoverished girls. One of the bags fell into a stocking hung on the hearth to dry. The popular 1842 children's story *Kriss Kringle's Book* portrayed Kriss

—Illustration by Thomas Nast

KRISS KRINGLE'S CHRISTMAS TREE

(Santa) leaving presents the German way—tucked in among the tree branches—rather than in stockings. Rather than choose between tree and stockings, Americans ultimately adopted both.

Meanwhile, as hundreds of wagons began to roll west, a certain someone tagged along, following the children. Santa Claus was on the move once again.

SANTA CLAUS WEARS THEM.

Yes, he wears the Alfred Dolge Felt Shoes and Slippers. That is why he is so jolly and noiseless, and he likes them so well he makes large use of them for Christmas gifts. They are warm, quiet, home-like, cozy, and good in all points. Send to Daniel Green & Co., Sole Agents, 122 East 13th St., New York, for illustrated circular, giving full information to those desiring to select Christmas gifts.

Santa soon became a pitchman for seemingly every product in America at Christmastime . . .

and every store in town claimed to be Santa's "headquarters."

THE HOLIDAY SPIRIT
IS HERE

We now push Holiday Goods to the front. Store is full--overflowing--from basement to attic. Never before have we made such a display of the right goods for Christmas presents. Impossible to publish all that is interesting on this page--What we mention are important.

BAZAR

On Second Floor
Remember in this you can find every fancy article made. Our counters are filled with handsome articles at popular prices. 50c and 75c Hand Painted Medallions, Fancy Gold Trimming, Bisque Ornaments, Colored and Plain Ink Wells, Wood, Metal, Silver and Gilt Hand Decorated Plaques Paper Weights, Opal Ware, Handkerchief and Glove Boxes, Pin Trays, Stationery, Smoking Sets, Atomizers, Glass Jewel Boxes, Pin Cushions, Candle Stick, Hair Pin Holders, at the popular prices.

MY HEADQUARTERS ARE AT Joslins'

Standard Patterns for January Now Ready

Holiday Ribbons.

For Neck Bows and Fancy Work
Tomorrow good lots of Ribbon prices silks are remarkable. Satin and Gros Grain Ribbons all pure silk, in all the new shades.
No. 5 cut price ..... 3c yard
No. 7 cut price ..... 4c yard
No. 9 cut price ..... 5c yard
No. 12 cut price ..... 6c yard
No. 16 cut price ..... 8c yard
No. 22 cut price ..... 10c yard
No. 40 cut price ..... 11c yard
No. 60 cut price ..... 16c yard
No. 80 cut price ..... 18c yard
5 inch all pure Silk, Satin and Gros Grain Ribbon, cut price 25c.

50c and 75c Each

Christmas Very Near.
Only Fifteen Days More for All the Planning and Buying.

BOOK DEPT. SPECIAL FOR MONDAY—Three lines of pretty
Gift Books, fancy binding; also, standard
line gilt top 12mos., fine Christmas presents—Monday only **25c**

254

O CHRISTMAS TREE

WE TAKE PICTURES of it, sing songs about it, lay gifts at its feet. It's hard to pinpoint why the Christmas tree holds such a lofty position in our hearts. For Americans, the love affair began in the mid-nineteenth century and has since grown into an enduring passion.

Most sources cite the Germans as the parties responsible for bringing the Christmas tree and its trimmings to America, though other theories abound. To be sure, the Germans did not invent the custom. Its roots (forgive the pun) are ancient. The particulars of its origin are difficult to determine. Some credit Martin Luther with having been the first to decorate the Christmas evergreen; others claim it's a descendant of the paradise tree used in the miracle plays of the Middle Ages. Druid priests decorated oak trees with apples and candles for winter solstice, giving them claim to part credit as well. The Romans also decorated trees, using candles to represent the image of the sun god, during the December celebration of Saturnalia.

At Christmastime in Germany, parents would set up in the house a large evergreen, which they decorated, surrounded with presents, and lit up with candles. Usually, presents and treats were hung on the tree itself; large gifts were set beneath or on tables nearby. When all was ready, the children were summoned to behold the spectacle and receive the gifts. By the 1840s, many Americans (as well as the British) had adopted the custom of the Christmas tree, and within a few decades, it was common practice in American homes. This tradition was then carried west with the emigrants along with whatever other remnants of civilized life they could hold onto.

On the frontier, some areas were devoid of evergreens, so settlers had to make do. Some brought in cottonwood branches, others sagebrush, depending

on what was at hand. Some resourceful pioneers fastened scraps of wood together in the shape of a tree. In 1867 *The Lady's Friend* suggested, among other things, burying presents in a barrel of sawdust or bran. "The sides of the cask can be ornated with colored paper and evergreens," it offered.

Manufactured ornaments became available around the mid-1800s. Glass balls were epecially popular. Near the end of the century, electric tree lights began to replace candles. In the West, however, among the generally underfunded settlers, most ornaments were homemade. Nearly anything imaginable could be pressed into this service.

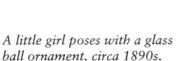

A little girl poses with a glass ball ornament, circa 1890s.
—Courtesy Colorado Historical Society

Some common and uncommon tree ornaments of the time included:

Bonbon bags (circles of lace, gathered and tied with
  bright yarn or ribbon and filled with candy)
Buttons strung together
Candles
Cigar butts, painted
Cookies—gingerbread and sugar
Cranberry strings
Crocheted doilies
Eggshells, halved, gilded, and filled
Fans
Flags
Framed pictures
Gifts
Honey cakes, decorated
Icicles (thin strips of foil)
Indian trade beads
Mirrors (small)
Nuts, covered with foil or painted
Paper cones filled with candy
Paper chains
Pictures cut from catalogs
Pincushions
Pinecones
Popcorn strands
Postcards
Soap cut into shapes
Tin cut into shapes
Toys, dolls, doll furniture, etc.
Wax figures and shapes

DRESSING A CHRISTMAS TREE
By Mrs. A. G. Lewis

A Christmas tree ought to be selected with special reference to the space it is to occupy; one with branches firm, not too broad, and quite tall is best. The upper branches should be decorated before the tree is set up, in case they are too tall to be reached by step-ladders. This can be managed by undoing the strands that confine the upper branches of trees as prepared for market, then tying upon the tips of the boughs white cotton batting snow-balls, short loops of popped-corn, strings of cranberries, glittering ornaments, etc., etc. The decoration of the tree may be more or less elaborate, as desired. To save expense, yet at the same time to insure a brilliant effect, it is a good plan to hang the gifts so that bright, contrasting colors may set off the tree. Bundles done up in brown paper are never pretty; but dolls, bright-covered books, gayly painted toys, bright silk handkerchiefs and white scarfs, sleds, wagons, etc., should be placed in prominent view.

When the gifts are all nicely arranged, take a liberal quantity of frost powder and a dozen, more or less, packages of gilt and silver fringe (these are sold at one dollar per dozen). Spread the fringe to ornament as much space as possible, and cover lightly the front and sides of the tree with it. Then sprinkle the glittering frost powder upon the tree branches. Under a brilliant light the tree becomes a veritable creation of fairyland. Santa as a dispenser of candy-bags and bonbons is always welcomed by the little ones. If he has a fund of Christmas rhymes, stories and songs to mingle with his gifts, he is all the more welcome.

—From *Ladies' Home Journal,* December 1892

Tinsel in the 1800s? Yes! Tinsel, that longstanding tree-tip favorite, was invented about the year 1610 in Germany. The original version was made of silver, which was stretched out thin by a device made specifically for the tinsel-making task.

A Christmas tree is only a shadow of itself if it be not lighted, so it is best to have it after dark. If proper precautions are taken, there is very little danger of fire. In the near future, when electricity becomes a little cheaper, incandescent lights will make a tree a blaze of glory, and there will be no fear of catastrophe. While we have to depend on tapers, care must be exercised in placing, and one person should be deputed to watch that nothing inflammable swings within reach of the light. There should be . . . a pail of water and an old blanket, or rug, to smother the flames should anything catch fire and spread. . . . If there is a carpet it is best to have a large, old rag spread under the tree for fear of accident.

—From *Ladies' Home Journal,* December 1892

HINTS AND HELPS FOR "MOTHER"

Rainy Day Amusements in the Nursery

"CHRISTMAS TREE DECORATIONS," INVENTED BY ADELIA BELLE BEARD

"I LIKE popcorn on a Christmas tree," was the sole comment of the boy of the family last year as he gazed rather wistfully at his glittering, glowing tree, overburdened with its tinsel ornaments from the shops, but bearing no popcorn, and showing no hint of the old familiar home-made decorations that meant Christmas to him. It was a severe criticism, and the suggestions I am giving here are in answer to the unconscious appeal of childhood for simpler, more personal, decorations, whose value is doubly enhanced because their manufacture is a part of the thrillingly happy Christmas preparations.

Fig. 1 is the photograph of a Christmas tree whose trimming is entirely home-made. The brilliant colors and shining gilt of the papers used, give a sparkle and life that is most captivating, and the ornaments are so easily made that the children themselves can do much toward decorating a tree in this manner.

At the top of the tree, shining above all other ornaments, is the Christmas star, and this is the way to make it:

From a piece of cardboard cut an oblong with the top and bottom edges five and one quarter inches long and the side edges just five inches long (Fig. 3). Now, exactly in the middle at the top edge make a dot (A, Fig. 3), then on each side edge, one and seven eighths inches from the top edge, make a dot (BB, Fig. 3). On the bottom edge, one inch from each bottom corner, make the dots CC. With the aid of a ruler draw the lines connecting these points, as shown in Fig. 3. This gives a perfect five-pointed star, five inches high. Cut the star out, cover its entire surface with a coat of paste, and lay over it a smooth piece of gilt paper, pressing out the fullness and creases. When the paste is dry, cut away the paper from the edges, and there will remain a gilt star, firm and stiff enough to stand up bravely.

FIG. I. THE CHRISTMAS TREE WITH HOME-MADE DECORATIONS.

164

But this is not all. There are to be a number of gold-tipped rays flaming out from the star to represent its spreading light. For these rays select ten broomstraws with two prongs. Trim the prongs off evenly, shorten the stems at the bottom, and spread the prongs apart. Now, cut twenty strips of gold paper half an inch wide and a little over four inches long. Lay one strip down, cover the wrong side with paste, place three broomstraws with their prongs resting on the paste side of the paper, and press another strip of gold paper over the first, inclosing the tips of the straws. This will give gold paper on both sides of the straws. Then, when the paste is dry, cut away the paper, leaving a gold triangle on the tip of each prong of each broomstraw. Fig. 4 shows one triangle cut out. Treat all of your broomstraw rays in this way, then cover with paste the center of the wrong side of the star up to the points, lay two straws in place, the stems crossing, as in Fig. 5, and over the stems press a short strip of white paper like D, Fig. 5, pasting it down securely. Adjust the other rays between the points of the star, and fasten them in place in the same manner.

To hold the star upright make a lighter from a strip of white writing-paper for a stem. Flatten the top of the lighter, cut it off evenly, and paste it on the back of the star between the two lower points, as in Fig. 5. Over the stems of the broomstraws and the end of the lighter paste a white paper lining that will reach part way up each point of the star. This lining should be made before the rays

FIG. 2. THE STAR

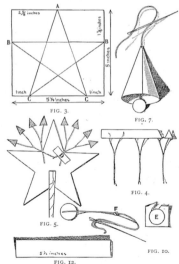

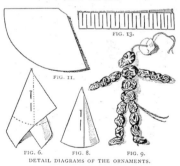

DETAIL DIAGRAMS OF THE ORNAMENTS.

are pasted to the star, by laying the star on white paper, tracing around its edges with a pencil, cutting out the white paper star and then clipping off about one inch of the points. The gold star will look like Fig. 2.

Not the least effective trimmings on the tree are the little Christmas bells that hang by strings from the tips of the branches and dangle alluringly. They are of different sizes, and some are made of gilt, others of colored paper. Fig. 15.

For a bell three and a half inches high (a very good size) cut a strip of paper three and a half inches wide and

DETAIL DIAGRAMS OF THE ORNAMENTS.

seven inches long, curve it into the shape shown in Fig. 6 and pin together. Cut off the point that laps over according to the dotted line, also the point that laps under, leaving a little over half an inch for the final lap. Trim off the bottom points even with the shortest part of the bottom edge, as shown by the curved, dotted line, and you will have Fig. 8. Fig. 8 opened out will give you Fig. 11, which will be the pattern for other bells.

As Fig. 11 lies flat on the table run the paste-brush along one side edge making the coat of paste as wide as the lap is to be, then curve the bell into shape. Make the bottom edges meet evenly and press the paste-covered edge over the other side edge. Hold a finger inside the bell while you do this to keep it from flattening.

The clapper is made of two round disks of gold paper with the string pasted between them. For the bell we are now making the clapper should be almost one inch in diameter. Fold a piece of gilt paper and cut out the two disks at one time (E, Fig. 10). Cover the wrong side of one disk with paste, lay the end of a string across the middle (Fig. 10), and press the other disk on top. Both sides of the clapper will then be gilt. Hold the clapper up to the bell by the string so that half of the clapper is below

FIG. 14. THE SNOW POCKET.

the bottom edge of the bell, then, bringing the string close to the point at the top of the bell, run a pin through the string to mark the distance. Where the pin is tie a knot (F, Fig. 10); this is to hold the clapper in its proper position. Thread the end of the string through the eye of a darning-needle and push the needle up through the point of the bell, the knot will keep the string from running up too far (Fig. 7). Allow eight or ten inches of string above the bell so that it may be hung high or low as desired. A bell should never be tied close to a branch, but should hang down far enough to sway with every passing current of air. The long string also adds to the decorative effect.

The snow pocket (Fig. 14) is another pretty ornament and is made with a few snips of the scissors.

Cut a strip of white tissue-paper five and a half inches wide and twenty-two inches long. Fold the paper crosswise through the middle, then fold it again and again, until your folded piece is one inch wide. The folds must always be across the paper from start to finish (Fig. 12). Now, cut slits in the folded paper, first a slit on one side, and then a slit on the other, as in Fig. 13. Let the spaces between the slits be one eighth of an inch wide, and cut each

slit to within one eighth of an inch of the edge. When this is done, carefully unfold the paper and spread it out flat, then lift the top edge with one hand, the bottom edge with the other, and gently pull the meshes apart. Gather the top edge into little plaits, and twist them together in a point; gather the bottom edge in the same way and twist that, then carefully pull the snow pocket out, and you will have a long, narrow bag of soft, white meshes. If it flares out too much, crush it together softly with your hand. Make a small, gilt paper star and fasten a narrow strip of white tissue-paper to its top point. Open the bag,

FIG. 15. THE CHRISTMAS BELLS.

slip the star inside, and suspend it half way from the top by pasting the end of the paper strip to the top of the bag. Make a loop of tissue-paper, fasten it to the top point of the bag, and then hang the snow pocket on the tree. The gold star gleaming through the frosty meshes is very pretty, but if you have several snow pockets there need not be stars in all.

Jocko, the monkey (Fig. 9), is not made of paper, but of delectable, sugary raisins. He is a funny little fellow, and will delight the children.

Thread a clean, cotton string in a large darning-needle, then select three of your largest raisins for the body and a suitably shaped one for the head. There must be three raisins for each leg, one for each foot, and three for each arm. Tie a knot in the end of your string and, beginning with one foot, string on three raisins for one leg, then the three for the body and, lastly, the one for the head. Tie a knot close to the top at the head and leave a long end to the string. Thread your needle again and string on the

raisins for the other foot and leg, then run the needle up through the lower raisin of the body, and fasten the second string to the first between the two body raisins.

String three raisins for one arm, run the needle through the middle of the top body raisin, where the shoulders should be, then string on the three raisins for the other arm and tie a knot at the end. Jocko is all right now, except that he is very limp. Put stiffening into his joints by running broomstraws through his legs, body, and arms. Use a raisin-stem for the tail, and fasten it on by pushing the largest end into the lowest body raisin. Make the eyes by running a short piece of broomstraw through the head, allowing the ends to stand out a short distance in the place for the eyes. Remember, a monkey's eyes are always close together, and they must be made so in order to look natural.

FIG. 16. JOCKO.

At this stage Jocko will resemble Fig. 9; but he must have clothes and a hat to give the finishing touches and make him look like the monkeys the children are familiar with. Fig. 18 is Jocko's hat, Fig. 17, his coat, and Fig. 19, his little skirt.

Cut all these from bright-colored cambric of a size to fit the monkey. Fold a piece of cambric for the coat, and cut it out as you would for a paper doll, with the fold at

the top. The skirt and hat are circular. Cut a round hole in the middle of the skirt for the waist, and slit it down the back. This furnishes the costume.

Now, thread the end of the string from the top of Jocko's head into the darning-needle and run the needle through the middle of the hat (Fig. 9), then push the hat down on

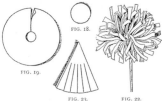

FIG. 19.　　FIG. 18.

FIG. 23.　　FIG. 22.

DETAIL DIAGRAMS OF THE ORNAMENTS

his head. Fit the skirt around Jocko's waist, and fasten it at the back with needle and thread; then put on his jacket and fasten that in front. It is unnecessary to say that Jocko is good to eat.

The chrysanthemum ornament is showy and pretty, it is also very quickly made.

Fold through the middle a piece of bright orange tissue-paper, six inches square. This will give you an oblong. Fold again through the middle crosswise, and you will have a smaller square. Bring the two opposite corners of the square together and fold like Fig. 24, then cut off the point curving the edge, as shown by the dotted line. The folded part of the triangle is at the diagonal in Fig. 24, the edges at the bottom. Now cut slits in your triangle like Fig. 23. Open it, and you will have Fig. 21. Make two fringed circles like Fig. 21, lay one on top of the other, pinch the center in a point, twist it, and draw the fringed ends together. Make a writing-paper lamp-lighter for the stem, cover the point of the ornament with paste, insert it in the large end of the lighter, and press together with your fingers until it holds tight. The result will be like Fig. 22. In fastening the chrysanthemum ornament on the tree stand it upright and run a pin through the stem into one of the small branches.

Strings of colored paper disks, looped from branch to branch, take the place of colored glass balls, and add materially to the beauty of the tree.

Fig. 20 shows how these strings are made. Red gold, yellow, orange, green, blue, and white, make pretty disks, and show off well on the tree.

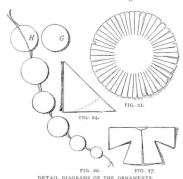

FIG. 20.　　FIG. 17.

DETAIL DIAGRAMS OF THE ORNAMENTS.

Cut your disks perfectly round, a pair for each disk; for they must be the same on both sides (G, H, Fig. 20). You can make the disks on some strings all of one size; on others they may graduate down to quite small ones at the ends. When the disks are cut lay one down, bottom side up (H, Fig. 20). Cover this with paste, then lay a white cotton string across the disk, directly through

TOYLAND

JUST AS TREE ornaments on the frontier were mostly homemade, so too were most toys and other gifts. Mothers knitted clothing, sewed rag dolls, and baked treats, while fathers carved dolls, blocks, and toy animals, and built dollhouses, wagons, and train sets. In very poor families, a doll might be fashioned from twigs, a corn husk, or even a potato. More affluent settlers might order store-bought gifts from a catalog or, if they lived in or near a town, purchase them at a general store. (Interestingly, wrapping gifts was not common practice until the 1880s.)

Most store-bought gifts were practical, such as pencils, handkerchiefs, aprons, and underwear. Books were always a welcome gift for those in the

MAPLE SUGAR CARAMELS.

Ingredients.
Two pounds of maple sugar,
One quart of rich milk.
Break the maple sugar into small pieces, and put into a pan on the fire with the milk. The pan must be deep enough to allow the sugar to expand as it boils; stir without ceasing. Test it in cold water, and when it is sufficiently brittle it is done. Then pour into square buttered pans, and score with a knife into small tablets. (1886)

CANDIED GRAPEFRUIT PEEL

Cut grapefruit peel in strips, then make a syrup of one cup sugar to one half cup of water; boil until sugar is dissolved, then drop in peel and cook until tender; remove and roll in sugar. This may be used as a confection; it also makes a delicious seasoning for custards and puddings, etc. (1897)

wilderness and were often passed from home to home to keep the winter blues at bay. Other popular store-bought gifts for adults included knives, sewing kits, slippers, scarves, cologne, cigars, silver or gold pens and pencils, boots, hats, teapots, and jewelry. For children, china dolls, doll furniture, toy trains, miniature tea sets, toy animals, small drums, music boxes, storybooks, playing cards, dominoes, candy, and money often filled stockings and lay among tree branches. The very lucky might find a sled or, late in the century, a bicycle leaning against the wall. Because of their rarity in winter, fruits, especially oranges, were a popular gift for both children and adults.

HOLIDAY ATTRACTIONS.

Robes de Chambre and Fine Smoking Jackets in the very latest Parisian styles.

Choice Neckwear, including the Langtry, Cloverton, Allaire, Leontine, and all the new style Velvet Scarfs. The finest assortment ever opened.

Silk Handkerchiefs, including Merry Christmas, New Year, Embroidered, Hem-Stitch and Fancy Bordered Handkerchiefs.

Suspenders—Embroidered Velvets, Plush, Silk and Satin Beads, Kid and Cloth Gloves, etc.

Balbriggan Underwear and Hosiery. Also, Fine Merino and Fancy Shirts and Drawers.

Night Robes, Fancy Percale and White Shirts, and all the Latest Novelties, at

J. KOHN'S,

THE LEADING CLOTHIER & HATTER,

Corner First and Morrison Streets.

Old Santy is no phantom prim—
The cheer he brings cures many ills;
Thro' dreamland's door we follow him,
And lose the thought of New Year's bills.

—From *The Sentinel*, December 1884

—From the *Daily Oregonian*, December 18, 1882

HOLIDAY TOYS

Furnishing for dolls' houses is carried to perfection this winter, and includes cabinets, pianos, and jardinieres in the drawing-rooms, library sets that are covered with leather, whitewood chamber sets upholstered with pale blue silk, dining-room sets, with buffet and extension table, and every article of kitchen furniture. Hammocks, statuettes, busts mounted on pedestals, transparent pictures for the tiny windows, mantels with mirrors set in them, gilded clocks, vases, lamps, and photograph albums are among the new articles of luxury, and a lady doll in full evening toilette of the present day, or else a powdered French marquise, is chosen to preside in the tiny mansion.

Among the walking toys is a cock that crows as it walks, an elephant that moves slowly, and an ape that clambers along most ungracefully; the musical ape and a most natural-looking cat are new this season; a pug walks around, a pig jumps out of a box, and an egg is put in at the top of a box, and a chicken comes out below. There are new musical rattles dressed as harlequins, with a music-box inside. Tambourines, lutes, mandolins,

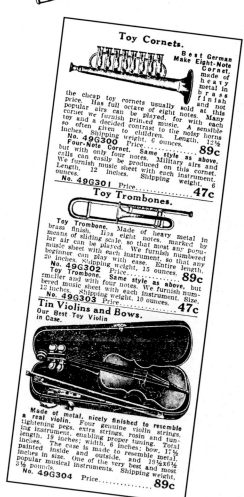

Toy Cornets.

Best German Make Eight-Note Cornet, made of heavy metal in brass finish and not the cheap toy cornets usually sold at this price. Has full octave of eight notes. Many popular airs can be played, for with each cornet we furnish printed music. A sensible toy and a decided contrast to the noisy horns so often given to children. Length, 12½ inches. Shipping weight, 6 ounces.
No. 49G300 Price..............89c

Four-Note Cornet. Same style as above, but with only four notes. Military airs and calls can easily be produced on this cornet. We furnish music sheet with each instrument. Length, 12 inches. Shipping weight, 6 ounces.
No. 49G301 Price..............47c

Toy Trombones.

Toy Trombone. Made of heavy metal in brass finish. Has eight notes, marked by means of sliding scale, so that most any popular air can be played. We furnish numbered music sheet with each instrument, so that any beginner can play with ease. Entire length, 20 inches. Shipping weight, 15 ounces.
No. 49G302 Price..............89c

Toy Trombone. Same style as above, but smaller and with four notes. We furnish numbered music sheet with each instrument. Size, 13 inches. Shipping weight, 10 ounces.
No. 49G303 Price..............47c

Tin Violins and Bows.

Our Best Toy Violin in Case.

Made of metal, nicely finished to resemble a real violin. Four genuine violin strings, extra strings, tightening pegs, enabling proper tuning and tuning instrument, rosin and bow. Total length, 19 inches; width, 6 inches; bow, 17½ inches. The case is made to resemble metal, painted inside and outside, and 19½x6½ inches in size. One of the very best and most popular musical instruments. Shipping weight, 3½ pounds.
No. 49G304 Price..............89c

MOLASSES CANDY.

Take equal quantities brown sugar and molasses, and one table-spoon sharp vinegar, and when it begins to boil skim well and strain, return to the kettle and continue boiling until it becomes brittle if dipped in cold water then pour on a greased platter. As soon as cool enough, begin to throw up the edges and work, by pulling on a hook, or by hand, until bright and glistening like gold; flour the hands occasionally, draw into stick size, rolling them to keep round, until all is pulled out and cold. Then with shears clip a little upon them at proper lengths for the sticks, and they will easily snap; flavor as you pour the candy out to cool. (1876)

and all the musical instruments used by the aesthetes in Patience are copied in toys, and some are decorated with paintings and gay ribbons.

New alphabet blocks have the letters painted on squares of different sizes that are piled up one within another. The Brooklyn Bridge and the House that Jack Built are new building blocks. The newest wagon is the great canopy-topped wagon of the prairies, and is labelled, Go West. New banks for savings represent all kinds of animals with open mouths for catching pennies, and ample bodies for holding them. Wooden animals, well carved and without paint, are in boxes for small children, while for larger ones are boxes of skin-covered animals. Menageries, stables, sheep, cats, dogs, show genuine skins and finely shaped creatures. New targets have four birds and a bull's-eye that can be knocked out when struck; a cannon or a rifle is sold with these. New tops work by electricity, and the colors change as you touch them while they spin. Telephones, telescopes, printing-presses, tool-boxes with a scroll-saw added to them, rubber balls, drums, trumpets, sleighs with real white Angora robes, bicycles, and leaping horses are the attractive things for boys.

—From *Harper's Bazar*, December 31, 1881

DOLLS

The eating doll is the novelty with which girls are delighted this year. A bit of candy is put in her open mouth, disappears, and comes out at the sole of her foot. Another new doll has music within herself, so that when wound she raises her hands and seems to sing. A third novelty, more valued for its durability than beauty, has the doll head cut from a solid piece of wood, and this wooden head can be banged about without breaking. The head moves, and the body, which is also of wood, is painted as the fine French dolls are; and some of these wooden dolls say "Mamma" and "Papa." In small sizes, such dolls, without the speaking attachment, are $1.25, and these are chosen for children whose bump of destructiveness is large. The well-known indestructible heads, with short hair of sheep's wool that will wash and comb, are made with prettier faces than when first introduced.

Brown-eyed dolls are in great favor this season, especially among the bisque dolls, that were formerly all blue in eye. The tiny doll entirely of bisque, with natural long blonde hair, eyes that open and close, and jointed limbs, is a favorite with little girls who do not think size everything; and these cost from 65 cents upward.

Mothers who want to teach their children correct ideas select each part of the doll with care, and have each article of clothing well made, so that it can be taken off and put on. First, the doll's head is selected. This may be of the composition said to be indestructible, and with short blonde curly hair of wool that is easily cleansed, and will cost from 30 cents to $2, according to size; or else it may be of French bisque, with eyes that are fixed

or with movable eyes, and hair of wool, but most natural-looking. These range from 70 cents upward, and among the more expensive heads are those with Titian red hair and brown eyes, or else golden yellow hair with a bang on the forehead and flowing behind. The wax heads are most varied of all and most natural-looking, but most perishable. They are shown as infants with bald heads or a scant bang, to wear caps; as short-haired boys, with Charles II flowing locks; and as ladies with elaborate coiffures.

The body is then chosen of either muslin or kid, and must be made up without wires, and stuffed with cotton to make it light, instead of the heavy sawdust that sifts through the cover. They can also be bought with the crying arrangement inside. The muslin bodies cost from 30 cents upward; those of kid are more expensive.

Mother Hubbard dolls are favorites this season, and as this consists in dressing them in a shirred cloak of cashmere or satin, with a poke bonnet or steeple-crowned hat of the same, they are easily gotten up at home. The imported dolls come elaborately arrayed in plush and satin costumes, but tasteful little girls prefer instead a doll dressed in the first short clothes with white muslin yoke dresses, skirts, and petticoats that may be taken off and put on, and over this a Mother Hubbard hard cloak, with hat to match. Every article of clothing may be bought separately for the doll, including rubber overshoes and hair-pins, and there are boxes with three or four different sets of clothing for the doll inmate.

Infant dolls in long clothes are accompanied by a furnished basket, and are completely dressed in white muslin, with a sash, and a cloak of white cashmere with double cape and quilted silk border. A . . . French bonnet with a cap can also be supplied.

—From *Harper's Bazar*, December 31, 1881

I N SPOKANE, WASHINGTON'S *Spokesman Review*, December 27, 1964, Edith L. Boyd remembered a Christmas from her childhood in the late 1800s.

In my father's hardware store on the corner of Howard and Main [in Spokane] he showed the usual shiny things and his specialties, ore cars and miner's supplies for the Idaho miners, and Garland stoves and ranges. Outshining all these, though, was the dearest thing of all . . . a little-girl-size Garland range and all the pots and pans that belonged with it. Children gathered before that window, fascinated and full of longing. Whether that identical one or another I cannot tell, but its facsimile came to my sister and me on Christmas morning. Such joy! Such rapture! After we had examined and admired all the parts and bits of it, the question arose . . . could we cook on it, really cook on it? Yes, that was possible, but wait until tomorrow.

When the stove was taken to our play-room upstairs, we got ready for the first excitement . . . lighting the kindling wood stuffed in the fire box. Yes, it caught, a little flame showed through the front grate. Also, a wisp and then a puff of smoke erupted from the open stove-pipe hole. No stove-pipe or chimney attachment had been provided: nor could be. When the smoke cleared away, our disappointment continued . . . we would have to do our cooking on the porch when spring time came. We did and liked it just as well.

CHRISTMAS GAMES

FOR MANY CENTURIES in Europe, Christmas was the only time that working people were allowed to play games. Parlor games remained a Christmas tradition in many countries, including the United States, through the nineteenth and early twentieth century. The hectic pace of the modern-day Christmas doesn't allow much time for party games anymore, but it might be a tradition worth reviving. Most of these game descriptions came from *Godey's Lady's Book*.

BLINDMAN'S BUFF

The blind man is placed in the middle of the room; the players stand around him in a ring. The blind man reaches out to touch somebody. If he succeeds, he utters three cries, which the person he touched must imitate. If recognized by the voice the person must pay a forfeit, and likewise take the blind man's place.

SNAP-DRAGON

Snap-dragon is traditionally played on Christmas Eve, but it can also be played on Christmas Day. Raisins, currants, or other dried fruit are heaped onto a shallow dish, brandy was poured on top of them, and, with the lights extinguished, the brandy is set on fire. The object is to snatch a piece of fruit out of the flames, blow it out, and eat it.

FLY, FEATHER, FLY

Ten or twelve young people sit in a circle. Somebody takes a tuft of cotton wool, or a downy feather, and lets it float in the air above the heads of the group, giving it a puff with his breath. The person towards whom it directs its descent must likewise blow it upwards and away. If it falls upon him, he pays a forfeit. A dozen persons so employed in chasing with their breath the common enemy compose a most amusing group, resembling the messengers of Aeolus, as represented in old mythological pictures. It often happens, as it is hard to laugh and blow at the same time, the feather finds its way into the throat of the intending blower, and, of course, the involuntary feather-eater pays a double forfeit as a penalty for his curious taste.

THE GAME OF ECHO

This game consists in telling a story which Echo is supposed to interrupt, whenever certain words (agreed upon beforehand) are pronounced. Each person present has to re-echo some given word, whenever it occurs. The words selected are those likely to occur most frequently in the course of the tale. If a military anecdote is to be related, appropriate words for repetition would be soldier, uniform, gaiters, rifle, sword, scabbard, bayonet, foraging-cap, haversack, etc. For instance: One morning a brave soldier *(soldier)* received orders to join his regiment; so he bade adieu to his friends, and set off on foot. After walking twenty miles, feeling a little tired, he sat down at the foot of a tree, resting his rifle *(rifle)* against its mossy trunk. Just as he was falling off into a doze he heard piercing cries of distress, at which he drew his sword *(sword)* from its scabbard *(scabbard)* and fixed his bayonet *(bayonet)* at the end of his rifle *(rifle)*. . . .

The yarn may be spun, *ad libitum,* to any length, calling forth responses from the surrounding echoes as frequently as possible. If they fail to take up the cue, a forfeit is their punishment.

SARDINES

In a darkened house, one player goes off to hide. Everyone else counts to one hundred, then spreads out to search for him. When players stumble into the hider, they join him, packing silently together like sardines. The loser is the last one to discover the crowd.

HOT COCKLES

The origins of the name of this game are lost in the mists of time. One person kneels in the center of the room, and is blindfolded. He then places one hand, with the palm uppermost, on his back. The rest of the company advance in turns, each administering a tap on the shoulder or a slap on the palm. The kneeler must discover, without looking, who it is who has given the slap or tap. If the guess is correct, the discovered player takes the place of the kneeler, and the game continues.

THE LOVE TEST

Join hands in a circle. One player, being blindfolded, goes into the middle. All dance around until the blindman holds out his hand, which the one immediately opposite takes hold of and enters the circle. The blind player then asks in succession the following questions: "Do you love me? Can you love me? Will you love me?" and he should endeavor to render his tone and attitude as ludicrous as possible in order to provoke a smile from the young lady or gentleman (as the case may be) whom he is addressing, for which those players forming the circle must carefully watch, the rule being, that in the answers given which should be in a feigned voice, the adverbs Yes and No are inadmissible, and no smile is allowed on the countenance. Otherwise, by way of penalty, they must kiss each other, and if the blind player can tell the name of the individual before him, they change places.

It should also be observed that those players who pass through the ordeal of the three questions without breaking the rules return to their places, and all dance around as before.

ALICE McNITT MONTGOMERY, the daughter of Colorado homesteader Orpha Baldwin McNitt (whose letter appeared earlier in this volume), wrote this fictionalized version of a childhood Christmas in the early 1900s. It is reprinted from *Prairie Christmas and Other Stories* with the kind permission of Alice's daughter, Emma Alice Hamm.

In it, a small rural community in the early 1880s comes together to create a memorable Christmas for their children. Popcorn balls, molasses taffy, and homemade toys make a humble prairie cottonwood into a "real Christmas tree." The Eleanor Ann of the story is Alice.

PRAIRIE CHRISTMAS
By Alice McNitt Montgomery

"Mother, will you tell me about Christmas trees? In the magazine Grandmother sends me, there is a beautiful picture. It's a tree in the center of a room, and there are dolls on it and other toys, and lights, and children standing around. They are dressed up and smiling, and under the picture it says, 'The Christmas Tree.' Did you ever see one when you were a little girl?"

"Yes, we had one every year, and I would like to tell you about it. We began getting ready for Christmas early, in December. We made presents for each other, and that took some time. When that was nearly done we popped corn and strung it on strings. Father always had plenty of cranberries from his own marsh, so we often strung three of four kernels of popcorn, then a cranberry and then more popcorn, until we had a good many yards.

"The older boys took the bob-sled and went out in the woods, and cut the prettiest evergreen tree they could find. They brought it home and set it up in the parlor, which was a room we seldom used. We girls made ropes of ground pine to decorate the room. The tree was trimmed with the popcorn and cranberry chains, bright-colored bags of candy and candles in gay holders. Then Mother came and placed a star in the very top and hung the Christmas Angel under it. I think it looked very much like your picture, only more beautiful."

This sounded like a fairy story to Eleanor Ann. She tried to imagine a tree that kept green all winter and a lot of happy children trimming it. Eleanor Ann was an only child and lived with her parents on a homestead on the Colorado prairie.

Mr. Mason, her father, was a surveyor, and Mrs. Mason and Eleanor Ann were often alone. They sometimes felt lonely, for the nearest neighbor was several miles away, but they were not afraid because, as Eleanor Ann said, "There was nothing to be afraid of."

Eleanor Ann found many interesting things to do every day, and when it grew dark she and her mother had pleasant visits together. Just now they talked about Christmas trees. The more they talked, the more Eleanor Ann wanted to see one. After she had quit talking and gone to sleep, her mother kept thinking and planning.

Father came home Saturday night, and Sunday afternoon, as usual, they went to the little schoolhouse three miles away to Sunday School. Afterward the children went out in the yard while the elders visited. It was then that Mrs. Mason said, "Don't you suppose we could have a tree for the children Christmas Eve?"

"I should say not, Mary Mason; don't you know that there isn't even a Jack pine within thirty miles?"

"Yes, I know that as well as you do, but there are plenty of cottonwoods over on the Platte River, and that isn't ten miles. We could trim it in some way. The children have never seen a real Christmas tree. They would not miss the evergreen."

"I have to go to Platteville for the mail tomorrow and I could bring you all a little tree," said a soft-voiced young man.

"And I know exactly how to trim it," responded Miss Lena, briskly.

"We have no money for candy."

"No, and we don't need any. We had a good crop of cane and so did you. We have plenty of sorghum molasses and we can make taffy for everyone."

"We have sorghum and popcorn, and I will make popcorn balls enough to go around."

"Now can we think of anything for presents?"

"I have a pattern and I can make each of the girls a doll if you want me to," said Miss Harriet.

"Why, Miss Harriet, that is the very thing! Let's see how many girls there are. Mary Jane and Esther and Annie, Margaret and Eleanor Ann; that is five. Can you make that many?"

"Of course I can. Mother will help me. You know, Aunt Anne left me her piece bag when she went back home."

"That settles the girls. Now what can we do for the boys?"

"I know," the young man of the Christmas tree spoke again; "I can make good balls with leather covers. That is, if some of you can find two old boot tops. I have one."

"That is splendid. Now is there anything else?"

"Yes. I would like to make some tapers to light the tree. I've helped Mother dip Christmas candles. It does not take much tallow for such little ones," said Mrs. Mason.

"I'll tell you something else to do," came a deep voice from one of the men. "You pack baskets and we will have a picnic supper."

This idea pleased everyone, and the afternoon before Christmas found them all in the schoolhouse again.

Miss Lena and her helpers were hidden behind a curtain stretched across one corner of the room. Everything was mysterious and interesting. The children were sent outdoors to play, but even their favorite games of Pull-Away and Prisoner's Base seemed dull and tiresome. After a long time they were called in to supper, but they were in too much of a hurry to see the Christmas tree to enjoy the good things from the picnic baskets. The grown people ate and visited and were in no hurry

Nebraska sod schoolhouse with students, undated. —Courtesy Nebraska State Historical Society

at all. At last they were through eating. The blackboard which had been used for a table was hung on the wall, the school seats were arranged in rows and they were ready for the tree. Lights began to glimmer in the corner, the curtain was taken away and the Christmas tree was in full view.

The shapely little cottonwood stood on a low table, around which were piled popcorn balls and bags of red mosquito netting filled with molasses candy.

The trunk of the tree and the larger branches were covered with cotton to look like snow, the small twigs were wound with tinfoil and tipped with tufts of cotton. Strings of popcorn hung in festoons. The dolls and balls danced from the branches. The white candles burned brightly. Altogether it was most satisfying. Even Eleanor Ann, who had thought and talked of little else for a week, decided no tree could be prettier.

Miss Lena read the Christmas story while they looked at the tree. The children were given their presents. The girls were delighted with their dolls, and just as the boys were finding it's too hard to hold a fine new ball and not play with it, popcorn and candy came around and everyone began eating.

Eleanor Ann could scarcely enjoy her popcorn for looking at the beautiful little tree and hugging her dolly, which she secretly thought the prettiest of all the dolls.

Grandfather Moore, who had lived in England when he was a boy, suggested that they sing Christmas carols; but as he could not carry a tune, and no one else knew any, they sang "Precious Jewels," which did almost as well, for it carried their thoughts from their own little ones to the Blessed Baby in His manger cradle in far-away Bethlehem on another starry December night.

The most wonderful evening the children had ever known was ended. Mothers gathered up lunch baskets and sleepy babies. Fathers brought buggies and wagons to the door. All the people climbed in, and joyous good-byes were called as they drove away, each one happier that the Spirit of Christmas had found a place on the wide prairie.

Butter the Size of an Egg?
Vintage Weights, Measures, and Kitchen Terms

WEIGHTS AND MEASURES

Early chefs didn't have the precise measuring utensils we use today. Instead, they often measured with everyday cups and spoons.

butter the size of an egg = ¼ cup

butter the size of a walnut = 2 tablespoons

lump = 2 tablespoons

dessert spoon = 1½ teaspoons

salt spoon = ¼ teaspoon

old-time teaspoon = ¾ modern teaspoon

old-time tablespoon = 4 modern teaspoons

tumblerful = 2 cups

coffee cup = 1 cup

2 coffee cups = 1 pint

tin cup = 1 cup

teacup = ¾ cup

gill = ½ cup

2 gills = ½ pint

wineglass = ¼ cup

dram = ¾ teaspoon

scruple (an apothecary weight) = ¼ teaspoon or ¹⁄₂₄ oz.

dash = ⅛ teaspoon

pinch = ⅛ teaspoon

pound of eggs = 8 to 9 large eggs, 10 to 12 smaller ones

EMPTY TIN CANS

Canned vegetables, fruits, and even seafood started to appear in the West around 1837. After the tins were emptied, they could be used for measuring.

#1 flat = ½ pound

#1 tall = 1 pound

#303 = 1 pound

#2 = 1¼ pounds

#2½ = 1¾ pounds

#3 cylinder = 2 pounds, 14 ounces

#10 = 6 pounds, 10 ounces

OVEN TEMPERATURES

very slow: 250°

slow: 300°

moderately slow: 325°

moderate: 350°

moderately hot: 375°

hot: 400°

very hot: 450° to 500°

Domestic Terms
from the Western Trail and Homestead

airtights: canned goods

barley coffee: coffee substitute made from barley

bear-sign: doughnut

blickey: small tin container

bodewash: dried cow dung, used for fuel in treeless areas; from the French "bois de vache"

calabazilla: a wild squash (*Cucurbita foetidissima*) used for removing stains from clothing and for medicine

canned cowboy: canned milk

Charlie Taylor: butter substitute made of sorghum and bacon grease

Confederate beef: mule meat

cook-all: iron skillet used for cooking and baking

cree (verb): to boil any grains into a porridge

dough keg: wooden barrel for storing sourdough starter

firkin: same as "dough keg"

freshening (washing): rinsing salt-preserved food in several changes of water to make it palatable

hog side: salt pork

hoop (garth): a deep ring of wood or iron used as a mold for large cakes

isinglass: gelatin made from sturgeon and dried into sheets; also used as a clarifying agent

lick: molasses

lively emptyings: yeast sediment in the bottom of a beer barrel; used in place of eggs in some recipes

pearl ash: a bicarbonate of potash used as an alkaline in combination with sour milk for leavening

prairie turnip (also, prairie potato): the root of a wild plant (*Psoralea esculenta*) often dried, pounded, and made into gruel

rock hominy: parched Indian corn pounded into a fine powder

saleratus: a more refined bicarbonate of potash that replaced pearl ash as a leavening agent. Today, baking soda may be substituted for saleratus in equal amounts.

samp: course cornmeal, boiled and eaten usually with milk and sugar

sea plums: canned oysters

searce (verb): to sieve or sift

tuna: prickly pear cactus fruit

wreck pan: a pan of water for dishwashing

Bibliography

BOOKS

Alderson, Nannie, and Helena Huntington Smith. *A Bride Goes West*. (n.p.: Farrar & Rinehart, Inc., 1942. Lincoln: University of Nebraska Press, 1969).

Annals of America, vols. 6 and 7. Chicago: Encyclopedia Britannica, 1968.

Baur, John. *Christmas on the American Frontier, 1800-1900*. Caldwell, Idaho: Caxton Printers, 1961.

Bennett, Larsen Cynthia. *Roadside History of Utah*. Missoula, Mont.: Mountain Press, 1999.

Brady, Cyrus Townsend. *Recollections of a Missionary in the Great West*. New York: Charles Scribner's Sons, 1900.

Butruille, Susan G. *Women's Voices from the Oregon Trail*. Boise, Idaho: Tamarack Books, 1993.

Chittenden, Hiram M., and Alfred T. Richardson. *Life, Letters and Travels of Father Pierre-Jean DeSmet, S..J., 1801-1873*. New York: Francis P. Harper, 1905.

Clemenson, Grace Johnston. *Grandmother's Stories*. Fairfield, Wash.: Ye Galleon Press, 1991.

Clyman, James. *Journal of a Mountain Man*. Ed. Linda Hasselstrom. Missoula, Mont.: Mountain Press, 1984.

Cody, William F. (Colonel). *An Autobiography of Buffalo Bill*. New York: Holt Rinehart & Winston, 1920.

Coffman, Lloyd W. *Blazing a Wagon Trail to Oregon*. Springfield, Ore.: Echo Books, 1993.

Cook, Jeannie, Lynn Johnson Houze, Bob Edgar, and Paul Fees. *Buffalo Bill's Town in the Rockies*. Virginia Beach, Va.: Donning Company, 1996.

Cox-Paul, Lori A., and James W. Wengert. *Frontier Army Christmas*. Lincoln: Nebraska State Historical Society, 1996.

Crossen, Forest. *Western Yesterdays, vol. 2*. Boulder, Colo.: Boulder Publishing Company, 1964.

Douglas, George William. *American Book of Days*. Bronx, N.Y.: H.W. Wilson Company, 1937.

Drury, Clifford M. *Marcus and Narcissa Whitman and the Opening of Old Oregon*. Glendale, Calif.: Arthur H. Clark, 1973.

Everett, Dick. *Vanguards of the Frontier*. Lincoln: University of Nebraska Press, 1941.

Fremont, Jesse Benton. *Far West Sketches*. Boston: D. Lothrop Company, 1890.

Funk and Wagnalls Standard Dictionary of American Folklore, Mythology, and Legend. New York: Funk and Wagnalls, 1972.

Gabriel, Ralph Henry, ed. *Pageant of America: The Lure of the Frontier.* New Haven: Yale University Press, 1929.

Hafen, Leroy R., and Ann W. Hafen, eds. *Journals of the Forty-Niners.* Glendale, Calif.: Arthur H. Clark, 1954.

———, eds. Rufus B. Sage: *His Letters and Papers, 1836–1847.* Glendale, Calif.: Arthur H. Clark, 1956.

Hafen, Leroy R., and Francis Marion Young. *Fort Laramie and the Pageant of the West 1834-1890.* Lincoln: University of Nebraska Press, 1984.

Horan, James D. *The Wild Bunch.* New York: Signet, 1958.

Journals of the Lewis and Clark Expedition. Lincoln: University of Nebraska Press, 1997.

Kingsley, Rose. *Christmas and New Year's in Colorado: Seventy-five Years Ago, 1871-1872.* Denver: Colorado Historical Society, 1946.

Logan, Mrs. John. *The Home Manual.* Philadelphia: H. J. Smith & Company, 1889.

Loutzenhiser, F.H., J.R. Loutzenhiser, and F.I. Trotter, eds. *Told by the Pioneers: Reminiscences of Pioneer Life in Washington.* 3 vols. Olympia, Wash.: Washington Pioneer Project, 1937-38.

Marcy, Randolph B. (Captain). *Prairie Traveler.* Franklin Square, N.Y.: Harper & Brothers, 1859.

McLoughlin, Denis. *Wild and Wooly: An Encyclopedia of the Old West.* N.p.: Barnes & Noble, 1995.

McNitt, Orpha Baldwin. *Letters from a Frontier Bride.* Private printing, 1993.

Monaghan, Jay, ed. *Book of the American West.* New York: Bonanza Books, 1968.

Monnet, John H. *Rocky Mountain Christmas.* Boulder, Colo.: Pruett Publishing, 1987.

Montgomery, Alice McNitt. *Prairie Christmas and Other Stories.* Private printing, 1993.

Myers, Rex C., ed. *Lizzie: The Letters of Elizabeth Chester Fisk.* Missoula, Mont.: Mountain Press, 1989.

O'Connor, Carol A., Martha A. Sandweiss, and Clyde A. Milner, eds. *Oxford History of the American West.* New York: Oxford University Press, 1994.

The Old West. Alexandria, Va.: Time-Life, 1974.

Peavy, Linda. *Frontier Children.* Norman: University of Oklahoma Press, 1999.

Reedstrom, Ernest L. *Scrapbook of the American West.* Caldwell, Idaho: Caxton Printers, 1990.

Reynolds, Edward B., Michael Kennedy, and Greg Patent. *Whistleberries, Stirabout, and Depression Cake.* Helena, Mont.: Falcon Press, 2000.

Roe, Frances M. A. *Army Letters from an Officer's Wife 1871-1888.* New York: D. Appleton & Company, 1909.

Schlissel, Lillian. *Women's Diaries of the Westward Journey.* New York: Schocken Books, 1992.

Siegert, Wilmer H. *"Old-fashioned Holidays."* Paper presented at a Westerners Spokane Corral meeting, Spokane, Wash., September 18, 1969.

Spring, Agnes, ed. *An Army Wife Comes West: Letters of Catherine Wever Collins 1863-1864*. Denver: Colorado State Historical Society, 1954.

Springer, Marlene, and Haskell Springer. *Plains Woman: The Diary of Martha Farnsworth 1882-1922*. Bloomington, Ind.: Indiana University Press, 1986.

Stiles, Alfred L. *Log of a Trip around the Horn to San Francisco in 1849*.

Stratton, Joanna L. *Pioneer Women: Voices from the Kansas Frontier*. New York: Touchstone Books, 1982.

Tennent, William L. *John Jarvie of Brown's Park*. Salt Lake City: Utah Bureau of Land Management, 1984.

Thompson, David. *Narrative, 1784–1812*. Ed. Richard Glover. Toronto: Champlain Society, 1962.

Trimble, Marshall. *Roadside History of Arizona*. Missoula, Mont.: Mountain Press, 1986.

Unruh, John D., Jr. *The Plains Across: The Overland Emigrants and the Trans-Mississippi West 1840-60*. Chicago: University of Illinois Press, 1982.

U.S. Works Projects Administration, Washington (State). *Told by the Pioneers*. Olympia[?]. Wash.: WPA, 1937–38.

Waitley, Douglas. *William Henry Jackson: Framing the Frontier*. Missoula, Mont.: Mountain Press, 1998.

Walter, Dave, comp. *Christmastime in Montana*. Helena: American Geographic Press, 1990.

Werner, Emmy E. *Pioneer Children on the Journey West*. Boulder, Colo.: Westview Press, 1995.

West, Leoti L. *The Wide Northwest*. Spokane: Shaw & Borden, 1927.

Wills, Mary H. *A Winter in California*. Norristown, Pa.: n.p., 1889.

PERIODICALS

The American Missionary

The American West

Annals of Wyoming

Atlantic Monthly

Buffalo Bulletin

The Century Illustrated Magazine

Colorado Tribune

Daily Argus

Daily Oregonian

Daily Sun

Denver Times

Field and Farm

Godey's Lady's Book

Greeley Tribune

Frank Leslie's Illustrated Newspaper

Harper's Illustrated

Harper's New Monthly

Harper's Weekly

Harper's Young People

The Holiday

Kansas City Journal

Ladies' Home Journal

Rocky Mountain News

Routt County Sentinel

St. Nicholas

San Francisco Call

San Francisco Chronicle

The Sentinel

Spokane Spokesman-Review

The Trail

The West

COLLECTIONS AND LIBRARIES

Bent's Fort, La Junta, Colo.

Buffalo Bill Historical Center, McCracken Research Library collection, Cody, Wyo.

Colorado Historical Society, CWA pioneer interviews, Denver, Colo.

Denver Public Library, Western History/Genealogy Dept. Will Ferril Collection; Menu Collection; Works Progress Administration Collection.

Fort Laramie Historical Association, Fort Laramie, Wyoming.

Library of Congress, Manuscript Division, Works Progress Administration Federal Writers Project Collection Life Histories, Washington, D.C.

Longmont Historical Society, Seth Terry Collection, Longmont, Colo.

Making of America Digital Library, Cornell University (http://cdl.library.cornell.edu/moa/).

Midwest Jesuit Archives, St. Louis, Missouri.

Mountain Men and the Fur Trade On-line Research Center (www.xmission.com/~drudy/amm.html).

Museum of Western Colorado, Loyd files Research Library, Grand Junction, Colo.

National Archives, Washington, D.C.

Northwest Museum of Arts and Culture, Spokane, Wash.

C. M. Russell Museum, Great Falls, Mont.

Park County Historical Society Archives, Cody, Wyo.

San Francisco Public Library, Main Branch, Magazines and Newspapers Center, San Francisco, Calif.

Spokane Public Library, Northwest Collection, Spokane, Wash.

University of Missouri, Ellis Library, Western Historical Manuscript Collection, Columbia, Mo.

Wyoming State Archives, Cheyenne, Wyo.

Wyoming State Historical Department, Works Progress Administration Manuscript Collection, Cheyenne, Wyo.

Thanks

BOOKS ARE NOT BORN, they are built. Each hand involved contributes to the strength of the whole. I must gratefully thank the following for lending their hands to this work.

Jeannie Cook, Park County Archives, keeper of history

Ann Marie Donoghue and Mary Robinson, Buffalo Bill Historical Center, for the smiles

The staff at Fort Laramie for allowing me to access their files and to photograph their ghosts

Nancy Merz from the Jesuit Archives for directing me to Father DeSmet

Paul Beck, University of Wisconsin, LaCrosse

Nancy Compau and the staff at Spokane Public Library

Jeff Creighton, archivist, Northwest Museum of Arts and Culture

Larry Eick

Dean Knudson, Scotts Bluff National Monument

Newman Myrah, Ricardo Perez, and the staff at Fort Clatsop

Kim Smith, Elizabeth Dear, and Duane Braaten, C. M. Russell Museum

Towana Spivey, Fort Sill Museum

Robin Urban and Virginia Jacobson, World Museum of Mining

Nancy Watts, Lewistown Public Library

Wyoming State Museum

The good folks at Mountain Press Publishing, for the tireless work and for taking a chance on a Christmas book

Lloyd Rich for his humor, legal counsel, and teaching me it's OK to walk away

My dear family, who never complained as I chased Santa Claus for four years—I missed you.

I also owe a great debt to the western families and individuals of the past whom I have never met, but with whom I have shared so many holidays.

About the Author

SAM TRAVERS is the owner of North Pole West, the nation's largest retailer of western holiday products, with a new store in Cody, Wyoming, and northpolewest.com, the company's online store and information resource. She also designs her own line of western Christmas merchandise and was one of the artists selected to create an ornament for the White House Christmas tree in 2001. She is a member of Women Writing the West and several historical associations, and the author of *Manny Claus: A Western Christmas Tail.*

A resident of Cody, Ms. Travers regularly travels the West in search of new resources and fresh ideas. She has been collecting Christmas memorabilia for sixteen years, resulting in "an impressive range of cookie recipes and ugly Santas." During the holidays, she invariably offers her services as a tree decorator, stocking stuffer, basket filler, or bell ringer. Her love of Christmas, big black cowboy hat, and petite stature have earned her the nickname "Spike, the Outlaw Elf."

Recipe Index

General Index

We encourage you to patronize your local bookstore. Most stores will order any title that they do not stock. You may also order directly from Mountain Press using the order form provided below or by calling our toll-free number and using your credit card. We will gladly send you a catalog upon request.

Some history titles of interest:

_____ _The Arikara War: The First Plains Indian War, 1823_	$18.00/paper	$30.00/cloth
_____ _The Bloody Bozeman: The Perilous Trail to Montana's Gold_	$16.00/paper	
_____ _Chief Joseph and the Nez Perces: A Photographic History_	$15.00/paper	
_____ _Christmas in the Old West: A Historical Scrapbook_	$28.00/paper	
_____ _Crazy Horse: A Photographic Biography_	$20.00/paper	
_____ _Encyclopedia of Indian Wars: Western Battles and Skirmishes, 1850 to 1890_	$28.00/cloth	
_____ _The Journals of Patrick Gass: Member of the Lewis and Clark Expedition_	$20.00/paper	$36.00/cloth
_____ _Lakota Noon: The Indian Narrative of Custer's Defeat_	$18.00/paper	$36.00/cloth
_____ _Lewis & Clark: A Photographic Journey_	$18.00/paper	
_____ _The Oregon Trail: A Photographic Journey_	$18.00/paper	
_____ _The Mystery of E Troop: Custer's Gray Horse Company at the Little Bighorn_	$18.00/paper	
_____ _The Piikani Blackfeet: A Culture Under Siege_	$18.00/paper	$30.00/cloth
_____ _The Pony Express: A Photographic History_	$22.00/paper	
_____ _Sacagawea's Son: The Life of Jean Baptiste Charbonneau_	$10.00/paper _(for readers 10 and up)_	
_____ _The Saga of the Pony Express_	$17.00/paper	$29.00/cloth
_____ _Stories of Young Pioneers: In Their Own Words_	$14.00/paper _(for readers 10 and up)_	
_____ _William Henry Jackson: Framing the Frontier_	$22.00/paper	$36.00/cloth

Please include $3.00 for 1–4 books or $5.00 for 5 or more books for shipping and handling.

Send the books marked above. I enclose $ _____

Name _____

Address _____

City/State/Zip _____

☐ Payment enclosed (check or money order in U.S. funds)

Bill my: ☐ VISA ☐ MasterCard ☐ American Express ☐ Discover   Exp. Date:_____

Card No. _____

Signature _____

MOUNTAIN PRESS PUBLISHING COMPANY
P.O. Box 2399 • Missoula, MT 59806 • fax: 406-728-1635
Order Toll Free 1-800-234-5308 • Have your credit card ready
e-mail: info@mtnpress.com • website: www.mountain-press.com